Nana Lena's Kitchen
Recipes for Life

A memoir in recipes

Amy Ostrower

First published by Dog Ear Publishing
4010 W. 86th Street, Ste H
Indianapolis, IN 46268
www.dogearpublishing.net

ISBN: 1-59858-056-6
Library of Congress Control Number: 2005936915

This book is printed on acid-free paper.

Printed in the United States of America

Nana Lena's Sayings:

"You have to pay for the space you take up on earth."

"Give a kugel, get a kugel, or sometimes you get a sweet potato pie."

"To hell with the expense. Give the bird another seed."

"It's a wonderful thing to dine under the stars because when you start thanking God for all his bounty, you feel that much closer to him."

"It is hope wrapped with promise, and sprinkled with love, or as your Papa would say, 'It's sweet, twisted and a little nuts, like my Lena.'"

"These are special cookies. Love cookies. Made with love, filled with love, for a day on which we celebrate love. It's not every day you get to go to your grandson's wedding."

"But your Nana's not modern. She's old-fashioned."

"I put eighteen cents in the *puske*, and I count my blessings. Eighteen, *chai*, for life."

"So you see, Amele, things just never die. People go on forever, and the stories go on forever."

"I adore you and I always will."

"Don't argue with your Nana. You want the world to think I didn't teach you any manners?"

"Make a *mitzvah*; it will come back to you."

"He's my brother, and I'm going to take care of him. I always have; I always will."

"Besides, you did a *mitzvah*. You reminded him of what it feels like to be young."

"Life has a funny way of ruining your expectations."

"We aren't born knowing how to hate."

"After the war, there were hundred of thousands of refugees who needed my help. Who was I to refuse?"

"So you ask yourself, what kind of game lets a jokester, a black man, a kid with a bum leg and a Jew, play ball together? Baseball…my kind of game."

"Dwell in the positive, and somehow you'll get through the negative. Or as Mama used to say, 'When life gives you lemons, make marmalade!' Fooled you, didn't I?"

"Come hell or high water, I'll be at your wedding. A little thing like death won't keep me away."

"That is what makes us human, how we value life."

"Because in a lifetime, you'll go through a lot of things and you need to be strong to get through them all."

Acknowledgments

I would like to thank my incredible network of family and friends who helped make this book possible. To my parents, sisters, brother, niece, nephew, and cousins for allowing me to use details of our personal lives as incidents in this book.

To my mother, who exposed me at an early age to the wonders of reading and who has always encouraged my creativity.

To my brother, for building my Web site, which you should all visit at www.nanalenaskitchen.com.

To my aunt, Felice Saks, who has always fostered my literary skills and who is the ultimate resource for all things literary or pertaining to grammar.

To my childhood friend, Terri Denison, for being the first to publish some of my chapters in the *Southern Virginian Jewish News.*

To Dorothy Grob, mother of another childhood friend, for kashering my recipes and correcting my Yiddish.

To my incredible friends who read each draft and watched this grow from a box of recipe cards to a short story to a Web site to the book you hold in your hands today.

To the good guys at Dog Ear Publishing, Alan Harris, Miles Nelson, and Ray Robinson, for guiding me along this self-empowering path of self-publishing. To Susan Christophersen for her precise copyediting skills.

And last but not least, to my grandmother, Lena Goodman Herzberg, who taught me to find the good in every person, the heart of every situation, and, most important, who taught me about love.

Table of Contents

A woman of valor who can find?

Her price is far beyond rubies

She opens her hand to the needy

She is robed in strength and dignity

Many women have done superbly

But you surpass them all.

Beth Sholom Auxiliary
Woman of Valor Award
to Lena Herzberg
May 21, 1998

Introduction

Nana Lena was my mother's mother, Lena Goodman Herzberg. Her real name was Ida Lena, but she would have none of that. From an early age I remember life in her yellow kitchen with the white Formica countertops, a room that had once seemed quite modern and now, like its owner, showed signs of age. There was always something bubbling on the stove, some scent wafting from the oven, and Nana Lena chopping, stirring, molding, and baking. Whether it was brisket and potato kugel on Sunday, noodle kugel on special occasions, gefilte fish and matzo ball soup on Passover, seven-layer cookies and pecan tassies for weddings and bar mitzvahs, there was always something cooking in Nana Lena's kitchen.

Everyone worked at Nana Lena's, even the children. It was hard work done willingly, because we knew that we would soon taste the fruits of our labors. We came for more than the food: We came for her company. Nana Lena was a great cook and storyteller. Every recipe had at least one story to go with it.

I grew up listening to her stories, modern fairy tales of a long-ago, faraway land called Berkley, a transplanted bit of the Old World that had once thrived in a rural suburb of Norfolk, Virginia. A world where everyone knew everyone and people didn't lock their doors at night. When I was older there were other stories: about life and death, about honesty, courage, faith, responsibility, and family. This was the way she taught me the important things in life—by example. And what an example she set. She used to say, "You have to pay for the space you take up on earth," and "Make a Mitzvah. It will come back to you."

I realize now how fortunate I was to have had her as a guide through the twentieth century. Nana Lena was born July 4th, 1912. She experienced many of the great challenges of the past century. She lost a sister and a favorite aunt in the 1918 flu epidemic. She met and married my grandfather, Myer Herzberg, during the Great Depression. She watched as three of her brothers and two brothers-in-law shipped out in World War II, and when they returned, she threw herself into humanitarian causes to help the thousands of refugees the war had left behind. She witnessed man's inhumanity to man, as well as man's will to survive. She experienced the great miracles of science and technology: indoor plumbing, the flu shot, the refrigerator, the telephone, man walking on the moon—all during her lifetime.

My grandmother was a proud, second-generation American born on the Fourth of July. Her mother's parents, Elka and Muttel Gustomilsky, were from Kiev, and her mother, Minnie Gustomilsky, was born on a ship coming to America. Her father, Morris Goodman, came from Kovno, Lithuania, in the late 1880s, through the port of Baltimore. In 1905, Minnie and Morris met and married in Baltimore and started their own family. In 1910, the Goodman family moved to Berkley, a small Jewish enclave across the river from Norfolk, Virginia. My grandmother was the fifth of ten children, eight of whom had survived. She grew up in a house filled with life. There were four Goodman brothers (Leon, Pete, Mike, and Sidney), three sisters (Goldie, Fannie, and Poogie), and her parents, Minnie and Morris: Ten people living in four rooms, often sleeping two and three to a bed. Just across the yard lived her father's parents in a house filled with aunts and uncles. Around the corner lived her father's mother's family, the Finestones, and more aunts, uncles, and cousins. The Goodman family lived one block from the *shul* and two blocks from the nearest streetcar, in an old Southern neighborhood with rocking chairs on the front porch; you could sit outside on a summer night and watch the world go by.

Lena's father, Morris, had a variety of businesses, as a man with ten children must. In the winter, he went up into the mountains of North Carolina and bought furs, which he sold from a large screened-in porch in the back of his mother's house. In the summer, he owned an ice business from which he or one of the boys delivered large blocks of ice to the wealthier homes in Berkley. Later he had a candy shop and was one of the first businesses in Berkley to offer curbside service selling "Snow Cream in Summer." Too bad no one in the family bothered to write down the recipe.

Lena's mother, Minnie, was what they call a real *balebuste*. Bubbie Minnie, as I called her, always reminded me of a little tornado, but I guess it takes that much energy to handle such a large family. As the children grew up, they were assigned tasks in the various family businesses, or in the kitchen, a world in which Lena excelled.

Nana Lena's food wasn't fancy; it was hearty, rib-sticking Jewish food: brisket and latkes and blintzes and kugel, that kind of thing; but I never heard any complaints, and there rarely was a drop of food left on anyone's plate. She was especially well known for her desserts: rugelach, strudel, mandelbrot, and my favorite, pecan tassies, little pecan pies. She was always baking something for an *Oneg Shabbat* after services, or for that nice girl down the block who just had a new baby, or for one of our family weddings or bar mitzvahs.

My grandmother and I shared a bond that is special to grandmothers and granddaughters, a kind of love that often skips a generation. From the moment I walked into her house, I knew that I was loved: the hugs and kisses, the favorite food that had been lovingly prepared, her undivided attention and praise—these were the gifts that I received in her kitchen, and every one of them came from the heart. Nana Lena never scrimped on love; she dished it out in bowlfuls.

After my Nana died, I looked for a way for keep her in my life. I took out all the old photos and letters that I had saved. Even though Nana was gone, they were a great comfort. I could still see her beaming from ear to ear as she held my newborn body in her arms, or how regally she stood beside me at my bat mitzvah celebration. I reread the letters telling me how much she adored me, and traced my fingers along the lacy edge of birthday cards she had spent hours selecting: the fancy ones with sentimental poems inside. Then I took out the audio tapes I had made, years ago, of Nana Lena telling stories from the old days in Berkley. At first, I played them just to hear her voice. Later I realized what a treasure trove of material I had managed to save, and I decided to write this book. Some of the stories come almost directly from the tapes; the rest I pieced together from fragments of memories, phone calls with my family, and diligent online research. Sometimes I would just start cooking a recipe and memories would come flooding in. If I ever got too far off track, I could hear Nana Lena's voice reining me in: "Amele, you know I would never say that. Your grandmother's a lady... most "of" the time."

As I was writing this book, Nana Lena came alive for me again. Sometimes I felt that she was right there in the room writing with me. I did not feel her hand on my shoulder, or see her standing beside me, but I could hear her whisper in my ear as she guided me along the way. At one point, I was struggling with how to tell the story about my mother's birth. I had gone to sleep exhausted when Nana dragged me out of bed: "It was snowing the night your mother came into this world." I heard my grandmother tell me and I began to type.

A brief word about structure. Each chapter is a unit unto itself. First, there is the recipe or cooking level: Nana Lena and I in the kitchen, making one of her specialties. Then there is the story level, where Nana Lena tells one or more stories from her past. I have tried to group the stories in an order that mirrors her life. On this level, Lena is a child as my book begins, and then a young woman, and then a bride, mother, grandmother, and so on. My own age jumps back and forth a bit, because certain stories were for children and other stories came when I was mature enough to understand. Nana Lena's stories also move back and forth in time. One minute it is 1919, and the next minute it is 1944, but in the end you would understand the connection. Sometimes you'd think she was telling you a story you already knew, and then she'd fill in a few more details and the story would take on a new meaning. And finally, there is the trick of time: Memories mutate and take on a meaning of their own.

I'm not saying that my grandmother was an authority on Jewish history and customs. Ever the Southern lady, she had those ribald jokes that she loved. What I do know is that in a hard life, a life that saw many deaths and great grief, she carried on for nearly eighty-seven years with great compassion and a nearly Pollyanna-like faith in the good she seemed to see in almost everyone.

Nana Lena's recipes are for more than just food: they are recipes for life. If you want a life filled with love and family, follow Nana Lena's recipes. Whenever possible, I have remained faithful to Nana Lena's stories and language. Sometimes I had to beat in an egg to hold it all together, but the basic ingredients are hers all the same: one part family, two parts love, a cup of faith, and a pinch of sass. Together they tell the story of a remarkable woman who spoke Yiddish with a Southern accent as she journeyed through the twentieth century, spreading her legacy of love, laughter, and good food.

For years, I have cherished her recipes and the lessons in life that I learned at her table. Now I want to share them with the world. I hope you enjoy Nana Lena's recipes.

P.S. For those of you who are unfamiliar with Yiddish, you will find a glossary of terms at the end of the book.

Nana Lena's Intro

"Amele, when I touch 'record', 'record' and 'play' went down together. Is that right?"

"Yes, Nana. It's like life: record and play often go down at the same time."

Nana Lena settled back in her chair and cleared her throat.

This is the beginning of a long-awaited project. Many, many years ago my precious granddaughter Amy asked me to please record any and all of the "I remembers" which I always managed to get into conversation. Procrastinator that I am, I never started the project. However, for this, my seventy-sixth birthday—oh, excuse me, my seventy-eighth—the girls bought me a Sony recorder, and I am now recording the project which I promised her many years ago. Of course, it will come in dribs and drabs. But she says that's okay, because she will put it together after I have finished the recording.

When I tell you that my electronic ability is nil, please believe me. I have sat with this little wonder-box for over fifteen minutes trying to wonder how to turn it on, and suddenly, I hit record/play, and it's going like magic. Anyhow, today is July the 4th, my seventy-ninth... Oh God, before I was behind, now I'm ahead. Well, that's wishful thinking. I hope I live to see my seventy-ninth.

Today, my seventy-eighth, I am in fairly good health, when I don't have the knee bothering me or the eye not seeing and the ear not hearing. But I'm not bad for an old broad, and not one to complain. Well, here goes. I don't know what will be uncovered in this taping; nothing that I would not want you to know. I'm not stupid. So, Amele, I hope you brought lots of tape. I have lots of stories to tell.

Poor Fish

I remember coming home from school. I was six, maybe seven years old. I was chasing my sister Goldie up the stairs when I heard the sound of laughter coming from the bathroom. I thought my brothers were taking their bath; so I was surprised, when I burst into the bathroom, to find Mike and Pete fully clothed, leaning over the edge of the tub poking at a very large fish, which was swimming nervously back and forth in Mama's new porcelain pedestal bathtub.

I knew how much Mama treasured her bathtub. Indoor plumbing had only recently been introduced into the neighborhood and Mama was proud to have one of the first houses in Berkley with an indoor bath. Mama regularly led tours of her new bathroom, for our less fortunate neighbors, so I was having a hard time imagining her approval of this situation. "Irving Goodman, you tell Papa to get that poor fish out of there before Mama finds out."

"Poor Fish," two-year-old Mike mimicked.

Four-year-old Pete turned to me and in the sweetest little voice said, "Mama says we're gonna eat him for Pesach."

"We are most certainly not."

"Yes, we aaaa-rre. Momma's gonna make Gefillupte-fish."

"Gefilte fish."

"That's what I said… you fill it up with…something."

"But Mama said…."

Just then, Mama called from downstairs, "Lena, Goldie, get down here and help me in the kitchen."

"I don't care what Mama said," I told my brothers. "We can't eat him; we know him. He's practically family. For gosh sakes, he's swimming around in our bathtub."

Goldie poked her head in the bathroom. "I see Mama got the fish."

"You knew about this?"

"Of course I did."

"She never brought a live one home before."

"We never had an indoor bathtub before." Goldie flicked a

towel at me and darted out of the room, cackling.

I turned back to my brothers, "We've got to think of something, or tomorrow he's gonna be..."

"Dead," Pete nodded sadly.

"Poor fish."

I joined Mama and Goldie in the kitchen. They were in the process of making horseradish. Goldie was seventeen months older than me, so Mama let her handle the more dangerous tools. Goldie grated the radish while I was assigned to baby duty, like crushing walnuts or sorting rice. This time it was raisins, good from the bad, dark from light. Mama preferred yellow raisins, so any raisin bold enough to turn dark or shrivel up had to be eliminated. I obliged by eating the dark ones and pushing the shriveled ones aside. I had completed my task and was presenting my handiwork to Mama when Goldie screamed, "Darn it!"

"Goldie! Such language!"

"What's the matter? "

"I cut myself."

"Run it under the water, quick." Mama dragged Goldie's thumb over to the sink and then squeezed it hard until it bled.

"Owwwwh. What you do that for?"

"To make sure the wound is clean." She looked at Goldie's thumb, which had two deep cuts from the grater, and shook her head. "This is not good. Lena, get me the iodine and a bandage." She turned her attention back to Goldie. "Now you won't be able to make the gefilte fish."

I ran to the pantry to fetch the iodine and then stood and listened to their conversation, breathless.

Goldie said, "It's just a little cut, Mama. I'll be fine..."

"You can't put your hands in the fish with a cut on your finger. Not in my kitchen and definitely not in your Bubbie Sareva's kitchen."

"But, Mama..."

"Lena will make the fish."

"Lena's still a baby."

"Not so much anymore. She will take your place."

"But, Mama...

"Lena will help this year. And next year, you will both help."

I stood there trembling, knowing how furious Goldie would be with me if I helped make the fish, and knowing what an honor it was to be invited to my grandmother's kitchen. Then again, there was Poor Fish.

That night at dinner, I noticed that the pan under the icebox was probably large enough to hold Poor Fish. My plan was to get the fish back out to the river and set it free. After everyone had gone to bed, I crept downstairs to the pantry to retrieve my mother's pan, and then went back upstairs to the bathroom, making sure not to step on the second stair from the top because it squeaked. I carefully closed the bathroom door before turning on the light.

There he was, Poor Fish, gills pumping, hardly moving, looking up at me with those sad fish eyes. I had to do something. After several attempts, I succeeded in capturing the confused carp and placing it in the pan; then I added some water so it could breathe. As I was lifting the tray from the tub, the fish flung itself out onto the checkerboard-tiled floor. Poor Fish lay there, mouth and fins gaping. I finally managed to pick him up and put him in the pan, when I slipped on a wet spot, and fell, making such a clatter that it woke everyone in the house.

Within seconds, my older brother Leon arrived, flashing his police badge. "Hold it right there, young lady!"

My other brothers and sisters arrived, along with Mama and Papa, and they stood in the doorway, pointing at me and laughing.

I can still remember Mama, standing there, hands on her hips, shaking her head. "Lena! That is not the pan for the fish. Look, Morris, how excited she is. She can hardly wait for the cooking."

I could have stood up to my mother and made a scene, as you young people say nowadays, about saving Poor Fish, but the truth was that as much as I hated that the fish had to die, I was greatly honored to be allowed to participate in preparing Passover with my mother and grandmother, in my grandmother's kitchen. And this time, it was no baby recipe. We were making gefilte fish.

I slipped the fish back into the bathtub and looked up at my mother for approval, but all she said was, "Clean it up and go to sleep."

The next morning, I joined my mother and my father's mother, Bubbie Sareva, and my Tante Fannie, my father's sister, in my grandmother's kitchen, in the making of gefilte fish, a family recipe handed down from generation to generation. This time it was my turn to learn.

The teakettle interrupted with a loud annoying whistle. "I'll get it, Nana. Where's the coffee?"

"In the cabinet, by the stove."

"You know, you should really keep it in the freezer to keep it fresh." I looked inside the cabinet, "You still use instant coffee?"

"There's nothing wrong with instant."

"Haven't you heard of Starbucks?"

"At three dollars fifty cents a cup? Are you kidding?"

I handed the cup of instant coffee to Nana Lena.

"I remember when it was a nickel a cup, and that was with refills."

I took a sip of the instant coffee and winced. "There's a reason we spend the money on the coffee, Nana."

Nana Lena handed me a cutting board, a knife, and a bowl of onions. "Save the skins." She walked over to the sink and began scrubbing her hands and arms. "Let me tell you, it's not so easy to make gefilte fish. First, we put on aprons and washed our hands and arms, like on that show you watch, the one with the cute doctors."

"You mean 'ER', Nana?"

"Yes, that one." Then she continued.

Bubbie Sareva inspected my hands and nails. She sat me down in front of a mound of onions and barked orders at me. "Peel them, and then cut them in quarters. Save the skins for the broth."

I began peeling onions while she and Tante Fannie went out back and separated Poor Fish from his head.

As I chopped and peeled the onions, tears pouring down my face, I decided that if Poor Fish had to die for our meal, then I was determined that the least I could do was to make this the best gefilte fish ever. I would make Poor Fish proud. So I continued chopping the onions and crying my eyes out. Some of my tears must have ended up in the recipe.

At the other end of the kitchen, Bubbie and Tante Fannie skinned and de-boned the fish, while Mama prepared a pot of boiling water, to which she added one stalk of celery, three onions with their skins separated, parsnips, carrots, and the fish head.

While this broth simmered on the stove, the women cleaned the rest of the fish and set up the grinder, inserting alternating pieces of fish, celery, and onions.

"In Galicia they use the sugar in the broth." Bubbie Sareva bent over the pot and skimmed off some foam.

"Tante Gussie sometimes used the beets, remember, Mama?"

"Not in my kitchen." Bubbie Sareva nodded her approval of the broth to Minnie. "So tell me, what happened to our Goldele?"

Tante Fannie leaned forward, concerned. "Is it a bad cut?"

Minnie shook her head. "I think she did it on purpose."

"No."

"She wouldn't."

"She hates the smell."

"Can you blame her?"

All three women made a face.

"We may not like how it smells, but we like how it tastes." Bubbie Sareva looked over at Lena, who beamed happily even though her face was streaked with tears. "What's done is done, and why Goldele chose not to join us is Goldele's problem. But this little one...."

"My Lena." Minnie beamed proudly.

Bubbie Sareva nodded her head, "She likes the kitchen. She is at home here." She waved to her granddaughter, "Come, Lena, let me show you how we make the fish."

Mama removed the fish head and strained the broth, which had now reached a beautiful golden-brown color. Lena watched intently as Tante Fannie handed her mother each of the items she mentioned.

"Now we add the eggs, a half an eggshell of salt, a *bisele*, just a little white pepper, not the brown, and a *yahrzeit* glass of matzo meal. Mix it together good, like this. Use a little more matzo meal if it's too runny. Let me see the hands. Are they clean?"

I nodded eagerly, waving them in front of her.

"Now wet your hands and take a handful of this and rub it into a ball, and then we drop it into the boiling broth like this!"

"Be careful when you drop it, so you don't splash and burn yourself." Tante Fannie warned me, as she gently tied my hair back, out of my face: Tante Fannie, whose hands always smelled like vanilla.

I pushed my sleeves up and dipped my hands into the mixture. It's cold and slimy, like a mud pie. I made a ball and dropped it gently into the water.

"Perfect. Her hands are just the right size."

I made another and dropped it in a little less gently. I made dozens of balls, dropping them in one after the other, until all of the mixture was gone, and dozens of little balls, about two inches in diameter, started bubbling to the surface of our witches' brew.

"Like I said, she's a natural." Bubbie Sareva patted her granddaughter's head. "In the old days, after the fish cooked, we used to wrap the balls in the fish skin and that's why we called it gefilte fish, because we filled the fish." She flashed her daughter and daughter-in-law a look. "Now we are in America. We don't need such a thick skin."

"Mama, if you want to keep the skin, we can keep it...."

"Your Tante Fannie wants to be a modern woman."

"Mother, if it really bothers you...."

Mama led me to the sink so that I could wash my hands. Then she squeezed lemon over them.

"Come, Lena, now is the best part."

"What, Bubbie?"

"Now we sit and drink a *glassl* tea with a touch of schnaps."

"But, Mama, she's only a child."

"She can make the fish, she can have the tea. She earned it."

They all nodded and patted me on the back. I earned it. And you know what was the best part? It was the best gefilte fish ever. I made Poor Fish proud.

"Ever since then, I've made gefilte fish for Passover," Nana Lena stood at the counter, up to her elbows in fish mush, as she formed the balls and dropped them into the bubbling liquid. "Not so big. Like this." She showed me her fish balls, smooth and uniform, about the size of a golf ball. I make them round, you see. But sometimes people make them like this." She reshaped the ball in a few strokes into a more oval shape. "Boat shaped."

"I'm not very good at this, Nana."

"You just need practice. Yes, that's much better. See."

"You're not just saying that?"

Nana Lena smiled and wisely did not answer.

"It seems like an awful lot of trouble to me."

"It's a lot easier now. You can buy fresh fish without having to kill it yourself. Sometimes you can even get the butcher to grind it up for you. *If you do it yourself, you know what you've got.* Remember that, write that down. I am telling you important things."

"Yes, Nana."

"I love you, my Amele."

"I love you too, Nana. But the jarred fish is good enough, and it's a lot less work."

"Good enough? Yes, I suppose it is good enough...for a stranger, perhaps. Good enough, when there is no time for anything else. But the way I look at it...is it good enough for my family? Is it the healthiest, freshest gefilte fish I can make? Is it as filled with love? Then...it's good enough, *farshtéyst?*"

I looked at my Nana, who, at seventy-five, had to be the wisest person on earth, dropping her little balls of love into the bubbling waters of life, and I nodded.

"Yes, Nana, I understand."

* * *

Gefilte Fish

This is a loose translation of Nana's fish recipe. It's an enormous amount of work, and requires a fish grinder, a tool not found in every modern kitchen. Nana didn't measure; she did everything by touch and taste. All I can say is that if you are brave enough to make this recipe, "Ess gezundhayt": "Eat it in good health!" And invite a lot of people. This recipe feeds 20–30 people.

Fish

Ask the nice man at the fish counter to filet 20 lbs of Rockfish, Trout and Pike. This yields about 9–10 pounds of fish meat. Keep the heads and bones, and scrape the remaining meat from the bones. (Don't be wasteful! This can yield up to another pound.) The fish heads will be used to prepare the stock and give it a strong flavor. If you aren't making the fish the same day, you can buy it in advance and freeze it, separating the fish filets between pieces of waxed paper. Make sure the fish is completely defrosted before grinding.

Stock

Fill a large 5-gallon pot about 2/3 full with water. While you are waiting for it to boil, add the following ingredients and let them simmer for about 1/2 hour.

   2 onions, cut up, including skins

   3 fish heads

   3 stalks celery

   4–5 carrots, peeled and cut into thick chunks

   salt and white pepper to taste

Skim off the brown foam that accumulates on the top of the water. After broth has achieved golden brown color, remove the carrots and set aside for later.

Carefully remove the fish heads, and strain all remaining items from the broth, twice. Return the clear broth to the large pot and bring to a boil.

Fish Mixture

3–4 onions (no skins!)	a dozen eggs
2–3 stalks celery (peeled)	2 cups water
fish filets from above, and bits of fish culled from the bones.	salt and white pepper matzo meal

Before you begin to grind the fish, check one more time for bones and bits of skin. Rinse each piece and squeeze off the excess water with your hands. Set up your grinder. Nana Lena had the old-fashioned kind you clamped onto the kitchen counter, the kind you could take apart and clean thoroughly before and after making the fish. You'll need a large mixing bowl positioned under the grinder, and a small pushing tool. Alternate inserting the three types of fish with pieces of onions and celery until all the fish has been ground. Mix it well so that there are no dark areas or white areas, just a uniform mixture of fish, onions, and celery.

Beat up a dozen eggs in the blender. It makes them fluffier this way. Alternate adding the eggs and the water to the fish mixture. Mix thoroughly. Salt and pepper to taste.

Now add 1/2 cup of matzo meal and mix well. Keep adding a little at a time until you feel that the fish is firm enough to shape into balls. Nana would pick up a handful, shape it into a ball, and, if it were too runny, she'd add a little more matzo meal until it was right. Somewhere between 1 and 2 cups, you will find the right texture.

Shape a golf-ball-sized "tester" and drop it into the boiling stock. If you see a flake or two rise to the top, that's okay, but if you see the ball break up into several parts, then you don't have enough matzo meal.

Keep a dish of water handy to dip your hands in between balls. Drop the balls in one at a time. At first they will fall to the bottom, but eventually they will rise to the surface. Bring to a boil. Cover and simmer for 2 1/2–3 hours. Shake the pot from time to time so that the balls don't stick.

Carefully remove the gefilte fish from the broth with a slotted spoon. Store in airtight containers in the refrigerator. Serve chilled with a slice of carrot and a sprig of parsley on top, and a dollop of horseradish on the side.

Noodle Kugel

I cracked the egg and watched it slide slowly down the side of the bowl, colliding with the other yolks, splitting one in two. The next egg cracked with a hollow sound. Instinctively I emptied it into a smaller dish. Inside the egg, a dead baby chick. It wasn't the first time I had seen death. It was the timing. I was making a noodle pudding to take to the Finestones, who had lost their daughter Rivka in the flu epidemic that was ravaging the country. Rivka and my sister Bertha were in the same class at school. Rivka and Bertha had been inseparable. Now Rivka was dead and poor Bertha inconsolable. As I stared at the dead chick, I thought of Rivka.

Mama always said that a good noodle kugel is the best thing for a *Shivah* table. It is good hot or cold, and if it's *milkhik*, you can eat it for breakfast. Sometimes she made a *fleyshik* one, when Uncle Yanks was in town. There are as many variations of noodle kugel as there are cooks. Tante Fannie and my mother disagreed on which fruit to add: apples or raisins. Bubbie Sareva favored pot cheese over sour cream. I liked my kugel sweet and cheesy with a trace of vanilla and a little cinnamon on top.

I opened the icebox and noticed that the tray underneath it needed to be emptied, but I was in a hurry and couldn't be bothered. Inside I found farmer's cheese, sour cream, and plenty of cream cheese. I mixed the good eggs with a teaspoon of vanilla and a cup of brown sugar. Then I added a cup of raisins, and waited for the noodles to drain. I greased mother's kugel pan, combined the noodles with the cheese mixture, and poured it into the pan, sprinkling cinnamon and brown sugar over the top.

It was rare to find this kitchen so empty. Bubbie Sareva was helping the *Chevra Kadesha* prepare the body for the funeral. Mama was with Tante Finestone, who was beside herself with grief. Tante Fannie was taking care of Bertie, whose eyes were red with weeping for her friend.

I had the kitchen to myself. I placed the kugel in the oven and smiled. Then I thought of why I was making it and my heart fell.

A week later Bertie still hadn't stopped crying. Only now you couldn't hear her, she was so weak with flu. She had been moved to a room off the porch, and Aunt Fannie had moved in with her. We, the children, weren't allowed to visit, for fear that we might catch the disease, but sometimes Aunt Fannie let us stand in the doorway to talk to Bertie.

Toward the end of the week, Bertie couldn't lift her head even to take a sip of water. Her skin was gray in color, her hair damp with sweat; her eyes didn't see us, her thoughts were in another time: "Yes, Rivka, I would like that. The pink one, in the pretty dress."

I remembered Bertie's last birthday, when Rivka and Tante Finestone had come to visit, and the look on Bertie's face when she first saw the doll, a brand-new doll in a pink satin dress, not a used doll that had been passed down from sister to sister and was missing an arm or a leg.

Aunt Fannie dabbed Bertha's forehead with a cool cloth. "She's not herself today."

"Is she mine, really?" Bertie smiled. "She's beautiful."

"I think you better go now, Lena. Bertie needs to rest." My eyes teared up as I turned to leave. Tante Fannie called after me, "Say goodbye to your sister."

I took a small step into the room, knowing I could go no further. "I'll see you in heaven, Bertie, one of these fine days."

"It was the tradition back then to wear uniforms to school," Nana Lena continued. I remember wearing a little white blouse, with a blue jumper, and big blue bows in our hair. The boys wore white shirts and blue pants. When word got out that Bertha had died, the children started arriving, dressed in their blue and white uniforms, standing silently in the yard. Public assembly was frowned upon back then: There was fear that it might spread the disease. I think her entire class gathered that evening in tribute to their friend. Their teacher, Mrs. Rabinowitz, stood there fighting back the tears. The Finestones opened their front door and stood on the porch across the way. We all came outside and stood on the porch, silently thanking them all for coming.

"For a moment, I saw Bertie standing there, in her blue and white uniform, holding that pink doll, with her other arm around her beloved Rivka."

"You actually saw her?

Nana nodded. "She was happy. She wanted me to know. It's comforting, really, knowing that the people you love will be with you when your time comes."

"Of course we'll be with you, Nana."

Nana Lena stood looking out the window for a moment longer. "God be willing." Then she clapped her hands and took charge in typical Nana Lena fashion. "All right, I need a pot of water for the noodles. Use the gefilte fish pot. We need to make a double batch."

"Who died? I don't want to know."

"Mrs. Kaminsky from the Temple Sisterhood, and the Thornes' son, Michael." She lowered her voice, "Suicide."

"My friend from across the street who I used to swim with when I was, I don't know, twelve?"

"Yes. Such a nice-looking boy."

"CiCi must be beside herself."

Noodle kugels aren't only for funerals. A good kugel is perfectly acceptable at a *bris*, baby naming, bar mitzvah brunch, or confirmation. Lena had made so many kugels over the years that there wasn't a home on her block that hadn't received one of those Pyrex dishes with her name on it. Neighbors knew that you could leave the empty Pyrex on Lena's back porch, or, better still, you could return it filled with some other dish, such as stuffed peppers or eggplant parmigiana. She looked out for the neighbors, and they looked out for her. She cooked a kugel, and they made whatever they liked to cook. It was a kind of food-based karmic exchange.

The concept of a kugel can be confusing, because in German, which Yiddish draws heavily from, a kugel usually means something round: a ball, globe, sphere, or bullet, as the case may be. Potato kugels *are* round because they are cooked in a round cast-iron skillet; at least that's how we do it in our family. Noodle *kugel* is usually made in a square or rectangular pan and cut into cubes. It can be served as a side dish or eaten as a meal. It's a comforting, Jewish soul food made from eggs and noodles, two foods that symbolize the continuity of life: eggs, round like life, and noodles, going on and on without end.

CiCi Thorne sat in the dark, chain-smoking cigarettes. A glass of scotch rested on the table near her. She looked up but did not recognize me.

"CiCi, it's Amy."

"Amy," CiCi's voice quivered.

"I'm so sorry."

CiCi stared into space, nodding.

Nana Lena lifted the casserole, "We brought you a kugel."

"A what? Put it over there." CiCi pointed to an empty space in the middle of the living room.

Nana shook her head sadly. "I'll put it in the kitchen for you in case you get hungry later."

I could see that eating was the furthest thing from CiCi's mind.

Nana Lena disappeared into the kitchen and returned. "You got people coming over here to take care of you?"

CiCi nodded slowly.

Lena lifted her glasses to rub her eyes. "Well, you call me if you need anything, you hear?"

I slammed the front door without meaning to. "She looks terrible."

"Can you blame her? I don't know *what* I'd do if something happened to your mother, or to one of you. It's a horrible thing to watch your own child die. It's not supposed to happen that way. In 1918, my Bubbie Sareva lost a child and a grandchild in the same year. She was never the same."

I took her arm as we walked home.

"More Americans died during the 1918 flu epidemic than in both of the great wars combined. Over a half a million Americans lost their lives, including my sister Bertha *and* my dear Aunt Fannie."

"Tante Fannie, too?"

"Yes, the poor dear. She was Papa's sister, the middle of nine children and the only one to never marry, which was quite a shame, because mothering was in her nature. She was a kind and gentle soul, with long beautiful hair, which she wore in braids wrapped around her head like a crown. After nursing Bertha, Tante Fannie got the flu and almost died of it. She recovered for a while, we thought, but two months later she was still in such a weakened state that she succumbed to tuberculosis. She was only twenty-three.

"She was pretty, her face pale, almost iridescent, as they brushed her long hair which reached down past her waist. The ladies of the *Chevra Kadesha* had come to clean and dress her, to prepare her for a proper burial, and to sit with the body until it was buried. I remember watching from the side porch, through a small hole in the screen, as they bathed her body and wrapped her in her shroud. She looked even younger in the long white gown, untouched, like an angel.

"If Tante Fannie had not played nursemaid to Bertha, would she have married and had children of her own? She knew the risk, yet she took it willingly. Oh, how Papa cursed himself for allowing her to stay. If it hadn't been Fannie, it might have been Mama, or Goldie, or me. I thought about her bravery, her selfless sacrifice. I decided I wanted to be like Tante Fannie when I grew up."

"Never break the noodles. Leave them whole," it says on Nana's recipe card, in her clean, neat handwriting, and I follow the directions, substituting applesauce for margarine, currants for raisins, using the ingredients I have on hand as I prepare a kugel for an Upper West Side *bris*. At least in New York I don't have to explain what a kugel is.

Every time I make a noodle kugel, I think of Nana Lena, Great Aunt Bertha, Great-Great Aunt Fannie, and the millions who lost their lives in the flu epidemic of 1918. I am grateful to be the one making the noodle kugel, rather than the one for whom it is being made. But then again, it is a kugel. You always begin and end in the same place.

"Give a kugel, get a kugel," my Nana would say. "Or sometimes you get a sweet potato pie."

* * *

Lena's Noodle Kugel

*There are as many kugel recipes as there are cooks. You can
pretty much interchange what dairy products you use, whether
you use applesauce, fresh apples, or crushed pineapple. I've
used currants or dried cranberries instead of raisins. Some
people prefer to cook their noodles first. Experiment! A
successful kugel can be made with pretty much anything.*

12-ounce package medium or wide egg noodles

6 well beaten eggs

2 cups milk

1/2 stick melted margarine, cooled

1 1/2 tsp vanilla

3 tsp lemon juice

3/4 cup sugar

3/4 cup raisins, steamed in a small amount of sherry, then
drained

1 can pie-sliced apples, drained, or 4 apples grated on medium
grater, or 2 cups applesauce

Boil noodles and drain. Or not. Lena boiled her noodles,
while her sister Poogie insisted there was no need to precook the
noodles, as long as the milk and egg mixture covered them.

In a large mixing bowl, combine the eggs, milk, margarine,
vanilla, lemon juice, sugar and raisins. To this mixture, add the
drained apple slices, grated apples or applesauce. Add the
noodles. Mix thoroughly.

Butter a 9x13 pan or Pyrex dish or two 8x8 pans. Pour the
kugel mixture into the pan. Sprinkle with sugar and cinnamon.
Bake in preheated 325° oven for one hour, or more, until firm and
golden brown on top.

This dish can be prepared in advance and returned to a 325°
oven for half an hour before serving. Also good served at room
temperature.

Elka & Muttel Gustomilsky, Lena's
maternal grandparents

Joseph & Sareva Goodman,
Lena's paternal grandparents

Minnie Gustomilsky & her
sister Ida in Baltimore 1905,
shortly before her wedding

Minnie & Morris Goodman, 1908

Lena & Goldie, 1914

Sidney (infant), Leon, Pete, Mike, Fannie, Lena, Goldie, 1920

Fannie, Lena, Sidney, Poogie, 1929

Lena & Sidney

A Berkley Thanksgiving

My grandfather Joseph Goodman, my *Zeyde*, lived with my Bubbie Sareva in a house located at a 45° angle across the street from our house in the block next to the synagogue. You could call over to their house from our back porch. Bubbie and Zeyde Goodman were from Kovno, a small town in Lithuania, the old world, and Zeyde talked with a thick accent. In the old country, Zeyde was known as Yossi der Viner, Joseph the winemaker. In Berkley, we certainly didn't have a vineyard, but Zeyde still liked to make wine for the holidays.

One day, Zeyde stood out on his porch and yelled over to me, '*Schick mir arayn mein Leike*' (bring me my Leike)." Now, Leike is my Yiddish name, so I thought he wanted *me*. I went over there to his house, and I said. 'Here I am, Zeyde.'"

"*Was is du gekomm'n*? (Why are you here?) Where is my Leike?'"

"But, Zeyde, I *am* your Leike."

"No, no, no. *Ich will mein **Leike**!*" Then he made a motion with his hands and I realized that he wanted his *funnel* to pour the wine into the bottles. *Leike* is also funnel in Yiddish.

Berkley was a community. Everybody was related or interrelated. When it came time for the holidays, Papa would go out to the country and bring back buckets of fresh river trout, a coop of chickens, crates of eggs, and mounds of vegetables. He would unload everything in the backyard and Mama would call the Kuzines and the Tantes and the Bubbies, and everybody would come and get their share. Papa would have *never* gone and bought just for Mama. It was the kind of relationship where you bought for *everybody*...all your kinfolk.

Berkley was the kind of place where if one mother was away, another mother, whoever was home, would nurse the baby when the baby had to be fed, and if anybody questioned it she would say, "Look, the baby was hungry. I gave him something to eat!"

If you baked on Friday, you never baked just for yourself. You always baked a *challah* for this one, a pan of *berches*—what you call sweet buns—for that one. It was an interchange. You always shared.

For the holidays, Zeyde used to make *med*. It's like beer, but it's made from honey. It brewed for a long time until it got the right taste. The first two quarts went to the family doctor, Dr. Irving Chapman, and one went to the man who ran the drugstore, Dr. Thompson. They always got the first bottle of beer and the first box of matzo. Papa took that to them each year. This was Papa's way of thanking them for helping him take care of his ten children, for keeping the medical care and the medicine flowing, even when the money wasn't. Life was like that, back then. You looked after each other, and somehow, we all got by.

One year, it was *Succos*, the festival of the fall harvest, a day of thanksgiving for earth's great bounty. Nowadays, we hardly celebrate it, but when we were kids, it was a night of magic. It was Indian summer and still quite warm. That year, Zeyde had decided to hold *Succos* in the barn behind our house. At first, Bubbie didn't think it was a very good idea, but on this particular year our family was going to be larger than ever, and the barn was the largest space where all of us could eat. Once Bubbie was resigned to using the barn, she launched a sanitation campaign to end all campaigns. All of us children helped.

The animals were moved to the pasture behind our house, and we began removing all straw and hay and animal droppings, sweeping until the dirt floor seemed to shine. We wiped down every surface of that barn until Bubbie was satisfied. Then the Aunts and Uncles started bringing out their dining tables. The kids helped by bringing the chairs. Pete was quite little, about five, and he was struggling to carry a chair that was twice his size. Everybody tried to help him, but he kept repeating, "I can do it. I can do it." And he did. He dragged it all the way over to the barn…all by himself.

We decorated the barn with pumpkins and corn and dried flowers and whatever else we could find to commemorate the harvest. We put candles on the tables because there was no electricity in the barn. We decorated the table with grapes and pomegranates.

The children went home to bathe and dress, while the women put the finishing touches on the food they were preparing and the men went to synagogue to say the evening prayers.

We gathered in the barn just before sunset to light the candles.

The sky was purple and the moon hung low on the horizon, shimmering, orange, a full Harvest Moon. We lit the candles. Then the barn was bathed in a golden light, which made everything that much more special. The Tantes and the Kuzines started arriving, everyone carrying trays of food. Bubbie Sareva made her specialty, rolled cabbage. Mama made vegetable soup. Tante Celia brought stuffed squash and stuffed tomatoes, and Aunt Belle had brought the strudel. Almost all of the items were stuffed, or filled, commemorating the harvest and times of plenty.

Pete and Irving chased each other around the table, waving the *lulav*, the dried branch made up of palm, myrtle, and willow that made a noise like a rattle. The barn had a lemony scent from the *esrog*, the special citrus that was brought in from Palestine for the holiday. An *esrog* is slightly larger than a lemon, and more bitter. The women stood around the table chatting, waiting for the men.

I remember sitting there at the table, hanging my head backwards over the chair, seeing the first stars twinkling through the cracks in the roof, and I knew Papa would be there soon. It's a wonderful thing to dine under the stars because when you start thanking God for all his bounty, you feel that much closer to him.

Zeyde, Papa, and his brothers arrived to boisterous greetings, exchanging hugs and kisses all around.

"Good *yontif*, Tante."

"Good *yontif*, Leon."

"Good *yontif*, Leike."

"Good *yontif*, Zeyde."

Then all the children lined up and Zeyde blessed each one. We recited the holiday prayer. Zeyde blessed the wine. Bubbie made the motzi. And then Zeyde said that since this was a day of thanksgiving, he thought we should go around the table and say what we were thankful for.

Zeyde started. "Tanks God for mein Family, and for my beautiful Sareva, the light of my life for almost forty years."

Bubbie Sareva's eyes misted up and she nodded happily. "I thank God for giving me another year with my family."

Pete thanked God and Bubbie Sareva for the rolled cabbage. Mike was grateful for the stuffed kneidlach. Goldie and I could only have been seven and eight years old; we said we were grateful for the new dresses that Papa had given us. And then

Yanks thanked Papa for his good wine, and his other brother, Al, thanked him for the great *med* Papa made last Pesach, and Mama thanked everybody for helping make the holiday a happy one.

Papa was silent a moment. Then he said, "I thank God that the Great War is over. I thank God that none of my brothers had to die in that war, and Minnie's brother Moe, may he rest in peace. I thank the United States of America, this country, my country, which took us in when we were no longer welcome at home. And for all the immigrants who have made it to these shores, I raise my glass. God bless the United States of America."

Everyone stood and raised their glass. "God bless these United States."

* * *

A world war later, three of my brothers were serving their country. Mike was in the Galapagos Islands; Pete and Sidney were stationed in Europe. Your mother and Myer and I shared *Succos* with your Bubbie and Zeyde on the back porch of our apartment on 36th Street. Elayne had colored drawings of *lulavs* and *esrogs*, and Myer had hung them from the lattice above. Mama and Papa arrived, and I could immediately sense that something was wrong. Papa looked so tired, like all life had been drained from him. He didn't even touch the chopped liver.

"Did something happen to one of the boys?" I asked Mama, and she just shook her head.

That night, Papa didn't start the familiar "what are we thankful for" game that we always played on *Succos*. Even Elayne, who was only eight, knew something was wrong when Papa finished the blessings and gave the official "let's eat," so she started it.

"Zeyde, haven't you forgotten something?"

"What, Elka, did I forget to say a *brokhe*?

"You know, Zeyde...what are we grateful for this year?"

"Oh, that." For a little while, Morris was silent. "I received, yesterday, a letter from your cousin Ruth in Cleveland. Her Uncle Hiam and her Aunt Sarah just arrived from Europe. The Department of Immigration tried to prevent them from entering, even though they had their sponsor letters, even though they had been told that they could enter the country, when they left Lithuania by way of Sweden over six months ago. From Sweden, they took a freighter, one hundred people packed in like so much cargo. When they arrived, they were held in detention, separated, threatened with deportation, branded as spies! Eventually immigration tired of that approach and turned them over to their family. *This* is how we are treated now! For *this* I should be thankful?"

"Morris, in front of *di kinder*."

"We're at war, Papa," Lena tried to reason with him.

"We are at war with Germany; we are at war with Japan. The Jews are not the enemy."

Myer agreed. "Morris is right. Less than ten thousand Jews have been allowed into the country since the war broke out, yet we send whole armies to Europe to fight for them. "

Morris slammed his fist on the table. "I am extremely disappointed in President Roosevelt. I thought he was our friend."

* * *

Many, many years later, my mother Elayne is grown and has four children of her own. We do not celebrate *Succot* anymore, but we celebrate Thanksgiving which is almost the same. So one year, we are sitting around the table, while my grandfather carved the turkey, when my mother started a new game. "Tell me, what are you thankful for?"

"Laney, you remembered? Like we used to play with Zeyde...."

"Of course I remember, Mama."

And Papa joined in willingly, "I'm thankful for my beautiful wife, the light of my life, my Lena."

Melissa wasn't talking yet, so she just banged her spoon on the highchair. David was thankful for his new bicycle, Donna was thankful for her new dress, and I was thankful for the good food.

My father said, "Amen to that."

Nana Lena's eyes sparkled as she looked out over her family. "I'm thankful to spend another year with my wonderful family. For this great *nachas*," she gave a quick glance toward heaven, "I will be forever grateful." She clapped her hands. "Eat up already, before it gets cold!"

* * *

Rolled Cabbage

Makes 20–24 cabbage rolls

For cabbage rolls

2 large heads of cabbage   1 cup matzo meal

3 lbs ground meat (lean)   1/3 cup ketchup

3 large eggs   1 cup water

3/4 cup diced onions   salt to taste

For sauce

Remaining cabbage, chopped   2 cans water

30 Ginger Snaps, crushed   1 cup brown sugar

2 large sliced onions   1 tsp Sour Salt

1/2 cup raisins   1/2 cup maple syrup

2 cans diced tomatoes   1/2 cup ketchup

4 Tbsp lemon juice

Core the two heads of cabbage, then either boil until leaves can be separated (and burn your fingers separating them) or freeze the cored cabbage overnight (and freeze your fingers separating them). Either way, you need about 30 large leaves. When you have finished separating the leaves, chop the broken pieces and smaller leaves and place them in the bottom of a 3x11x17 pan, or a large covered baking dish. Top with one thinly sliced onion. Cover with crushed Ginger Snaps.

Mix the meat, eggs, water, matzo meal, ketchup, diced onions and salt. Place a large meatball sized portion on each leaf, starting on the thicker end, and folding up the sides as you roll. Seal by placing the end flap down when you place it in the pan.

Place cabbage rolls on top of the cabbage mixture. Sprinkle with raisins.

To make sauce, combine all remaining ingredients and pour over the rolls. Cover with tough outer leaves. Cover tightly with foil or roasting pan lid. Bake at 350° approximately 3 hours.

Break Fast

It was Yom Kippur morning, I was six years old, and I had spent the night at Nana Lena's. Usually by this time, she would have prepared breakfast, which would consist of eight ounces of milk, six ounces of orange juice, a slice of challah, a *schmear* of margarine, and a flat-top eggie. Now, a "flat-top eggie" is not a traditional Jewish dish, nor is it a Southern concoction. A flat-top eggie was just another of the ways that Nana made us feel she was treating us special. It was only a thin egg pancake, made in a blintz pan, but to me it was the thinnest, tastiest egg in the world and she had made it just for me. This morning was different: breakfast wasn't waiting on the table. It was Yom Kippur.

Nana was already dressed, in a neat skirt and a silk blouse, with her gold Hadassah pin on the collar. "You'd better get dressed for *shul*. Don't forget to brush your teeth."

"But, Nana! The rabbi said…"

"I don't care what the rabbi said. No granddaughter of mine is going to have a mouthful of cavities. You heard me. Go on." I turned to go, knowing there was no use arguing. "Check on your Bubbie. See if she needs anything."

I had been raised in a Reform congregation, where some of the prayers were in Hebrew but most of the service was in English. It was an A-frame concrete and wooden structure, with wooden benches, rather like a church. Nana Lena attended a Conservative congregation in Norfolk. Although it was unlike the Orthodox synagogue Nana grew up in, the stained glass windows and the ornate eternal light were far more exotic than anything I had ever seen. The men wore *taleysim*, prayer shawls with fringes, and carried them in small blue velvet bags. The congregation was much larger than ours, and every seat was full. Nana seemed to know everyone, and everyone seemed genuinely happy to see her. I was sitting in Bubbie's seat. She had stayed home.

On more than one occasion, one of Nana's friends stopped next to our seats and exclaimed, "That doesn't look like Minnie

Goodman to me."

"Say 'Good *yontif'* to Mrs. Weinraub, Amele."

"Good *yontif*, Mrs. Weinraub."

"Good *yontif* to you, too, *zisele*."

"Good *yontif*, Sara." I could see Nana sit up, just a little prouder, as she reached over to put her arm around me.

I fell asleep, lulled by the rhythmic droning of the foreign-sounding songs. When I woke up, I found Papa's *tallis* draped over me.

Back at her house, it was hard not to gravitate toward the kitchen, which was where we always congregated. I stood in the doorway, looking into the darkened, empty room.

"I'm hungry, Nana."

"Let me fix you something to eat."

"But it is Yom Kippur; the rabbi said we aren't supposed to eat. We're supposed to fast."

"You're still a child, Amele. Children, the sick, and the elderly; the Bible says they should eat."

"But you're old, Nana."

Nana laughed at my eight-year-old impertinence. "I'm fifty-two. I hardly call that *old*. Your Bubbie is seventy-eight."

"She's *really* old. Where is Bubbie?"

"She's taking a nap in her room. How about you, *sheynele*, do you want to take a nap, too? It helps pass the time until we eat."

Nana Lena was seated on the sofa in the living room, and I was lying stretched out with my head in her lap. She smiled and reached down to stroke my head.

"I'm too old for a nap."

"Let me tell you something I've learned: You're never too old for a nap."

"Oh, Nana."

"You may not think so at your age, but a nap can be a very fine thing."

I'm not persuaded. "I have an idea. We need the box."

"The box?"

"You know, the story box."

"You mean my picture box? What a good idea!" Nana Lena got up and retrieved a large gold dress box from Smith and Welton's that she kept on a shelf in the closet.

I sat up, making space on the couch, and she returned with the box of photos.

"Um, um, um, every picture has a story. Pick one, any one. It doesn't matter where we start."

I selected a photo of a man loading a large container of milk onto the back of a wagon.

"That's my grandfather Joseph Goodman, my Zeyde. Zeyde had a couple of cows in a barn out back, and a horse. Zeyde made milk and cheese and sold them all around the community. Sometimes he would sell the bags the feed came in. Housewives used to buy them to make curtains. Sometimes he would hitch up the wagon and drive way out in the country, down to Campostella, to one of the farms out there, and he would pack a picnic and take one of us kids along. Now a picnic consisted of Bubbie's homemade pickles, three or four slabs of thick pumpernickel bread, and a *flaschl wasser*, a bottle of water. Bubbie used to make the best kosher pickles, which she kept in a barrel under the stairs. It was the first place we ran to when we entered the house, if Bubbie didn't catch us first and make us wash our hands.

"A good sour pickle and hunk of pumpernickel bread. I tell you, my mouth still waters just thinking about it."

"Stop, Nana, you're making me hungry!"

"I'm sorry; that wasn't very thoughtful of me considering we are *fasting*."

She produced a photo of her grandfather dressed in a white *tallis*.

Zeyde was a very religious man. He always wore white on Yom Kippur. He enjoyed going to synagogue, surrounded by his family, his wife, his nine sons and daughters, Mama and Papa, and the eight of us children. We made quite an impression when the Goodman clan filed into *shul*. Now this was a real Orthodox *shul*. The women sat on the third floor and the men sat on the second, with the *bimah* in the middle. The lower level was used for Sunday school rooms and offices. Mama, Goldie, and I sat upstairs with the other women and children. Papa and Zeyde and the men remained downstairs and prayed. While the men *davened*, the women traded recipes and gossip. Only the children were allowed to wander back and forth between these two worlds.

Zeyde went to *shul* three times a day, and if he did not fast on Yom Kippur, he was surely going to hell. Papa's brother, Zeyde's youngest son, Yanks, loved the bottle, and Zeyde knew that every year on Yom Kippur, Yanks would slip home and do the unthinkable: Not only would he break the fast, but he would do so by drinking.

The windows on one side of the *shul* faced the street where Zeyde lived. He could stand at a certain window and look across the street and see his house. This particular day, Yom Kippur, the Day of Atonement, when we are supposed to be fasting and praying for our sins, Yanks said to Zeyde that he had a headache from not eating and that he was going home to lie down for a little while. Zeyde told him not to be gone long, and above all, "*Ess nichts und trink nichts!* (Don't eat or drink anything!)."

Yanks give Zeyde a sheepish look, "You know, Papa, I would never do such a thing."

A little while later, Zeyde was looking out the *shul* window when Yanks came out of the house spitting and spitting, like he was trying to get an awful taste out of his mouth. Zeyde had urinated in a bottle, mixed it with a little schnaps, and left it where he knew Yanks was going to drink, to teach him a lesson, so Yanks wouldn't drink anymore on Yom Kippur!

Nana Lena laughed so hard, I could see her back molars. "Can you believe that? That's the kind of person my Zeyde was."

"Where was Zeyde from?"

"Zeyde was born in the old world, in Kovno, Kovna Gubernia, and by the way, so was your Papa's family, but that is another story. Bubbie's family was from Kiev." Nana Lena shows me another photo. "Here is the house over on Rockingham Street where I grew up. And here is Bubbie and Zeyde's house and the synagogue. These were real places. Not just stories I make up."

"And your father, what was he like?"

Nana found another picture in the box, of a neatly dressed man standing proudly in a candy store. "Oh, Papa was the most agreeable soul in the world. Anybody that treated his children right was all right with him. He might have had only two bucks in his pocket, but if his children needed it, he took it out of his pocket and gave it to them. He was the cream of the earth. He really was."

She handed me a tiny photo of Great-Grandpa Morris as a

young man, surrounded by six women in long skirts. "Papa was the oldest male of nine children, five girls and four boys. But the three boys were born over twenty years after Morris was born, so Papa was basically raised by six women: his mother Sareva, and his sisters, Esther, Minnie, Belle, Fannie and Celia. He was extremely close to his sister Fannie, the one with the braids here in the picture."

"Is that who Aunt Fannie is named for?"

"Yes, my *sister* Fannie was born July 24, 1918, three weeks after *Aunt* Fannie died. Papa named the baby for his sister."

"Who are these little girls? Is that you and Goldie?" I showed her a photo of two small girls in long winter coats with beautiful fur collars.

"It sure is. Just look at us. That was 1922. Papa was in the fur business. He was gone all week buying hides and furs in the hills of North Carolina. He bought the traps and gave them to the farmers, and they, in turn, sold him their furs. They would catch muskrats—Papa called them "ratz"—and they also caught raccoons ("coons") and every once in a while a mink or an otter. Papa would bring them back, put them on boards to stretch and dry them, and place them in my Bubbie's house on the tremendous upstairs porch. Then a man would come from Delaware on Sunday mornings and buy the furs."

"Goldie and I had a sixth and seventh grade education, and we thought we were great mathematicians, so when the buyer would come, we'd go over there with Papa to multiply. Papa would say, in a thick accent, "One hundred thirty-five ratz at forty-five cents a piece and seventy-six coons at eight-five cents," and we would multiply. Papa would have given the man the figure in an instant; he could do it so fast in his head, much faster than we could with our pencil and paper."

Nana Lena handed me back the photo. "We thought we were something."

"Can I have a coat like that, Nana?"

"I don't think they make them like that anymore."

Nana Lena pulled out another photo, this one of a horse-drawn wagon with children chasing after it, and smiled. "In the summer, Papa had an ice business. He delivered blocks of ice to the stores and to some of the wealthier private homes in the community. Leon, Mike, and Pete made the deliveries when he was out buying furs. The boys had quite a reputation. You know, the other day, I was at a party, and this woman sat down next to me said, "You're a Goodman, aren't you?"

"That's the name I was born with."

"Your Papa and brothers used to deliver ice?"

"Yes, they did."

"Hoo, boy, my Mama used to yell at me and my sisters, 'Alice, Clarice, Daisy, get inside this house. The Goodman boys are coming!'"

"Oh, no."

"Oh, yes she did!"

She and I laughed together for a while, and then I told her about the man who lived across the street from us; he was the town's only barber. Nice old man, great big, heavyset, Italian, bright, sparkling eyes. His name was Patsy Nuzzo. He lived in a big house with his wife and seven kids.

Leon was delivering ice that day. I don't know how old he was; sixteen or seventeen. I guess he was feeling his oats that particular day, because he got it in his head to pinch Mrs. Patsy Nuzzo. I don't know if he pinched her breast or pinched her behind, but that night, we were having dinner, and Patsy came over.

"Morris, I'm sorry to interrupt your dinner, but could we talk?"

Papa went out on the back porch with him, where he told Papa what Leon had done. Papa came back in, let Leon finish his dinner—we called it supper in those days—and then told Leon he wanted to see him in the backyard. There Papa took out the horsewhip and told Leon to start running.

Leon screamed, "What are you beating me for? I ain't done nothing!"

Papa beat him every time he made a turn. Papa really put the whip on him. Mrs. Robbins, the next-door neighbor, came to the fence and hollered, "Mr. Goodman! What are you doing to that boy?"

Papa said, "Mrs. Robbins, you live over there and I live over here. You take care of your business, and I'll take care of mine."

Finally, Leon said, "What you beat me so hard for? I didn't do nothing!"

Papa exploded, "Pinching tits and asses ain't *nothin'*?!"
Leon didn't ever pinch Mrs. Patsy after that.

Nana Lena fished out a photo of Leon in uniform. "Funny,
Leon went on to become the first Jewish policeman in Norfolk. I'll
tell you something else interesting about Leon. Did you ever hear
the story of John Dillinger? You know who John Dillinger was? It
was 1933, and the police captain was having his daily briefing, you
know, giving the officers their assignments, telling them what's
what, and this was at the time that Dillinger was on the loose. The
whole country was looking for Dillinger."

The police captain said that morning, "Men, I want some
quick answers from you."

Nana Lena whispered to me, "This is going to be ugly." She
continued in the Captain's voice: "What would you do if you saw
Dillinger? Okay, Brown, what would you do?"

Brown said, "I would pull out my gun and I would say, "Stick
'em up!"

(Nana Lena informed me, "The police didn't say 'freeze' in
those years.")

The captain said, "Okay, Saunders, what would you do?"

Saunders rose and demonstrated: "I would turn and I would
shoot."

"Very good, Saunders. Now, Goodman, what would you do if
you saw John Dillinger?"

And Leon said, "Sir, I would shit in my pants!"

"My turn." I shuffled around in the box and pulled out a
photo of a young man in a bow tie and glasses, holding a small
trophy. "Who's that?"

"Why, that's your Uncle Mike when he was a boy. He worked
with Papa, in the summertime in the ice business, and in the
winter with the furs and hides.

"Mike had a beautiful voice; he sang beautifully. One night,
Mama was having her card game and we were all listening to
some contest on the radio. All of a sudden we heard:

"The next contestant is Irving Goodman from Berkley,
Virginia, better known as Mike."

We started screaming, "Mama, Mike's on the radio! Mike's on
the radio!"

The card game stopped. Everyone gathered around the radio.

The host asked him what he would sing. "I would like to sing *Autumn Leaves* for my mother, Mrs. Minnie Goodman, but I really don't know it well enough."

We all laughed, as audiences across America did. Mama sat there smiling with tears just streaming down her face. Then he sang *You'll Never Walk Alone* and had us all crying. He won the second prize that night."

"No, really?"

"He most certainly did."

The next photo was of a tall, thin boy in a hat, pulled down over one eye. "That's Uncle Pete, isn't it?" I asked Nana Lena.

"It sure is. Wasn't he handsome? Pete skipped school one day. He went to the old Wells Theater. He was outside ogling the movie posters when he saw Mama coming. Mama liked going to the movies. About the only time Mama had for herself was when all of us were in school. Pete saw her first, pulled his cap down, and tried to slink away before she noticed.

"Milton Goodman! What are you doing here?" Milton was his birth name, and Mama only used it when she was really mad.

Pete pretended he didn't know her. He wouldn't look her in the eye. Minnie got right up in his face. "Wait till your father gets his hands on you!"

"Get away, woman," he told her. "I don't know you."

Mama hauled off and slapped him. "You know me now? I'm your mother. You know me now?" Ohhh, Mama was mad.

I found a photo of a horse with three kids astride, surrounded by three older kids, one of whom is holding an infant. "What's this, Nana, a birthday party?"

"No, we didn't have parties like that when I was a child. That's me and Leon and Pete and Mike and Goldie and Fannie and Poogie and Sidney and Frank."

"Frank? I never heard about an Uncle Frank."

"He's not your Uncle, honey; Frank was our horse. Papa had an ice business, and he had a horse named Frank, who pulled the wagon. He lived in a barn behind the house. That reminds me, there was the time Leon shot the horse. No wait, it was Pete…no, it was Goldie."

"Goldie shot the horse?"

"One day, I was fourteen, Goldie, fifteen, and Goldie thought she heard a noise in the backyard. Goldie was always afraid of her shadow. So was I. She grabbed Papa's rifle and then she went upstairs to the boys' bedroom where the window faced the barn. Pete was taking a nap, Mike was downstairs, and Leon was in the bathroom getting ready for work. When Goldie looked out, she was sure that something was moving behind the barn. "Somebody's stealing the horse! I've got to do something!" She rested the rifle on Pete's head and fired the gun. Pete didn't even flinch."

Nana Lena cannot control herself. "Goldie came *that close* to killing the horse. All of us went running down the street chanting, 'Goldie killed the horse. Goldie killed the horse,' although she didn't really. It was great growing up in a house with all those children. Everybody was crazy, you know, *meshuge*."

Nana Lena glanced over at the clock. "Well, look at that. It's almost time to break the fast. Are you still hungry?"

"Not anymore."

"I'll go ahead and set the table. Your parents will be here soon. You'll clean this up?" Nana Lena asked without having to.

I gently gathered up all the pictures of Bubbie, Zeyde, Papa, Leon, Goldie, Mike, and even Frank the horse, and placed them carefully in the box. "See ya'll next year," I said, as I returned the story box to its proper place. Then I skipped off to help Nana Lena set the break fast table.

* * *

Flat-Top Eggie

1 serving

Beat 1 egg lightly with a touch of milk. Add butter to preheated 6-inch skillet or crepe pan. When butter sizzles, add egg mixture. Distribute egg evenly so that it heats uniformly. Salt and pepper to taste. Using a spatula, flip egg over and cook briefly on other side. Remove to plate. Serve with bread.

Can be served with 2 slices of challah and a slice of tomato, as an egg sandwich.

Rugelach

"Place the cream cheese, butter, sugar, salt, vanilla, and lemon zest in the Mix Master. Add flour and mix until the dough is soft." My sister Melissa put the recipe card down. "A Mix Master, Nana? I thought you made everything by hand?"

"It's a poor substitute for four sisters, but it will do in a pinch. Your old Nana's hands aren't what they used to be."

Melissa tied on her apron. "That's what we're here for, Nana. We're here to help."

I took a bowl out of the cabinet, "And to learn."

My other sister, Donna, opened the fridge. "And to eat!"

"Here, here," we all agreed.

"It's so nice to have my granddaughters here with me, the three roses in my garden. I remember, back in Berkley, one time when the four of us girls helped Mama make the rugelach. My Mama, your Bubbie Minnie, wasn't such a good cook, like Tante Fannie, or my Bubbie, but Mama had a recipe for rugelach that was the best in Berkley."

Every year we would help Mama make the rugelach for the Jewish New Year and on Papa's birthday. We'd make hundreds of them and store them in tins that Papa had brought home from the candy store. One tin was for Papa, one for Mama's card games, the others were for special occasions, like weddings or bar mitzvahs, and one tin was always left as an anonymous gift at the door of the Rabbi. Though I don't know how anonymous it was since the *Rebbetzin* always knew where to return the tin.

It was the spring of 1930. Poogie was seven, Fannie eleven, I was almost eighteen, and Goldie had just turned nineteen. Leon was at work, Mike and Pete were out back playing ball, and Sidney had gone with Papa to deliver the ice.

Mama took the bowl of cream cheese and the butter that she had let soften near the stove and added two cups of unsifted flour. Then she handed the bowl to Goldie. "Stir."

"Poogie, let's get started on the filling. You're in charge of the walnuts. Break them up into little pieces like this."

"Fannie, when you've finished sorting the raisins, soak them in water for fifteen minutes."

Mama slapped Poogie's hand. "Stop eating the walnuts. We won't have enough for the filling."

When Goldie finished adding the flour, Mama shaped the dough into large balls and put them into the icebox to chill.

"Lena, get the jam out of the cupboard. Lena?"

My mind was elsewhere. An old friend of mine, Mitzi Laden, whose Uncle Jacob owned a haberdashery at the end of Granby Street, had decided one day that we would walk down to see her uncle during our lunch break. She was buzzing around the store like a bee, and I propped myself upon a table full of men's pants, stacked high on either side. Mitzi ran out of the store and then I saw her talking to this tall, good-looking, rather lean young man who looked like he'd just stepped out of a glamour magazine. He asked who I was. She told him I was a good friend of hers, and he said, "Call her out. I'd like to meet her."

Well, being a come-after-me-if-you-want-me type, I said, if he wants to meet me, he'd better come on in. And he did. We were introduced, but a few minutes thereafter, I had to go back to work, as did Mitzi. He asked which way I was going. I crossed my arms, indicating either direction.

And he said, "Looks like you're going my way." It didn't matter which way I was going; he was going my way. I liked that. Myer was from Lynn, Massachusetts, and he worked on a steamship that traveled back and forth between New York and Norfolk twice a week. He ran the concession stand on the ship. He asked if he might take me to lunch the next time he was in town, which was on Mondays and Thursdays. I said yes, and sure enough, when I came out of work on Thursday, there he stood, eager and ready to buy me that thirty-five-cent blue-plate special across the street.

"It's not like your sister to not enjoy the cooking." Mama knew that more than any of her children, Lena seemed to prefer the kitchen over the outside world, but today her thoughts were obviously not on baking.

Goldie raised her eyebrow and smiled. "I bet she's thinking of that fella of hers."

"A fella? My Lena has a fella?" Goldie had been dating for

two years now, but Lena hadn't so much as looked at a man.

"According to Mrs. A.J. Legum, he's a very pret-ty fel-la."

Minnie smiled.

I knew that in about three hours Myer would be waiting for me at the ferry and dozens of tins were waiting to be filled, so I threw myself into the work. I spread flour over the kitchen table, divided the dough into balls, handing one to each of my sisters. We rolled the dough into circles about six inches wide and one-eighth of an inch thick. Over this, we spread the jam—apricot, strawberry, or raspberry are best—and then the chopped nuts and raisins. We cut the covered dough circles into wedges, the outside edge only one inch wide. I showed Poogie how to roll the wedges starting at the outside, over and over until you reached the center. Then we rolled the rugelach in sugar and cinnamon and placed them on baking sheets. With five pairs of hands, the process was done in under two hours.

Poogie and Fannie helped Goldie carry the last of the tins to the pantry while I finished washing the dishes. After the last dish was put away, I ripped off my apron. "I told Mitzi I'd meet her at the moving pictures at two."

"What's playing?" Goldie tested.

"That new Marx Brothers film, *Animal Crackers*."

"Wasn't that last week?"

I twisted and squirmed. I was like a puppy dog scratching at the door to get out.

Finally, Mama gave in. "Of course you shouldn't keep *Mitzi* waiting."

I raced upstairs and returned a few minutes later, wearing a pretty blouse, with my hair nicely combed.

Goldie and Mama exchanged knowing looks.

"A lady should always look presentable. Isn't that what you always say, Mama? I'll be back by suppertime," I promised.

"If you know what's good for you!" Mama wagged her finger.

On my way out the house, I ducked into the pantry and grabbed a handful of rugelach.

From the other room, I heard Mama call out, "Leave the rugelach alone."

"Yes, Mama," I said as I wrapped the pastries in a napkin and skipped happily out the door.

The ferry floated from the backwater of Berkley to the booming metropolis of Norfolk. I stood at the front railing, enjoying how the downtown buildings seem to grow even larger as the boat glided into the harbor. Myer waited on the wharf, dressed in tan knickers, green socks, and a green sweater, with a tan cap, real New-York-in-the-thirties. I waved to him as I waited for the walkway to be lowered.

We strolled along the waterfront. Several men tipped their hats to me. One man called out, "How's that beautiful blonde-headed sister of yours?"

"Oh, she's fine."

"Be sure to tell her I asked for her."

Myer looked worried. "It seems like you know everybody."

"It's a small town, and I've lived here my whole life. I'm sorry I was late."

"I wasn't sure if you were coming."

"I almost couldn't make it. Sunday is Papa's birthday. We were making rugelach. It's his favorite."

"My sister Pearl makes a pretty good rugelach."

"My family makes the best rugelach in all of Berkley."

"Is that a fact?"

"It most certainly is. As a matter of fact, I have some here, if you would care to sample." I handed him the napkin, which I had tied with a piece of yellow ribbon.

"What have we here? A present? What a pretty ribbon." Myer opened the gift and took a bite. His face dissolved in utter bliss. "You made this?"

"My *family* made this."

"Then I guess I have to meet the rest of the family."

He popped the other half of the rugelach into his mouth and did a little happy dance. "I can't believe you made this."

*   *   *

Nana Lena watched proudly as her granddaughters rolled the dough into small circles and sprinkled them with cinnamon and sugar. "Melissa, pass me the raisins. Donna, get the jam out of the refrigerator. Amy, turn the oven on to three-seventy-five?"

"Nana, tell the story about the first time Papa came to Berkley." I turned to my sisters, "You know the story?" Donna shook her head no. Melissa winked. Of course, we've heard the story before, but we loved to hear her tell it.

The first time Myer came to Berkley, Mama knew that he was coming at a certain time. Just before three Mama said she had to run across the street to see Bubbie Sareva but I knew Mama was going across the street because the streetcar stopped up on the corner of Liberty Street and our street, and she wanted to see what my fella looked like when he got off.

When he stepped off the car, she walked right up to him and said "Moishe, how are you?"

He said, "I beg your pardon, Madame."

Mama was impressed. She said. "Oh, I thought you were my brother-in-law. I'm so sorry."

"I can't believe she did that."

"Mama sure was slick." Nana Lena laughed, "Then he tipped his hat and said, 'So am I.'"

And she said, "I know you're a stranger around here. Who are you looking for? Maybe I could help?"

"I am looking for Miss Lena Goodman at 911 Rockingham."

Mama smiled up at the tall, dark gentleman. She was all of five feet tall and Myer was over six feet. "Nice to meet you; I'm her mother." And she pointed down the street. "She lives right that way."

Nana Lena stood at the counter, pointing and laughing. "Mama was so afraid he wasn't going to find me."

"But he did and that's the important thing." I said.

"Thank the good Lord." Nana took two trays out of the oven and put two more in. "We had tea with rugelach, and Myer swore it was the best rugelach he had ever had. After that, Mama always made an extra tin just for him."

"I tell you, it worked on your father, too. Ask him what's his favorite food that I make and he'll say it's the rugelach...*and* the chopped liver...*and* the kugel, I know. But the rugelach will do it every time."

"Do what, Nana?"

"Seal the *Shidduch*. Cement the match."

"Why is that?"

"It is hope wrapped with promise, and sprinkled with love, or as your Papa would always say, 'It's sweet, twisted, and little nuts, like my Lena.'"

* * *

Rugelach

Yields 48–64 pieces

Dough

   1 cup butter

   8 ounces cream cheese

   2 cups unsifted flour

Cream butter and cream cheese. Add flour. Knead until the bowl is clean. Refrigerate 2 hours or overnight.

Filling

You can use any kind of jam or spread. Traditionally, strawberry, raspberry, or apricot jam is used. I prefer the apricot because it doesn't turn dark in color when cooked. I have also heard of using orange, cranberry, or currant jam, or a thin chocolate spread. Look in your refrigerator and see what you have and use that.

Jam or spread of choice	1/2 cup finely chopped
1 1/2 cups sugar	walnuts
1 tsp cinnamon	1/2 cup golden raisins

Divide the dough into 4 parts. Keep the other parts in the refrigerator until you are ready to use them. Roll out each part on waxed paper to 8-inch rounds. Trim circle. Spread dough with jam of choice. Sprinkle with 2 tablespoons of the sugar and cinnamon mixture. Then sprinkle the nuts and raisins around the outer edges of the circle. Leave the center clear.

With a sharp knife, divide the circle in half, then again into quarters, and again into three or four pieces depending on size of dough. You will end up with 12 or 16 wedges. Work quickly, because as the dough softens it will be harder to roll.

Roll up from the wide end to the center. Curve to form a crescent.

Space slightly apart, pointed side down, on greased cookie sheet or on parchment paper.

Bake at 375° until lightly browned, 20–25 minutes. Using a wide spatula, remove to wire rack to cool. If you use parchment paper, they will just *slide* off the tray.

Roll in powdered sugar and store in cookie tin or tightly sealed plastic container. Can be frozen. Re-roll in powdered sugar before serving.

Myer (right) enjoys a drink in Havana

Myer carried this in his wallet. On it he had written "whoopee."

The beaming bride

Myer & Lena on the day they eloped

Wedding Cookies

I entered the kitchen carrying two stacks of cookie tins, attempting a delicate balancing act, knowing that at any second they could come tumbling to the floor in a clatter.

"The light? Did you turn out the light?"

"Of course, Nana. Do you think this will be enough?"

"It's a big wedding."

"I'm just kidding. And why isn't the caterer making the dessert?"

"What do they know about wedding cookies? I'm making the wedding cookies. Tassies, date bars, lemon bars, seven-layer cookies, strudel, rugelach, and raspberry swirls. Did I leave anything out?"

"And we're going to make all of that today?"

"We already made the rugelach."

"Then we'd better get to work."

"We'll start with the tassies."

"Why do you call them tassies, Nana?"

"That's what we call them. Pecan tassies. Little pecan pies."

"Is that a Yiddish word?"

"No, I think it's Southern." Nana Lena took out the cream cheese and butter and left them on the counter to soften. "Your Papa had never heard of pecan tassies before he met me."

"When exactly *did* you meet Papa?"

"We met on April the twenty-sixth, 1930. It was The Great Depression, and not a time for people to be falling in love. Businesses were going bankrupt. People were losing their fortunes. But we didn't care. We loved each other. We knew that. Whenever I attempted to broach the subject of the possibility of my marrying your Papa, my Papa would become furious."

"Now is not the time to get married!" He would say. "This man of yours, what kind of job does he have? In the paper it says that the shipping companies are laying off workers. How will he take care of you when he has no job?"

"But, Papa...."

"Has he asked you to marry him?"

"No, Papa."

"And you know for sure he will?"

Lena was silent, knowing full well that he already had proposed, but she did not want her father to know yet. "He will, Papa, I'm sure he will."

"And his people? What do we know from them? Are they good Jewish? Or are they bad Jewish, like the Schindlers, the ones who sell the shellfish? What kind of Jew sells shrimp?"

"They're good Jews, Papa. Miriam, Pearl. Ernie, Freddie. Don't they sound like good Jewish names? They live in New York City. You know how many Jews live in New York?"

"He sounds like a Damn Yankee to me."

"But, Papa."

"Enough, Leike. Enough of this talk. You are not marrying a *Damn Yankee!*"

* * *

Nana Lena removed a stack of mini-muffin tins from the cabinet and handed me a dish cloth. "Wipe them out good."

"Didn't you wash them before you put them away?"

"Of course, but they've been in the cabinet for a long time. I like to be sure they are clean."

"Good point." I began wiping.

"Now Mama and Papa, my parents, came to the United States in the late 1880s and ended up settling in Virginia; what did they know from Yankees? They were assimilated Southern Jews, and they had adopted Southern ways."

The doorbell rang, and Nana got up to answer it. My sisters Donna and Melissa arrived; and Nana began her hugging and kissing ritual.

"Thank God, more help."

"Sorry we're late."

"No, you're just in time. She's telling the Nana Papa story."

"The Nana Papa story?"

"You know, Romeo and Juliet in the *shtetl.*"

"She's making your old Nana sound even older then I am. Berkley was not a *shtetl.* It was a neighborhood. We were Jewish, and we were proud to be Americans. How else can you explain my father's ridiculous insistence on calling your grandfather a 'Damn Yankee?'"

"Too much schnaps?" I suggested.

"Very funny. Don't talk about your great-grandfather like

that. Take the dough out of the Frigidaire. It should be ready by now."

We took the dough, made out of cream cheese, butter, flour, and a touch of lemon zest, and formed it into little balls, the size of marbles. Then we pressed the balls into pregreased mini-muffin tins that were narrow at the bottom and wide at the top, like miniature pies.

"It's important to use as little dough as possible. That keeps the crust thin. Smooth it all around with your thumb like this, and pinch off any extra. Where were we?"

They had obviously heard this before. "Papa should have known better...."

"Right." She began to fill the shells with the nut filling, remembering:

Papa should have known better. Telling me *not* to marry was like waving a red cloth in front of a bull. On March the fifteenth, 1934, we got real brave and decided we would elope. The elopement was that he, his best friend Julie Lowenthal, and me and my best friend Mitzi Laden, would all meet at the rabbi's home at 621 Princess Anne Road to be married there, very, very quietly.

We were sitting in the Rabbi's living room, Mitzi with a corsage, me with a corsage, both men with little flowers in their lapels. The rabbi was in his study. After a few minutes, the door to the rabbi's study opened, and who should emerge but my Uncle Zachariah, who said to me, "Lena, *vus tust du do?*" (Lena, what are you doing here?)

I said, "Oh, we've just come to see the rabbi."

"The rabbi? Is something the matter?"

Then I got real nervous. "Uncle Zachariah, can you keep a secret?" I leaned in real close and whispered in his ear. "My friends are getting married and I'm here to be their witness. Promise me you won't tell?"

Uncle Zachariah winked. "And you promise you won't tell your Papa I took his last *flaschl* schnaps?"

He left, and then the Rabbi called in a man named Eichelbaum and his son; and Mrs. Steinbach and Julie Lowenthal held up the four corners of the *chupah* right there in the rabbi's living room, and we were married. Then we went out, oh, I guess six or seven miles from there, to the Pine Tree Inn, where we had dinner, listened to sweet music, and devoured each other with our eyes.

When it was time to go home, we thought, now what do we do? We were secretly married. We didn't dare *do* anything. Julie Lowenthal lived in a hotel, and the four of us went up to Julie's room for a while. When the party broke up, the boys took us back to the home of Mitzi's aunt, from which we had eloped. I stayed with Mitzi, and the boys stayed together that night. I don't know of many people who had a wedding night like that. But that was ours, and it's the truth."

"I love that story."
"So do I."
"What were you doing in that hotel room, Nana?"
"Nothing that I can't tell my grandchildren about, at least not *that* night."
"Nana!"
"Lena G!"
"After all, I was a married woman. It had to happen, eventually...."

On Mondays and Thursdays, we met at the Preston Hotel on Boush Street. Myer always got there first, and he would request room 315, which was our wedding date. I would sneak in the side door, making sure that no one could see me, and take the stairs to the third floor. The elevator was too risky, because I might run into someone I knew and then how would I explain why I was there? After all, I had my reputation to think about. We continued meeting that way, twice a week for some time until one day, about six weeks after the wedding, when I woke up feeling sick to my stomach.

I asked Goldie when was the last time we had our cycle, because the two of us always used to get our menses at roughly the same time each month.

"Last week." Goldie's eyes grew big as saucers, "Why, Lena Goodman! Are you...? I'm gonna tell Mama."

"You may be my big sister, but this is *my* mess, and I'll figure out what to do and whom to tell, you hear?"

"Lena G."

"Lena H. now, for six weeks."

"You sly fox. You've been married all this time without my knowing."

Goldie swore, on her favorite dress, that she wouldn't say

anything to Mama. Now it was up to me to tell them what I was sure they did not want to hear.

My friend Mitzi came over, and we were working on what I would say, putting all our little ducks in a row. I put on my wedding band. Myer had paid $22.50 for that wedding band. I still have it. I put on my wedding band, and I took the dinnerboard that I had taken from the Pine Tree Inn; Papa had written several things on it, and so had Julie Lowenthal. And I took my marriage license and the little silk bag with the broken glass, my crushed bouquet, and his crushed corsage, and I went downstairs to face Mama.

Mama was in the kitchen making blintzes. I hesitated a moment, and then showed her my ring.

"Get the hell away from me with that ten-cent ring."

"No, Mama, it's real."

"Then you tell him, this man of yours, that when he's rich, he buys you a *good* ring, with a *real* diamond, one I don't have to put my *glasses* on to see!"

I handed her the marriage license and the *ketubah*.

"Papa will be furious. How will we tell him?" I said.

Mama said, "You leave that up to me."

That night, from the next room, the four of us girls listened to Mama and Papa fighting through the wall.

"Wait till I get my hands on her!"

"You won't hurt her, Morris. I won't let you."

"That she could do such a thing! It's a *shande*. A *shande*, I tell you."

Goldie wagged her finger at Lena, imitating her father. "It's a *shande* I tell you."

Minnie sighed, "She could have done much worse."

Fannie chimed in, "Much worse."

"He's a good man, Morris. He will take care of her."

"What kind of husband will he make for my Lena? He spends half his time at sea, and he's a Damn Yankee to boot!"

Poogie giggled. "Papa said a bad word. What's a damn *Yankee*?"

My sisters and I laughed and hugged. What I didn't know was that on the other side of the wall, our mother and father were doing the same thing, laughing and hugging, as they pretended to make a scene for my benefit, and that Morris was whispering to

Minnie, "One down, three to go...." Then, with a sparkle in his eye, "Come, Minnie, let's get under the featherbed."

Elayne arrived bearing more cookie tins. "Looks like I'm just in time." She made a beeline for the pecan tassies. Her eyes rolled back in her head as she savored the taste. "God, these are good."

"Leave some for the wedding."

"How do you plan to get all these tassies to Florida, Nana?"

"Don't you worry. I have a plan."

We stacked the tassies in the tins, in between layers of waxed paper. As Donna washed the dishes and Melissa and I carried the tins down to the freezer for storage, Nana took out the ingredients for the next treat: date nut bars.

"Elayne, could you chop the dates?"

"Why don't you put them in the food processor, Mother?"

Nana just gave Elayne a look.

Elayne sighed in resignation and reached for the knife. "Has anyone seen the cutting board?"

Nana Lena returned to her story.

Ten months after our wedding, your mother was born. By that time, Myer and I had moved into the room off the back porch of my parents' house. It was the middle of January, and it was miserably cold. Papa was so worried that the house was not warm enough for the baby that he chopped down the fence that divided the house from the barns, to keep the fire going all through the winter.

While Papa worried about the cold, Mama worried about what the neighbors would think. After all, we were a good Jewish family, and if word got out that I was in any way promiscuous, she would have a hard time marrying off my sisters. The Goodman boys, on the other hand, had their own reputation, but that is another story.

A few weeks later, it started to thaw. Mama took the baby and me from house to house in Berkley, with the birth certificate and the marriage license, to prove that the baby was "good."

"Good? As in legitimate? Really?" I asked Nana Lena.

"If it were me, I would have died," my mother said.

"Your mother hates that story." Nana teased her.

"I do not."

"That's the way it was back then. Your Bubbie was a very proud woman, as I am, and your mother is, and all of you should be. She did what she did so that she could hold her head up high, and show that she had done a good job, been a good mother."

"How did it make you feel, Nana?" Melissa asked.

"All I remember is having to pee."

"Mother!"

"Nana!"

Everybody cracked up laughing. "Hush or you'll make me pee in my pants. Could one of you give me a hand?" Melissa helped Nana Lena get up from the chair. "And while I'm gone, Laney, chop the dates. Donna, chop the walnuts. Melissa, grease two Pyrex, and Amy, hand me a paper towel in case I don't make it to the bathroom in time."

* * *

Weeks later, I pulled into the driveway of Nana's house and honked the horn. We were on the way to the airport, on the way to Florida for David's wedding, and I had stopped to pick up Nana Lena.

She was waiting in the doorway, standing next to two rather large suitcases.

"So much stuff."

She shrugged, "Not really."

I picked up the first relatively light suitcase and took it to the car. The second case weighed a ton. "What's in here, Nana: bricks?"

"The wedding cookies; I just took them out of the freezer."

"I can't wait to see their faces when they x-ray your luggage. You've got enough metal inside to set off all the alarms."

"So I'll show them what's inside and I'll give them a little *taste,* and I will tell the officer, 'These are very special cookies, *love* cookies.'"

"I can just see the headline, 'Grandma busted for drug smuggling.'"

She triple-locked the door. "Made with love, filled with love, for a day on which we celebrate love. It's not every day you get to go to your grandson's wedding."

* * *

Pecan Tassies

yields 36

> *Pecan tassies are little pecan pies, made in mini-muffin tins.*
> *They take time to make, but one bite and you'll be hooked. I*
> *double this recipe and freeze some for later.*

Dough

1 stick unsalted butter

3 ounces cream cheese

1 cup flour

1/2 tsp grated orange or lemon peel

Cream butter and cream cheese together. Add flour and orange or lemon peel. Knead together until bowl is clean. Cover and refrigerate overnight.

Filling

2 beaten eggs

2 Tbsp melted butter

1 1/2 cups light brown sugar

a pinch of salt

1 1/2 cups chopped pecans

Using your thumbs, press a marble-sized ball of dough into miniature muffin tins. Use only enough dough to cover the bottom and sides of each cup, removing any excess dough with the side of a spoon for a good edge. Spoon a heaping teaspoon filling into each cup. Fill about 2/3 full. Batter will rise slightly. Bake 20–25 minutes at 325°.

Damn Yankee Pot Roast

"The key ingredient to a good brisket is…patience. After all, a brisket is one of the toughest cuts of meat; it comes from the forequarter, the chest, and if it isn't prepared properly, it tastes like shoe leather. A good brisket takes time, and Lord knows I have plenty of that these days, ever since your Papa died."

"I know you miss him. I miss him, too."

"I miss him with all my heart. He was such a good man, your Papa, such a *good* man. He never got to finish his education, he started working when he was fourteen, but he was a smart man, street smart. He used to say he went to Harvard, 'in one door and out the other.' Or sometimes he'd say that he had attended the 'School of Hard Knocks.'

"Myer loved Pot Roast. He always raved about his mother's pot roast. And we, we never knew from pot roast. Mama made brisket. Basically, it's the same thing, meat, slow cooked, in a savory liquid. I remember the first time Myer tasted my brisket, we were already married, but we hadn't told anyone yet, and I had invited him over for *Shabbos* dinner with my family. I made the brisket, with the roasted potatoes and carrots, you know how I make it sometimes, and Myer took one bite and shouted, 'Damn. This is *better* than my Mama's pot roast.'

"Mama and Papa looked at each other in shock. I think Sidney and Poogie started to giggle; then Papa started laughing and pretty soon we all joined in. After that my family called it 'Damn Yankee Pot Roast' and Myer called it brisket."

"Amele, take the pan out for the brisket and turn the oven on to three twenty-five."

I followed orders, placing the pan in front of her. "I remember coming to your house every Sunday, when we were little, for brisket and potato kugel, and when it was time to go, Papa always gave each of us a crisp dollar bill, which I would inevitably lose to my brother David playing dollar poker on the ride back home. I still have some of those silver dollars Papa gave us on special occasions."

Nana Lena removed the brisket from the refrigerator. "I

found a whole box of those coins hidden in the back of the medicine cabinet, when he died. They must be worth a lot by now."

"I bet they are."

Meanwhile, Nana Lena rinsed the meat and patted it down with a paper towel, as I assembled the familiar ingredients: an envelope of Lipton's onion soup, a cup of Heinz ketchup, a half-cup of Heinz 57 sauce, and four cups of water. It was hard to imagine a more Jewish dish made out of such All-American products. "I bet Bubbie Minnie didn't make it this way."

"No, back then we peeled the onions and chopped the tomatoes and grated the carrots. There were always plenty of helpers in the kitchen. Rub some of the onion soup into the *fleysh*. It gives the meat more flavor."

"And the jokes he would tell. 'Lynn jokes,' we called them because his family came from Lynn, Massachusetts. Like 'What do honeymooners eat on their wedding night?' 'Lett-uce alone.' Or the time Donna asked for a banana split and Papa brought her a plate with a banana split in two. That was Myer."

"I remember the trip we took to the World's Fair in New York."

"Do you remember how excited you were when you first saw Manhattan?"

"I hit my head on the ceiling of the car!"

"The first time I saw New York, they nearly had to scrape me off the sidewalk. Papa and I had taken the train to New York, so my first glimpse of Manhattan was when we stepped outside the Pennsylvania Station. Now in Norfolk, we had a few five-story buildings, but in New York the buildings were like giants blocking the sky. Then he took me over to that new skyscraper, the Empire State Building, and I became dizzy looking up at it and watching the steady flow of people, of every shape and color, stream through that revolving door."

"When was this?"

"It was 1934. Just after we were married. I was pregnant with your mother. We had gone to New York to live with his parents. We lived on 164th and St. Nicholas. You know where that is? Near the Presbyterian Hospital? It was such a fine Jewish neighborhood then."

"It's Dominican now. Things change."

"It was during the Depression; and it was, to say the least, depressing, being so far from my family for the first time in my life, in a strange city, and the baby on the way. My mother-in-law was a good woman. She was very kind to me, but I was terribly homesick. I remember one day, Myer and I walked all the way up to 181st Street to see a movie for twenty cents' admission, and when we arrived in front of the movie theater there was a car parked a little bit away and it had a Virginia license. I walked closer to look at it, and it had a Norfolk city tag. Well, I refused to go inside the theater. I wanted to see who came out, because it would *have* to be someone I knew. So we waited and we waited and we waited—and finally a great big burly black man came out, and it was somebody I *didn't* know!

"And Myer said, 'I thought you knew everybody?'

"By the same token, I got in the elevator one day in the apartment building where we lived, and I heard the elevator operator say to the black woman standing in the back, 'This is the lady I told you about; she gets mail from Norfolk.'

"And the woman said, 'She ain't from Norfolk, she's from Berkley. That's Miz Minnie's daughter!'"

"I had found a friend, and after that, when I got lonesome, I went up to the sixth floor where she worked and we talked about home."

"How long did you live in New York?"

"From June until December. Papa was working on the train then, so he was traveling back and forth all the time. He wasn't home much. He came up in December and he decided it would be best if I came home to have the baby. I can't tell you how relieved I was. I wanted that baby to be born in Berkley.

"So we moved back home. Just after Christmas, when the stores were having their after-Christmas sales, I picked up the paper one morning and I saw that L. Snyder Department Store had Birdseye Diapers on sale for eighty-eight cents a dozen, and I figured that I needed about three dozen. I waited until somebody came back from school and I got their book of school tickets, which you used in those days to ride on the streetcar. You'd get twenty-four rides for a dollar; otherwise the fare was ten cents. I took the book of tickets, and there I was two weeks away from having a baby, and I pulled myself and my big belly up onto the streetcar, and the conductor (his name was Mr. McGlowan; a cute little old

Irish man) looked over his glasses and said, 'Miss Goodman, they are going to have to *burn* that school down to get you out.'

"I laughed so hard I nearly needed diapers myself."

"Nana! You changed it. You usually say—"

"I was telling the PG version, for your recording. Apropos of that, this past Christmas, there was a big story in the newspaper about the McGlowan family, and how they get together for Christmas every year and how meaningful it was for them. The article mentioned that William McGlowan was a streetcar conductor, and I thought, My God, that's the same Mr. McGlowan. As I read the story, I saw that they were going to meet at one of the daughters' houses; I don't remember which one. I got the phone book and I called the woman and I said, 'Mrs. So and So, my name is Lena Herzberg, which probably doesn't mean anything to you, but I've just been reading that beautiful, sentimental story in the morning paper. I have to tell you there's some nostalgia there, as far as I'm concerned.'

I told her that her brother Britten had worked for my father, Morris Goodman."

"Oh my God," she exclaimed. "The snow cream man!"

"That was us." (You see, Papa made snow cream. It wasn't ice cream, it was snow cream, and I don't know why none of us ever bothered to write down the recipe, but it was a very special recipe and people came from all around, even from Portsmouth and Norfolk, which was quite a distance to come in those times. He had a shop on Liberty Street, and all of us kids worked there from time to time. We were never home alone. We were the first shop in Berkley to have curbside service. Papa had seen it up in Brooklyn and thought it was a good idea.)

Mr. McGlowan's daughter added, "Oh, I remember it well."

And then I said, "I have to tell you a story about *your* father, which you probably don't even know." And I told her the story about what her father had said to me that day on the streetcar. She said, "You know that sounds just like Daddy. He would have said something like that."

"So you see, Amele, things just never die. People go on forever, and the stories go on forever, as long as we keep telling them."

"Your Papa was a very sentimental man, filled with emotions.

I remember the first time he met me, at the clothing store, he asked me for my number. And I said 352J, in my best Southern drawl. Among the things I found in his wallet when he died was a yellowed piece of paper with the numbers 352J. He'd kept it all those years."

"How romantic."

"That's the way he was."

"You only had four numbers?"

"Some people only had three. We were one of the first families in Berkley to have a telephone. I can't tell you how many people on our street romanced on our phone. Boyfriends would call and we'd go out back and yell over the fence. 'So and so, your boyfriend's on the phone, but don't be long because I'm expecting a call from *my* boyfriend.' Sometimes I waited and waited all night and the call wouldn't come through."

Nana Lena covered the brisket with two pieces of heavy-duty aluminum foil, and I helped her lift it into the oven. I pressed the oven light and peered in through the door. "How long does it cook?"

"At least two hours, maybe more, depending on how thick it is. You want the meat to simmer in the juices until it is tender. Then we'll take it out, let it cool, slice it, and put it back in the juices to simmer for another hour."

"It takes a long time to make a brisket."

"Anything worth having is worth waiting for. Like your Papa."

Nana Lena hoisted the potato sack from under the kitchen sink and removed seven or eight large ones. We sat at the kitchen table, peeling potatoes and dropping them into a large yellow bowl filled with cold water to keep the potatoes from turning black.

"We dated on and off for four years, because of distance. On two or three occasions, we decided, I twice, and he once, that we wouldn't see each other any more, and on each occasion we made up and came back. We went on and off like that from April 26th, 1930, until March 15th, 1934. A few days before that he said to me, "You're pretty brave, aren't you?"

"Yeah."

"I dare you to meet me at the marriage license bureau."

"When?"

"Tuesday."

"I thought about it and I thought about it, and on Tuesday I said I would. It was very depressed times. There was no money on his side of the family, and there was no money on my side of the family. It would be wrong to get married *here* and not let his people see, so we decided to elope.

"Incidentally, just the other day when I was in the hospital for the radiation treatment, there was this man, and he was growing impatient, waiting for the doctor. He was pacing back and forth, and then he saw me and he walked over and sat down next to me, and I heard him say something like he was going to go sit next to 'Miss Pretty Legs from Berkley'."

"I said, 'I beg your pardon?' Not that I was really offended. It had been a long time since a man had affectionately referred to my legs, and I said, 'Do I know you?'

The man looked at me and smiled. 'I don't remember your married name, but your maiden name was Goodman. I used to work at the marriage license bureau, and one day I received a phone call from this mysterious young woman. She wanted to know if it would be possible to obtain a marriage license without publishing an announcement in the newspaper, as was the norm in those days, and it still is, except now they charge you for it. I said it depended on who was calling. And she said she would make herself known to me at the appropriate time."

"Very mysterious." I said.

"An hour later, you appeared in my office and identified yourself as the woman I had spoken to earlier, and I said, 'For you, Miss Pretty Legs, I think it can be arranged.'"

"That man's name was Bullock. Such a nice man."

"Every man's a nice man to you, Nana."

"Are you calling your grandmother a loose woman?"

"No, you just always seem to find the good in people."

"And that's a bad thing?" Nana Lena put down the peeler and reached for the grater. "I had the license. Now I needed a Rabbi. I called the rabbi, who had confirmed me, Rabbi Alex Alan Steinbach, and I asked him if he would perform a *secret ceremony*.

"And he said, 'Do I know you?'

"Yes, you confirmed me, Rabbi."

"Then why do you want to get married secretly?"

"The main reason is that we don't have money for a wedding."

"I see." Then: "I have to ask you a personal question. Are you in trouble?"

"I said, 'I'm not in trouble, Rabbi. We just want to get married.' So, of course, I told him who I was, and he agreed to do it."

"And the rest is history."

"History? It's just *my* story. Did I ever show you the picture of Papa and me on our wedding day? I wore a brown and white silk two-piece dress, with this big collar. I could have been wearing a potato sack, I was so happy. And Papa, he looked so dashing, in his dark brown suit and fine silk tie. We had our whole lives ahead of us."

"It's a beautiful picture. You look *so* happy."

"Oh, I was, and after that, I had forty-three wonderful years. It wasn't always easy, mind you, but the longer our marriage simmered, the better it tasted."

"I always wondered why you didn't have more children, Nana. Both of you came from such large families; didn't you want more children?"

Nana sighed deeply and reached over to put her hand on my shoulder. "It wasn't for lack of trying, or lack of love. Yes, Papa and I wanted a big family, but that's not what was meant to be. A few years after your mother was born, Papa got the mumps. I had the mumps as a child; all of us did. But Myer was a full-grown man when he got the mumps. He had a very high fever, and after that, the doctor said he was sterile. When Myer told me that we couldn't have any more children, I was crushed. He asked me if I could still love him or if I wanted a divorce. I answered, 'I don't love you. I *adore* you.' And he added, 'And I always will.' And that's what we said to each other after that. When things were good and especially whenever things were rough, I would say 'I adore you.' And he would say, 'And I always will.'"

Nana Lena wiped her eyes. "I still talk to him sometimes. I'll see him standing in the doorway, checking up on me. "

"Like a ghost?"

"More real than that. I can almost touch him. And we talk. You know, before he died, he told me that the hardest thing about dying would be not being able to take care of me, and I told him that a little thing like death wasn't going to keep us apart." She stopped grating for a moment. "Papa was in and out of hospitals that last year before he died. You were in Germany then."

"I remember. I was in class one day, and all of a sudden I started to cry. The teacher asked me what was the matter, and I told her my grandfather was in the hospital. I don't know why I said that. It just came to me out of nowhere, but when I got home from school that night, Mom called to tell me that Papa had been taken to the hospital. It was amazing the way I just knew."

"He hated the hospital and its inhuman procedures. He hated the backless gowns and lack of privacy and the beeping monitors and countless interruptions. He made me promise that I would die at home, with my family around me, in peace and dignity. And I told him I would, that when it was my time, it would be in my own bed, in my own home, with my family around me, when I was good and ready."

"Nana, please, don't talk about dying. The doctor said you're in remission."

"So I have a few more years left. That's *wonderful*. But when the time comes, that's how I want it. Will you *remember*?"

"I'll remember."

"And besides, I'm not going until they get electricity down there. You know how afraid I am of the dark."

Just then the oven timer went off. "Take the brisket out of the oven and put it on the cutting board to cool. We'll slice it later. You can rinse the grater."

"Why won't you use the food processor Mom bought you?"

"It's too complicated. I'm afraid I'll cut myself."

"I'm afraid to do it the old-fashioned way. This looks more dangerous. "

"I remember the day I bought that grater."

"You would, Nana. You remember everything."

"In memories, you live again and again."

I leaned over and kissed her.

"What was that for?"

"Just because."

"Because what?"

"Because I *adore* you."

Nana Lena leaned over and kissed her granddaughter. "I adore *you*, and I always will."

"Is that a promise, Nana?"

"That's a promise!" Lena looked at her watch. "Come on, it's time to set the table for dinner."

* * *

Many years later, my sister Donna decided to elope on Valentine's Day. She called me the day before. After my initial shock, I asked her if she had told Nana.

"I'm afraid to."

"You're afraid of Nana?" Then I reminded her that Nana had eloped for some of the same reasons: lack of money for a wedding; not wanting to offend either side of the family; for the pure romance.

She promised to call Nana on Valentine's Day.

I waited until the evening of Valentine's Day to call Nana Lena. After the usual chitchat I asked her if she had heard from Donna lately. There was a longer than usual silence before she answered.

"Yes."

"And?"

Then in a restrained voice, she said, "It is not what I would have wanted for my granddaughter."

"Nana! Why?"

"Because he doesn't have any money."

"Did Papa have any money when you met him?"

"Well, no. And he's a musician; what kind of life can he offer?"

"Remember, Papa was a graduate of the School of Hard Knocks."

"Yes...but...."

"So?"

"He isn't Jewish."

"He has agreed to raise the children Jewish...."

"Children?"

"There are no children yet. I'm talking *theoretical* children."

I heard a great big sigh from the other end of the phone, and then I laid into her. "You know, Lena Goodman, you sound just like your father."

"My father? I do not!"

Changing my voice to sound like my great-grandfather

Morris, "He sounds like a Damn Yankee to me!"

Nana Lena repeated "Damn Yankee" and then she started to laugh, and I laughed with her. "I can't believe it. I sound just like him. I just want Donna to be happy. That's all."

"That's what we all want, Nana. Look, the next time you speak to Papa, ask him to keep his eye on Donna, too."

"Oh, he's been doing that for a long time. He's the first one that told me she was married, but I didn't believe him. Next time, I'd better listen."

That night I dreamt about my grandfather, only it was more a memory than a dream. I was five years old and it was Sunday and Nana Lena was putting the brisket on the table.

Papa rubbed his hands together. "Just look at this. A little slice of heaven."

Nana Lena beamed as Papa began to serve me. Then, helping himself to a heaping portion, he paused for a moment, looked around at his wife and his family, and smiled from ear to ear. "Brisket is sweet and sour, like life. But damn, it's good!"

* * *

Brisket, a.k.a. Damn Yankee Pot Roast

Brisket, at least 2 lbs

1 cup ketchup

1/2 cup steak sauce (Heinz 57 was Nana's choice)

1 packet dry onion soup mix

4 cups water

salt and pepper to taste

Put brisket in roasting pan. For sauce, mix 1 cup of ketchup, 4 cups of water, 1/2 cup of your choice of steak sauce, and 1 package dry onion soup mix. Warm until mixed. Pour sauce over brisket and cover. Cook 2 hours at 325°. Uncover, baste, add more water if necessary. Cook 1 hour more or longer until tender. Remove meat from pan. Let cool 10 minutes. Slice against the grain in long thin slices, and return meat to remaining sauce in pan. Return to oven for at least 1 hour before serving. If the meat is chewy, it hasn't cooked enough. Eventually, it softens so that you can cut it with a fork. Remember, the longer it simmers, the better it tastes.

Variation

Add peeled potatoes cut in wedges, thick slices of carrot, fresh minced onion, and a can of crushed tomatoes. Use at least 3 cups of water to start. Set the meat on top of the vegetables and let it steam. Keep an eye on your pan; make sure that there is always enough liquid so it won't burn.

Cream Cheese and Jelly

It was snowing the night your mother came into the world and I remember it like it was yesterday. We were sitting around the house killing time playing Kalookie. Myer was there, and Mama, and Pete and Mike and Leon and Sidney; Pete was winning. I had an urge for a cream-cheese-and-jelly sandwich. Myer said he would make it for me, but I said, no, I needed to get up and stretch my legs, but that I wouldn't refuse a little help getting up. He gave me a hand and I went into the kitchen to make my sandwich. I was standing in front of the open refrigerator, reaching for the cream cheese, when I wet myself. I think I must have dropped the jelly, because Myer rushed into the kitchen. I was standing there crying looking at the growing puddle forming on my clean linoleum.

"Jesus, Lena, what happened?" Myer asked.

The boys followed him into the room all talking at once. "Lena?" "What's the matter?" "What the hell happened?"

As soon as Mama saw the puddle, she smiled and clapped her hands together. "*Mazel Tov!* Your water broke."

"Is that what? I thought I wet myself."

Myer was all concerned. "We better get you to the hospital."

Mama made one last attempt. "You sure you want to go to the hospital, Lena? Why don't you just have the baby here at home, like I did?"

"Mama, we already went through this. Myer and I agreed. This baby is going to be born in a hospital."

"There's nothing wrong with you, and you were born at home."

"That may be true, Mama; I know you had all of us at home, except Sidney and Poogie. They were born in the hospital."

"And look what good it did them," Pete said.

"We're going to the hospital, Mama."

"All right, Leike. Whatever you say. It's your baby. Don't listen to your mother, who is older and wiser than you."

I gave Mama a stern look and headed toward the doorway. I was going to the hospital no matter what she said. Then I had my first contraction. Mama saw my face, and she started barking orders: "Mike, get her suitcase. Pete, get the coat, Leon, you get the car, and crank the heat up. We'll be down in a minute."

Myer said, "What should I do?"

"You can clean up the floor. Someone could slip and fall on this."

Myer was a bit shocked at his mother-in-law's tone, but he went ahead and wiped it up. Then they bundled me up, and we poured down the stairs to the car.

Leon had pulled the car practically onto the sidewalk. He was pacing back and forth nervously until, seeing us, he rushed over to help. Everyone was talking at the same time, bumping into each other in their excitement. It reminded me of a Marx Brothers comedy routine. It was decided that Myer should ride in the back with me, Leon would drive, Mama would sit up front. The boys wanted to come too, but there was no room inside, so they rode on the running boards, all the way to the hospital.

When we got there, Pete jumped off the running board and grabbed a wheelchair from an orderly who was assisting another patient into a car. "Hey, buddy, what the heck?" But Pete didn't pay him any mind. He rushed over with the wheelchair. Myer and my brothers lifted me out of the car and into the chair. Then they all wheeled me into the maternity ward, with Mama right behind them. Norfolk Protestant Hospital had never seen anything like the Goodman family.

My sisters, Goldie and Fannie, were already there. They came straight from work.

"Lena? How are you feeling?" Goldie asked anxiously.

"I'm fine, Goldie. I'm going to be fine."

"Are you scared, Lee?" my sister Fannie asked.

"Of course she's scared. I know I'd be scared shitless."

"Goldie!"

Everyone was talking at the same time and I could hear a voice saying, "Excuse me. Excuse me. Could everybody pipe down a second so I can help the young lady here."

Pete blurted out, "It's about time we got some attention."

The nurse gave him a surprised look, but bit her tongue. Coming out from behind the desk, she took my wheelchair and leaned over and whispered in my ear. "Looks like you could use a little peace and quiet." Then she turned and addressed the others. "The rest of you can just wait out here."

The nurse (her name was Jackson; I could see it plainly on her name tag) wheeled me into the examination room. She asked me my name, and I told her.

"Am I glad to meet *you*. Your mother has been calling here almost every day for the past month. Probably every time you left the house."

"I wouldn't doubt it."

"Alice Lou," she called over to one of the other nurses, "look who we got here. We got Lena Herzberg."

"Thank God, her mother will stop calling."

"See what I mean?" Nurse Jackson took my blood pressure and measured my pulse.

"Mama's out in the waiting room," I warned her. "I promise you, you haven't heard the end of her yet."

"How close are the contractions?"

"About every fifteen minutes."

"Oh, then we have some time"

Outside, in the waiting room (I heard all about this later), Papa and Poogie had arrived, too, so that by now all my brothers and sisters were there, along with Mama and Papa, and Myer. Naturally, everyone was on pins and needles. Fannie rattled on nervously, "I don't think she looked good. Do you think she looked good, Mama?"

"She's scared. She doesn't know what to expect."

"Well, don't look at me. You think I know?" Goldie arched her brows.

"This is our first baby in the family. My first grandchild. *Keyn eynhore*," Minnie beamed.

"You think it's going to be a boy or a girl?" Poogie asked.

Goldie announced with certainty, "It's a girl."

Fannie said, "Looks like a boy to me."

"A boy, a girl, either way I'll be a Bubbie." Minnie turned to Myer. "You're the husband. Why don't you find out what's going on in there?"

Myer, glaring at Minnie, marched out. Minnie started pacing. After a few minutes, Myer returned. "Well?" Mama asked.

"The doctor is examining her now."

"It's about time! Leon, go find out what the doctor said."

Myer took a stand. "Minnie Goodman, I just told you, she's with the doctor."

Leon did not even resist. He did as he was told. As he approached the nurses' desk, he spotted a pretty one and sidled up to her. He looked at her name tag. "Cora Lee: that's a pretty name. My name is Leon Goodman."

"Yes, Mr. Goodman. How can I help you, sir?"

"My sister, Lena Herzberg, we just brought her in a little while ago, and I was wondering, how is she doing?"

"I believe she's with the doctor now."

"Could you find out for me, please, Cora Lee? I don't know if you've ever met my Mama, but she won't let up until she finds out."

Cora Lee blushed. "I'll see what I can do." She disappeared behind the swinging doors.

Leon took a seat behind the desk, looked at his watch, picked up the phone, and dialed. When Cora Lee returned, she thought she heard him say, "Put twenty on Lucky Girl in the Fifth." But she could not swear by it.

Back in the waiting room, the Goodmans had pretty much taken over the place. All the other families had left, and the Goodman family had spread out all over the room. Millie and Sidney were doing their homework. Papa *davened*. Mama and Myer paced back and forth. Mama paced one way, and Myer the other, and every once in a while they would pass and Mama would give him a "Hmmpfh," which would rile Myer even further, and he would roll his eyes at her.

Leon returned to boisterous greetings.

"So what did the Doctor say?" Mama was right up in Leon's face.

"It could be a couple hours, or it could be all night."

"See, you take her to a fancy hospital and a fancy doctor, and they still don't know *nothing*." Mama exclaimed. "Pete, Mike, see what you can find out."

This time a pert blonde nurse emerged through the maternity ward doors and reported to Mike and Pete, who were eighteen and twenty at the time and quite good looking. Of course, I'm partial. I'm their big sister.

"Oh, she's doing just fine, Mr. Goodman and Mr. Goodman." The young nurse batted her eyes.

"I'm Mike, and this here is my brother Pete."

"Can we see her?"

"We'll let you know when the time comes."

"How about I buy you a soda sometime?" Pete asked.

"That isn't necessary. I'm just doing my job."

Mike jabbed Pete. "Maybe she don't like soda. Maybe she'd like a beer."

"Beer? What do you know from beer, you little *pisher*? You ain't old enough to drink beer."

Mike shrugged, and both brothers turned to face her.

"I never drink while I'm on duty," She winked as she disappeared behind the swinging doors.

Mike said, "Did you see that?"

"See what?" Pete answered nonchalantly. "Did I see her wink at me?"

"What makes you think she was winking at you? She had her eye on me. She did."

Mama's reconnaissance mission and my brothers' pursuit of all the young pretty nurses continued for hours, wearing thin the patience of even the most patient of nurses, and driving Myer battier than hell. By the time Nurse Jackson emerged to announce my delivery, Myer was a nervous wreck.

"Mr. Herzberg. You have a baby girl."

"My Lena had a girl." Minnie beamed proudly.

"A girl?" Papa asked.

"It's a girl?" The Goodman clan was ecstatic. They started hugging and kissing each other, including the nurse.

Myer was stunned speechless.

Goldie said. "See, I told you so. I told you it was a girl."

The boys patted Myer on the back. Morris shook his hand.

The nurse asked. "Would you like to see her? Mr. Herzberg? Sir?"

Myer was in shock. Finally, nodding, he followed Nurse Jackson into the delivery room, where she helped him into a surgical robe and mask. Myer peered over the mask at me. I smiled as best I could and directed my head over to the infant in my arms. She had a full head of curly hair, like his, but the doctor had had to use forceps to get her out, so her head was kind of flat. The doctor said it would fill out in a few days and I was not to be alarmed. I was just going to tell Myer, when he took one look at her and ran screaming from the hospital. He ran all the way down Granby Street until he reached the waterfront. He was terrified at what he thought he had seen: With her flat head all covered in fur and what appeared to be grape jelly, she looked more like a bear cub than a baby. But when they laid her down on my chest and I held her hand and felt her little heart beating, I knew there was nothing wrong with my little girl.

A few hours later, Myer came back, his heart still pounding. He stood in front of the nursery window, scanning the cradles for his daughter. The cradle labeled "Herzberg" was empty. For a moment, he panicked. Then a kind nurse noticed and smiled at him, rocked her arms, and pointed down the hall to my room.

Myer entered, hat in hand. I was so relieved to see him I didn't even scold. Instead I offered him his daughter, who had been all cleaned and dried. Her head was already beginning to fill out like the doctor said. "Isn't she beautiful?"

Myer inched closer.

"Don't you want to hold her? I think she has the Herzberg hair."

"Really?"

"Most definitely. And the Goodman eyes."

"How can you tell?"

"They seem to be making fun of me."

Myer sat gingerly on the bed next to me. I handed him our girl.

"Hello, Elka. We'll call her Elayne, right?"

"Of course. Elayne, Laney, for my mother's mother, Elka Gustomilsky. Don't forget to tell the rabbi."

"Don't worry, I'll take care of it."

"She's a pretty little thing. Look at her."

"I'm so proud of you, baby." Myer leaned over and kissed me, and I nearly passed out with happiness. Here we were the three of us, our new little family, *my* family. My life was forever changed.

"Can I get you anything, Mrs. H?"

"No, I can't think of anything, Mr. H. Come to think of it, you sure can. I would kill for a cream-cheese-and-jelly sandwich."

"Cream cheese and jelly? My favorite. You want some-thing to drink with that?"

"A glass of milk."

"Mind if I join you?"

"Mind? Why would I mind? You know, I adore you."

"I adore you and I always will."

"Myer?"

"Yes, love?"

"Don't be gone long."

Myer dashed out of the room and almost ran smack into my father who was on his way to visit me.

"Myer. *Mazel Tov*! I just came from the *shul*."

"I'm on my way over there shortly, to name the baby."

"It isn't necessary."

"To name the baby? Why?"

"I already did."

Myer was miffed. "Morris, why would you go and name my baby? It's *my* baby!"

Morris shook his head and answered apologetically. "Minnie says jump, I jump. I don't ask how high." Papa handed Myer a cigar.

"Is that the secret to a good marriage, Morris?"

"That," Papa winked, "and a good featherbed."

* * *

Cream Cheese & Jelly

Take 2 slices of challah or rye bread. Spread with cream cheese— whipped works the best. Add a dollop of strawberry, raspberry, or cherry jam or jelly. Whatever you like. Cut sandwich in half so you can share it. It always tastes better shared.

Lena, 1935

Myer Herzberg, 1935

Elayne Herzberg, 1935

4 Generations: Lena, her father Morris Goodman, (right), daughter Elayne seated on lap of her great-grandmother Sareva Goodman, 1937

Elayne & Lena, 1941

Lena serves the troops– 1944

Lena, Myer, & Elayne,
Ocean view, 1940

Myer & Lena, 1944

Mike & Sidney

Pete & Sidney

Sidney & Pete in Germany

Freddie Herzberg,
Germany 1945

A World Without Sugar

"Honey, would you mind filling up the sugar jar for me? That five-pound bag sure feels a whole lot heavier than it used to."

"Is there anything else can I do for you while I'm here, Nana?"

"Oh, I'll think of something."

"I'm sure you will."

As I poured the sugar into the canister, Nana Lena got that faraway look in her eyes. I could feel a story coming on.

"You know, during World War II, we had to ration sugar, which made it hard to bake sweet things."

"Sugar? You're kidding, right?"

"I'm not kidding. We had these little ration booklets: one for flour and one for sugar. Once a month, you were allowed to use one of those coupons. It was the war years. Things were different then. One day, Mr. Alex Ferebee, a local realtor, came over and said, 'Mrs. Herzberg, you want to give me a hand?'

"'What can I help you with, Mr. Ferebee?'

"'We need some people down at the ration board, and we need *honest* people. '

"I was flattered and I said, 'Thank you, sir, I'd be glad to.' And I did. I went down to the first floor of the city jail and I rationed liquor tickets, and later I rationed automobile tires and gasoline. I was tempted to take a few of those tickets myself, but I didn't. My conscience wouldn't let me. That's who I am, and the kind of person I want my grandchildren to be."

I smiled as she kissed me three times on the cheek. I was so used to her displays of affection that I didn't comment. "How did you cook without sugar, Nana?"

"We used applesauce, bits of fruit, honey, whatever we had. I remember one year — it was 1944—Myer and I took your mother to Baltimore and put her on a train to Camp Louise in Western Maryland. Myer and I took one thousand dollars out of the bank, and we were going to go as far as one thousand dollars would take us. That was a lot of money in those days, and we went all over New England. Coming back from Maine, we stopped in Boston, where one of your Papa's cousins was a regional manager for a large grocery chain.

"And he asked Papa, 'Myer, how are you fixed for sugar?'

"And Papa said, 'We're hurting.'

"'Myer, how are you fixed for flour?'

"'We're hurting.'

"All the cousins shook their heads in pity, and then he filled our trunk with bags and bags of flour and sugar.

"The trunk was so weighted down. I'm telling you the honest-to-God's truth, it really slowed us down." Nana Lena started laughing. "It took thirty-five trips to get all the stuff up the stairs when we got home. Then we were *hurting*—boy, we were hurting."

* * *

Nana Lena, my mother, and I were sitting around the kitchen talking as we chopped the ingredients for strudel.

My mother stopped dicing candied fruit for a second, and then she said, "All I remember about the war was a sea of white. Everywhere you looked when you went downtown was a sea of white sailor caps. Norfolk was always a Navy town, but during the war, it seemed like everyone was Navy. I was a child during the war."

"A real beauty, too, a dark-haired Shirley Temple with dimples to match."

"Oh, Mother, you're partial."

"As a mother should be. She won a beauty contest the year she was four. I still have the picture."

"That's because you never throw anything away, Mother." Elayne leaned in to explain. "The only reason I won was because my uncles stuffed the ballot box. They kept voting and voting, and I had a lot of uncles. During the early years of the war, my uncles used to take me out with them to pick up girls."

"They didn't!"

"Oh, yes, they most certainly did."

Nana Lena teased. "They always had better luck picking up girls when they had their Monkey along."

"Monkey?"

"That's what they called her."

"This is very useful information." I turned to my mother and taunted her, "Monkey."

My mother chose to ignore me, as she asked Nana Lena, "Where was Leon, during the war? I don't remember."

"Leon was home; he was too old for service. So was your father. Leon was a policeman, and Myer was regional blackout warden. His job was to make sure that blackout was upheld. He used to patrol the neighborhood and check to make sure that every house was sealed up tight, with no visible lights, and if someone forgot to pull down the blackout shades, he'd rap on their door three times as a warning. I used to love to make the rounds with him. We'd stroll along, arm in arm, through the streets of a darkened city. It was quite romantic."

"Your Papa was so tall and handsome, and I loved the way he made me feel parading me on his arm. If we happened to run into someone, he'd tip his hat, 'Good Evening, Mrs. So and So, Good Evening, Mr. So and So.' And he'd say, 'Have you met my lovely wife?' Oh, he was a charmer, your Papa. I thanked the Lord that He let him remain by my side throughout the war. With three of my brothers over there, and two of your Papa's, not to mention all the other Goodman cousins, I had enough people to worry about and enough letters to write.

"I had taken it upon myself to launch my own campaign against the Germans by strengthening the morale of the American soldiers, at least the ones that I was directly related to. Together with my sisters and my brothers' wives and friends, we got together once a week to write letters to our loved ones. Across both oceans, our husbands and brothers did the same. I still marvel that we were able to keep in touch, despite the fact that the war kept them constantly on the move and half our letters went astray.

"When I think back on those times, I can remember how excited we were to get each V-mail. Not e-mail, like you have today, but V-mail. About halfway through the war, the United States started using V-mail as a way of reducing the amount of airplane space needed to carry paper mail to all our soldiers overseas. The letters were photographed and transferred to microfilm for shipping. The rolls of film were sent to locations where they were printed four to a page, so they ended up about one quarter of their original size. These postcard-sized letters were then delivered to the addressee. It was very advanced technology for our time. I kept most of the letters. Mostly letters about writing letters, but it is quite amazing when you think our entire family was able to keep in touch throughout most of the war, and everyone, *Halevai*, lived to tell the tale."

Nana Lena handed me a stack of what appeared to be postcard-sized photocopies of letters from 1944 to 1945, but closer examination revealed them to be photographs of letters, remarkably well preserved, and filled with family history.

"One thing I found interesting is what the letters did *not* say. Pete, Sidney, and Freddie ended the war in Germany. They witnessed the ultimate horrors, yet they barely refer to it in their letters home. Instead, they talked about mundane, day-to-day details, and about not getting enough mail."

Belgium, 3–16–44

Dearest Lena, Myer and Elayne,

No mail from you for a few days, but I guess I'll get some soon. I am getting along swell now and sure do hope to hear the same from you all at home. How is Leon doing on the ice truck? Just fine I hope. How is Myer getting along? Has he plenty of work? I hope so. Tell Monkey she still owes me a letter.

Love,
Bro Pete

"Before he was sent to Europe, Pete was stationed in New York. He called home one day to tell us he had decided to get married that weekend. I told him there was no way he was going to marry someone I had not met. It was my responsibility as his older sister to at least look her over. So Pete invited us all up to New York. Because Myer didn't have a car at the time, I burst into tears. I cried and cried until Myer asked his friend Al to drive us up to New York. And he did. We drove up to Brooklyn to meet his bride-to-be, Thelma Rothman, a tall, thin reed of a girl, with long dark hair. What the boys called 'a real looker.' Despite the fact that she talked with that funny New York accent, I took to her from the start. The next day they were married."

My mother interrupted, "And that night your Nana proceeded to drink all the men under the table."

Nana Lena protested, "I did not."

"Mother, you know you did. Don't deny it."

"All right, I'll admit, I did have a little something to drink that night. After all, it's not every day your brother gets married." Nana Lena's face melted from happy to sad. "But, you know, life has a way of throwing a curve ball sometimes. Pete shipped out two days later. He was only married for two days! That's how it was for a lot of the boys back then. I think some of them got married so that they would have someone to write to."

England, 7–23–44

Dear Lee [Lena], Myer and Elayne,

Just a few words to let you know I am still in England and getting along as well as can be expected. Lee, I want you to do me a favor. I want you to buy an anniversary gift for Thelma from me as my anniversary is August 22nd and let me know how much it costs. I'll send you the money as soon as I get paid. Please buy her something nice and I won't forget it and someday maybe I will do you a favor. What's new around Berkley? Is Mama feeling alright? Has Mike left yet? If he has, send me his address so I can write to him. Tell my favorite niece to write her lonesome Uncle. Love to all the Goodmans and Herzbergs.

Your Bro
Pete

Somewhere in England,
August 11, 1944

My Dear Sis, Bro and Niece,

Just a few words to let you know your Bro is doing all

right. Had letters from Goldie, Poogie and am expecting some from you and Fannie very soon and if I don't get any I am going to give you both a spanking as soon as I get home. How is my darling Elayne? Is she still as mean as ever or has she suddenly changed her way of living. Tell her to write me a few lines as I really do miss her.

Your Bro Pete

Nov 5, 1944,
Germany

Dear Lena, Myer and Elayne,

No mail in over a week, but I am writing to you anyway as I know how it is when you get mail from someone you don't have a chance to see. I had a very nice letter from Mike in which he says he is getting along okay. I want you to remind my niece she owes me a letter and to hurry up and write me before I come home and give her a good spanking, or is she too big to be spanked? How is Myer making out? Has he got work? Is he still in the same business or has he got himself a softer racket? I will close now as time is limited. Love to all the G's and H's.

Your Bro,
Pete

"The next letter I received from Pete was dated December 15th, 1944, from the 19th General Hospital Medical Department. He never mentioned what had happened that had caused him to be hospitalized. Pete had seen duty in the Huertgen Forest. He survived the 'Green Hell,' as he called it. He was one of thousands of soldiers who lost or almost lost their feet and legs to the mud and cold of the forest, and to the lack of adequate boots or clothing for the cold German climate. The Huertgen Forest was southeast of Aachen and was part of the Rhineland Campaign, the first major Allied incursion into Germany. The Germans were well entrenched and well supplied. During the fall of 1944, over 24,000 Allies died or were wounded on this seventy-mile strip of land. But Pete wrote nothing about it. Maybe they did this to protect us. Maybe they were afraid they might reveal strategic information by relaying what happened, and their letter wouldn't make it past the censors. Maybe they just couldn't talk about it."

Dec 15, 1944, France

Dear Lena, Myer and Elayne,

Another day and still no mail. I sure hope I get some soon or else I guess I'll get transferred to the nut ward as I sure as hell will go nuts. Have you heard from Sidney recently? I sure would like to know where and how he is. I would also like to know where Mike is and how are his chances of getting back to the States. I'm getting along pretty good now. I guess they'll send me back to the front. I love and miss you all a lot.

Your Bro Pete

"Later, when he got home, Pete told me he had been taken to an Army hospital just west of the German border, in France. The doctors were assessing the condition of each patient. Many of the soldiers suffered from trench foot, where the foot, after long-term exposure to cold, wet, and unsanitary conditions, begins to rot and often had to be amputated.

"The Army doctor examined Pete and shook his head. 'I'm sorry, Private. The right one has to go.'

"Pete raised himself up from the bed and said. 'I have a gun, Doctor, and I'll *kill* you if you cut off my leg.'

"'If you feel that strongly about it, Private, we'll see how you're doing in a few days.' They did not amputate, and eventually he healed. When Pete was able to walk again, he was sent back to the front, this time even further into Germany."

* * *

We had finished chopping the candied fruit, pecans, and raisins and were ready to move on to the next stage in the strudel preparation: the dough, which is a mixture of flour, butter, and sour cream that Nana Lena had prepared the day before and allowed to refrigerate overnight. She dusted the cutting board with flour before rolling out the first ball, as thin as possible, into a long rectangle. She brushed the dough with melted butter before applying a thin layer of candied fruit, nuts, and raisins in a smooth, uniform pattern, along the longest edge of the dough.

"My brother Sidney was a medic, and he was stationed in eastern France at the time, just behind the advancing Allied front. As the Allies marched into Germany, they were met with fierce resistance. As the German soldiers defended their Fatherland, the casualties were extremely high. Since the medics were always closest to the casualties, they were close to danger. I prayed every night for Sidney and for Pete and Mike and Ernie and Freddie— prayed that God would protect them and bring them safely back home."

Dec 10, 1944,
somewhere in France

Dearest Sis,

I hope that this letter finds you, Myer and Elayne and the rest of the family in the very best of health and happiness.

Last night I heard a lot of artillery fire and some of it was hitting pretty near us. I haven't been in actual combat yet. The Germans also respect the Red Cross so I don't think they will fire on the medics. You see we don't carry any weapons. We just wear our Red Cross armbands for protection and PRAY.

Love,
Sid

Dec 15, 1944, France

My dearest Sis,

I received your letter today as well as mail from Goldie, Mike, the Salzbergs, Evelyn and Ellie. It was the first mail I have received in twelve days. I certainly am glad to hear that all at home are okay.

Sis, I am feeling fine and getting along just swell. Please don't worry about me. I am living in a French home that was once occupied by the Germans. This was a well to do home at one time. If my letters are few and far between it will be because we are constantly on the move. I will write home as often as I can. Love to all. Kiss Elayne for me.

Love always,
Sid

France
12/30/44

Dearest Sis,

I received your letter dated 12/11/44 today and was really indeed very glad to hear from you. Say sis, I'm not trying to start an argument, but I think I am writing you more often than you are writing me.

I know just what hospital Pete is in but it is too far for me to make a trip. I had a letter from him dated 12/7.

Glad to hear that Mike is getting a furlough. Perhaps he will remain in the States. I certainly do hope that he does.

Love,
Sid

"Pete and Sidney met up twice during the war. It was 1945. They were both over in Germany. They shouted and waved to each other as their convoys passed, one heading east, the other heading west. A few days later, Pete found out where Sidney was, and it wasn't very far away. The soldier who relayed the message said that Sid's unit was low on meat, so Pete got a jeep and he filled it with meat, and he took it over to Sidney's men. Wasn't that just like Pete to look after his baby brother like that? Even with a war going on?"

Nana Lena rolled the dough over the filling, careful not to let it tear. "Mama used to roll the strudel in a greased and floured dishcloth, but I do it like so." She finished the roll and then reached for a knife. "You see, you trim the end like this. Then you place the roll on a well-greased cookie sheet. I usually put two on a sheet. We'll have enough for two pans. Now you try."

I rolled out the second ball of dough with no problem.

"Make sure it's real thin."

I sprinkled the filling and began to roll the strudel. Bits of nuts kept breaking through, causing the dough to tear.

"Not to worry. You can pinch off a piece from the ends and use it to fill in any holes." Before continuing with her story, she demonstrated how to make the repairs.

* * *

"Your Papa's brother Ernie was also a medic. He was the third person to be drafted in New York State after the US joined the war. He was a corporal and medic and had been stationed in Brooklyn until he was shipped out in 1944 to be part of the Allied invasion of Africa."

Somewhere at sea, 1944

Hello Everybody,

Yo folks, this is me again. Things are a bit quiet just now so I thought I'd drop you a line. Of course I can't mail it, but what the hell. We're sailing along nice and peacefully right now and I sure hope it keeps up. We ran into a squall the other night and it really ruined the boys. Every damn one of them was sick as a dog for a couple of days. Just about everything in the hospital that was breakable was broken. This tub will match any destroyer roll for roll and pitch for pitch. We manage to keep pretty busy in the hospital, but we also have plenty of time to ourselves, if you know what I mean. Otherwise I'm okay and holding up pretty well. I earnestly hope that all is well with everyone in Norfolk. I guess that's all for now.

Love, Ernie

Nana Lena checked her watch, "It's been a half hour, Elayne; turn the oven down to three-fifty."

"Yes, mother. Your Nana would have made a good drill sergeant; I can just hear her."

"No doubt about it." I saluted my grandmother and started to sing an army marching song:

Chop the dried fruit nice and small

We don't want no pits at all.

Mince those pecans really fine

Roll that dough, it's strudel time!

Sound off. One. Two.

Sound off. Three. Four

Sound off.

One Two... Three Four!

By this time, my mother and grandmother were howling with laughter. "Come here," Nana Lena ordered with a stern face, and I obeyed. Then she leaned over and gave me another triple kiss, Nana Lena style.

"Papa's youngest brother, Freddie, was only eighteen years old when he joined the Army. Freddie was a tall, good-looking red head. He had a crush on me ever since he was a little boy. He told me so years later, but I already knew. Freddie was the *Wunderkind* in the family, and boy, was he smart. He went to college when he was fifteen years old. Myer was furious when Freddie enlisted in the army. When Myer asked him why he had signed up, Freddie was the first to tell him. 'Ever since I was a kid growing up on 155th Street and St. Nicholas, I was a fighter. That's what they need over there in Germany: a few tough Jewish street fighters like myself.' Freddie was a Sergeant in the 42nd Rainbow Division during the final months of the war."

Germany, March 6, 1945

Dear Myer, Lena and Elayne

I received two more V-mails from Lee today. I wish I could be in Virginia for ten minutes so I could kiss her. Lee, your letters have been coming very regularly and I can't tell you how much it means to me to hear about how things are at home often enough so I don't begin to worry. I'll see what I can do about getting in touch with Pete. Tell Mom and Pop I miss them very much and to please take care of themselves.

Love,
Freddie

Germany, March 7, 1945

Dear Myer, Lena and Elayne,

Every day I can I am writing a letter to each of you in Norfolk. Yesterday I even wrote two to Mom and Pop besides yours.

You wrote about Shirley coming to live in Norfolk in May. I hope so. It would mean a lot to me.

Things here are rotten. In the midst of all this killing and suffering, there is still that cheap pettiness of the American soldier. I can't understand it myself, but there is more to it than fighting in combat. I'll explain later what I mean.

I'd like to hear more news from Ernie. You sent me his address once, but I lost it in the moving. I keep an address book now. I'd really like to have a long letter filled with news of home. V-mail may be faster, but it has its limits, as I have reached the end of this page.

Love, Freddie

"That spring, we heard from Pete for the first time in months. It was just around *Pesach*, when the entire nation was grieving for its Commander-in-Chief, President Roosevelt. We knew Pete had been in Germany, so we were quite relieved to see the Belgian postmark."

April 7, 1945
Belgium

Dearest Lena,

Just a few words to say hello and let you all know I'm getting on okay. I go to services every Friday night, as I have since I got to Belgium. After what I've seen, I can't seem to pray enough.

I received your care package with the strudel and I can't tell you how much I appreciated it. The strudel tasted a little salty, because I cried with every bite. Just kidding. It was swell to receive a little piece of home.

How is Elayne doing in school? Very good I hope, or I should say, very good *I know*. Miss you all very much, especially my Monkey.

Love, Pete

"A week later we received this letter from Freddie."

April 18, 1945
Germany

Dear Myer, Lena and Elayne,

Finally some rest. Just in time to enjoy a peaceful birthday. It is really wonderful. Can wash and sleep and write. I haven't been able to write for so long. So much has happened. My company, I can't recognize, even our commanding officer was killed, the one I told you about in the States, right in front of me. We lost all our officers and practically all of the original men of my company. I can never hope to describe those days. I pulled through okay. My nerves were shot, and I don't think I could have stood much more. This rest was a godsend and as I said, I am okay and feel much better after sleeping and washing. I received the bronze star medal the other day.

Love, Freddie

"'I received the bronze star medal the other day,' he wrote so matter-of-factly, like the Bronze Star had no meaning. Maybe Freddie didn't feel that being the only one in his unit to survive deserved a medal. Instead, he felt guilty for being the survivor. 'Why me? Dear God, why did You chose me?' The answer came a few days later.

"It was the end of August, and Freddie's unit was fighting in the mountains of Bavaria when it came to the attention of General Hibbs that Freddie spoke Yiddish, French, and Italian. Freddie was transferred from the battlefield to a small town outside Munich—a town named Dachau—where there was an urgent need for translators. He later told us the following story:

"The incomprehensible brutality that was revealed inside those gates caused even the gentlest man to snap. The SS guards were quickly rounded up and shot, and no one gave it any thought after the box cars of dead bodies, the rows of ovens, the piles of human ash. If you took an SS prisoner, what were you going to do with him? 'Take him to regimental headquarters and be back in a minute.' In other words, shoot the son of a bitch.

"We were carrying out the bodies with typhus. I was white with DDT, which was supposed to protect us from the typhus. It was a mess at the end of the war. The horrors that occurred! The military was corrupt. It was absolute chaos. There was no food. No medical supplies.

"I remember running around delirious with typhus, wild-eyed, ranting, with a white silk scarf wrapped around my neck, taunting the Germans, *'Ich bin Jude,* and I'm in charge, goddammit.'

"Dachau became a POW camp for Germans, and I was put in charge of Freimann, a Polish camp nearby. The U.S. Army didn't recognize Jews as a separate people—they were Poles, Germans, Slavs, or Romanians—and the Jews just got dumped in where they came from. I was in charge of the Jewish D.P.s—the displaced persons. I was second in command.

"At this camp, who did the AMG put in charge of a group of mostly Jewish Poles? They put a priest in charge, an emissary of Pope Pius XII, who had collaborated with the Germans. I needed medicines, and he's coming with his long robes and swinging his incense. I turned to him and said, 'We need doctors.'

"'There are none, we only have a veterinarian.'"

"We need medicines."

"'Do the best you can. It is in God's hands.'"

"The Jews in the camp found out I was Jewish and came to me and asked if they could get some extra food for the holidays. It was coming up on Rosh Hashana. I had enough rations for seventy five people, and there were only nine of us Army, so we gave them a big banquet, and I was the guest of honor. None of them spoke Yiddish, but some of them spoke perfect English. One of the D.P.s introduced himself and told me he was a doctor. I was surprised because the priest had told me there were no doctors in the camp. 'How many other doctors are there?' I asked, and seventeen people raised their hands.

"The next day, the priest arrived in his big black car, filled with crosses. The camp is overrun with typhus, and he brings us crosses.

"I dismissed the guards, and I turned to him. 'How come I just found seventeen doctors, and you only told me all we had was a vet?'

"The Polish priest answered matter-of-factly, 'Oh, we don't want Jewish doctors treating our own.'

"I cannot remember what happened after that. All I remember is that I blacked out, and when I returned to Fort Dix after the war, my file had been lost, along with my memory."

"Do you think Uncle Freddie killed the man?" I asked Nana Lena.

"I don't know. I don't want to know. All I do know is that it took him a long time to recover after the war."

Nana Lena took out a large knife and began slicing the cooled strudel roll into one-inch pieces. "When Jewish people talk about the war today, they often remember the six million Jews who died, but they often forget about those brave Jewish soldiers who marched *into* Germany. I can't tell you how proud I was of my brothers, and of all those men, of every race and nationality, who fought by our side, and for the lessons they taught us about courage, endurance, strength, and dignity. As each of my brothers returned, I put eighteen cents in the *pushke*, to thank the Lord for bringing them home. I still do that, to this day, for every important occasion: I put eighteen cents in the *pushke*, and I count my blessings. Eighteen, *chai*, for life."

* * *

Lena's Strudel

makes 4 dozen bite-sized pieces

Dough

1/2 pound melted butter	1 cup sour cream
1 Tbsp sugar	2 1/4 cups flour, sifted
3/4 tsp salt	

Mix together. Stir until it forms a ball. Roll in waxed paper and refrigerate for an hour.

Filling

1 lb dried citrus fruit, diced	1 small can flaked coconut
1/2 box of golden raisins	2 lb chopped pecans
3 lemons, rinds and juice	sugar, to taste
6–8 oz jar strawberry preserves	

Chop dried fruit, coconut, raisins, and pecans by hand into small pieces. Combine in bowl with remaining ingredients.

Remove dough from refrigerator. Put a little oil on your hands and start working the ball. Divide it into four parts. Roll it out 1/8 of an inch thick, about four inches wide and 12 inches long. Trim the edges of the rectangle with a knife. Save excess to patch holes.

Spoon the filling down the middle of the roll. Fold one edge over filling and shape evenly. Try to pack the filling in as closely as possible. Fold other edge over middle, sealing the log by smoothing out the dough, pinching off any extra. Place logs sealed-side-down on a greased and floured cookie sheet or on parchment-lined baking sheet. Leave a little space between the rolls; they should not touch the sides of the pan.

Bake at 325° for 30 minutes. Let cool. Roll in confectioner's sugar. Slice into one-inch pieces.

Sweet and Sour Meat Balls

I love my country. I'm even born on the fourth of July. So it came as quite a shock to me to have people point their fingers at me and call me a "dirty Jew." I remember the first time I heard it. We had pulled into the gas station on a Sunday afternoon in December, 1941. The U.S. was finally in the war now. Pearl Harbor had made it abundantly clear that remaining on the sidelines was no longer an option. It was a warm day for December, and your Mama said she wanted a soda. Myer gave us ten cents, and we were headed over to the newfangled soda machine when the mechanic, a man covered in grime and sweat, looked me right in the eye and called me a "dirty Jew."

I looked at that man, and if my eyes could have burned a hole through him, I would have, but I didn't want Laney to notice. I steered her over to the soda machine, separating her from him with my body as best I could.

He stood there, in the shadows, a heavy tool in his hands, feet apart, in a threatening posture, and said, "This whole damn war is *your* fault. Damn dirty Jews."

Laney retrieved her soda, and we headed back to the car, my back straight, my head erect. I tried not to let his ignorance offend me. He stood there staring at me until we got in the car and left the station. As we pulled onto Granby Street, Myer asked me what I was in such a stew over because he could see something was wrong. I was going to tell him but didn't want to alarm Elayne, so I shrugged my shoulders.

Elayne chimed in. "She's mad at what the man said."

"What man?" Myer asked her.

"The man in the gas station. He called her a dirty Jew."

"He did what?!" Myer stopped the car right in the middle of Granby Street. 'I'll kill the sonofabitch!'

I tried to diffuse the situation as best I could. "He must not be right in the head, Laney, because he was the dirty one, right? You should have seen his clothes." But I could see the damage was already done, and the hatred that was seeping through Europe had reached our shores. Here it was, right in front of me, in my hometown. I'm as American as red, white, and blue, and in that man's eyes, I was the enemy. That is the true meaning of the war at home.

All in all, we counted ourselves amongst the fortunate ones. One by one, each of my brothers returned. Ours was about the only house in Berkley that didn't have a gold star hanging in the window. A gold star signified a soldier who had died in the war. Some windows had more than one star. Mama had lost her brother Moe in the first World War, so she prayed and put eighteen coins in the *pushke* until each of her sons came home. Mike made it back first, then Pete, then Myer's brothers Ernie and Fred. Sidney was the last one home.

As each of the men returned, we learned of more atrocities. The rumors were no longer rumors; they were fact. A madman had wiped out almost all of the Jews in Germany, Poland, Russia, Austria, Czechoslovakia, Hungary, Belgium, Holland, and France. Many of these nations had willingly turned over their Jews to the Nazis for extermination. Six million Jews, at least seventeen million people, lost their lives because Hitler decided to play God. He decided who should live and who should die. I decided to devote my energies to the living, to help provide for those who had lost almost everything during the war.

I had always been an active member of Hadassah, the Women's Zionist Organization founded by Henrietta Szold before the first World War, mainly for its commitment to Jewish social causes. After the second war, there were thousands of refugees living in Displaced Persons camps; many of these camps had been set up on the grounds of the very same concentration camps where the refugees had been held. Where could they go? They had no homes to return to. Their villages had been burned to the ground; their possessions seized by their neighbors. Some of these neighbors were the very same people who had reported them to the Gestapo. There was no question of returning home. There was no question of remaining in the camps. What should be done with the Jews of Europe?

Shadows filled the room as the sun set over the creek behind Nana Lena's house. "Lordy, look at the time," Nana Lena said. We better get dinner started. Papa will be home soon. Amele, take the ground beef out of the refrigerator, and take out two eggs and a couple of onions."

"What are we making?"

"Sweet-and-sour meatballs. You know how Papa loves my meatballs. Your father, too."

"We all do."

"Tell you the truth, half the time I make them because they are so easy to make."

"And the other half?"

"For the 'Oh, Nana's. Oh, Nana this is good. Oh, Nana, I love that.'"

I kissed her on the cheek.

"Amele, beat up two eggs and mix it with a half a cup of water while I chop up these onions real fine. Then we'll mix it all together, a half a cup of the minced onion, a teaspoon of salt, a quarter teaspoon of pepper and a half a cup of matzo meal, or flour if I'm out of meal. Check on the door of the refrigerator."

"Got it."

Nana Lena began mixing the ingredients, working the meal into the mixture to achieve a uniform color. "Now take my large pot and throw in the rest of this onion, a cup of lemon juice, a cup of water, one and one half cups sugar, and two cans of tomato mushroom sauce. If you don't have that, you can use a tomato soup and a can of sliced mushrooms. Or you can use fresh ones if you like. That's how I make it. Poogie doesn't make it that way." Nana Lena turned on the burner and let the sauce simmer.

Back home in Norfolk, I stayed busy with fundraisers and bake sales and bond rallies and we raised quite a lot of money. There were hundreds of thousands of refugees who needed my help. Who was I to refuse? Actually, a Jew is forbidden to turn away anyone who asks for help. It is a great *mitzvah*, a good deed, to show compassion, and above all, help one's fellow man. We call this *tzedakah*, or righteous behavior. The highest form of *tzedekah* is to help a man to help himself.

Now I'm going to tell you a story that not many people know. There was a group of Norfolk businessmen, twenty gentlemen who shall remain nameless—I think most of them are dead now, anyway. These men did something remarkable. They each put up five thousand dollars, which was a lot of money in those days, and they bought an old ferry from the Old Bay Line. The President

Warfield was once a luxury ferry that carried passengers and automobiles back and forth between Baltimore and Norfolk. During World War II, it was used to transport tanks and troops from England to the coast of France. It had been sold for scrap, and they purchased it from the shipwrecking company for one hundred thousand dollars. This ship was later renamed the Exodus. Leon Uris wrote a book about it. Have you read it? It's a goodie.

"The Exodus was outfitted in Baltimore and took to sea in February of '47, but a severe winter storm caused some damage and complete loss of cargo. The Exodus had to be towed into Norfolk Harbor to restock and regroup. We, the women of Hadassah, put the word out, and everyone came down to the pier with blankets and pillows and bags of food. The press got hold of it, and there were articles in all the papers. The British tried to keep the ship from leaving port, but they were unsuccessful. The Exodus left Norfolk over one month later on the first leg of its journey to southern France, where a boatload of Holocaust survivors eagerly waited passage to the Promised Land. The rest is history. You know the story. The British followed the ship from America to France and then to Italy, where the boat was detained for nearly seven weeks. Then, under cover of night, the Exodus returned to France where they smuggled aboard four thousand five hundred refugees—eleven times the ship's normal passenger load—and set its course for Palestine. Twenty miles from Haifa, the British attacked the Exodus using Chinese firecrackers to create noise and confusion. The refugees fought back with cans of food, buckets, and bottles—whatever they had. Three refugees were killed, and more than two hundred were injured.

The Exodus was towed to Haifa Harbor, and the refugees were transferred to British transport ships for their journey back to France. When they arrived in France, most of the refugees refused to leave the ship. The French government would not allow the refugees to be forcibly landed, so the remaining passengers were taken to Hamburg, Germany. The world watched as the British took these poor, ravaged souls from the shores of their new homeland back to the very hell which they thought they had escaped. This was the straw that broke the camel's back. This was the event that shook up the world and allowed for the creation of Israel in 1948.

The sauce began to boil as Nana Lena dropped in balls of meat, about the size of a golf ball. "We'll let this simmer at a slow boil for about an hour. But you've got to keep your eye on it, so the bottom doesn't stick."

"That looks like an awful lot of meat balls."

"We're making a double batch, one for tonight, and one for the freezer for another day."

"That's a good idea."

"It takes the same amount of time, and you get two meals instead of one. I always cook that way. One for the table, one for the freezer. Before I went to Israel the first time, you should have seen my freezer. I left Myer enough food for a month, and I was only going to be gone for ten days. Every container had a tape on it with the contents and the cooking instructions. When I came back all the sweet-and-sour meat balls were gone, and all the noodle kugel."

The first time I went to Israel was in 1962. I was following in the footsteps of great Jewish women like Henrietta Szold. She found her calling in 1912, when she decided to expand a small study circle in New York, into the largest women's Zionist organization in the world. Hadassah, the Women's Zionist Organization of America, was named for Queen Esther, the heroine of Purim. The goal of the organization was to bring modern health care to the Promised Land. Henrietta Szold ran a Nurses Training School, later known as the Henrietta Szold School of Nurses, and was the guiding force behind the creation of the Hadassah Medical Organization. With the creation of the Hadassah Hospital on Mt. Scopus, a world-class hospital that would provide quality care to all who needed it, regardless of race, religion or creed, Henrietta had achieved one of her major goals.

With the rise of Nazism and the worsening situation in Europe, Henrietta turned her attention to the plight of Jewish children. In 1934, she became the director of Youth Aliyah, and for the next fifteen years, she rescued thousands of Jewish youth from Nazi Germany and from wherever they were threatened in Europe and brought them to the Promised Land. She was a remarkable woman, I tell you. She spent her entire life trying to make the world a better place.

So here I was, many years later, on a Hadassah mission,

making my pilgrimage to the Holy Land surrounded by all the good deeds this woman had done. First, we were shown the Hadassah Hospital on Mount Scopus, and then the new facility in the western part of Jerusalem, The Hadassah-Hebrew University Medical Center in Ein Kerem. In the center of this modern medical complex, they had built a synagogue, and the famous Russian artist, Marc Chagall, had been commissioned to design a series of stained glass windows.

The first time I saw the Chagall windows I began to cry. These magnificent windows with their vibrant jewel colors depicted the twelve tribes of Israel. They made me feel peaceful and at the same time exhilarated. Three windows lined each side of the room: Reuben, Simeon, Levi, Judah, Gad, Asher, Issachar, Zebulon, Naphtali, Joseph, Dan, and Benjamin: The twelve sons of Jacob, and his four wives Leah, Rachel, Bilhah, and Zilpah. To have more than one wife was not unusual at the time, but Rachel was the wife he loved. You may recall Jacob worked for seven years to marry his beloved Rachel, only to discover after their wedding night, that he had been married to her older sister, Leah, instead. Then Jacob worked for seven more years before he could marry Rachel. Bilhah and Zilpah were Leah and Rachel's handmaidens. It was the tradition for a wife to offer her handmaiden to her husband to bear more children in her name. These four women were the mothers of the twelve tribes of Israel, two Jews and two Canaanites, and they lived together and multiplied in peace until one day, when their children sold their brother Joseph into slavery. Why? Because Jacob doted on his second-to-youngest son, Joseph, the son of Rachel, and had given him a beautiful new multicolored coat.

What is the moral of this story, you may ask? Simply, that jealousy can tear a family apart. Why did Chagall chose to depict this story in his windows? And how does this apply to Israel today? The land of Canaan, or Palestine, or Israel, whatever you want to call it, has always been a land of different cultures, different tribes. At the same time, we are family. We are all the sons and daughters of Abraham and of Jacob, Jews and Arabs alike. Our families have been intermingled for centuries. The struggle over Israel is simply a family squabble that has gone on far too long. That is why the Chagall windows are so important. There, in that one room, all the tribes live together in peace.

Later, we piled onto a tour bus, and we were shown hillsides covered in small trees. I wondered how many of those trees I had planted. For as long as I can remember, we had given money to help plant trees in Israel. From the little *pushke* Mama had in the kitchen back in Berkley to the Tu Bishvat fundraisers and the Sisterhood donations when someone died... now I was seeing the result. I imagined a time when all of Israel would be green again, and the desert would be reborn.

The most exciting part of our itinerary was an invitation to a *kum sitz* with David ben Gurion. *Kum sitz* is Yiddish for 'Come sit,' an informal get-together where people could talk, tell stories, get to know one another. Only this time, it was with the Prime Minister of Israel. I was a little nervous about meeting Ben Gurion until we actually met. He was a small man, smaller than myself, and he had a head of white hair like Albert Einstein. It went every which way. He had a warm smile and a feeling of *mishpokhe*—you know, family. I took a liking to him right away.

Ben Gurion said, "The people of Israel will always be grateful to the women of Hadassah."

"Why thank you, Mr. Prime Minister." I don't know what made me say it, but I said, "That reminds me of a joke."

Ben Gurion nodded. "I could use a good joke for my next Knesset meeting."

"I use this one at fundraisers all the time."

"I'm listening."

A busload of Hadassah women journeyed to the Promised Land, and they went over a cliff and died. Instead of going to heaven, they ended up down below.

Eventually, Saint Peter got wind of this and made a call to the Devil. "There seems to be a mistake. A busload of Hadassah women were headed my way and they seem to have disappeared. Have you seen them?"

"A mistake you say?" The Devil laughed. "A mistake that should have been made a long time ago... Those girls have only been down here two days and already they've raised enough money to air condition the place!'"

Ben Gurion laughed heartily. "Maybe next, the good women of Hadassah could see what they can do about air conditioning the Knesset?"

And then I said, "We'll get right on it, Mr. Prime Minister."

That night, Papa arrived carrying a small rectangular package wrapped in silver paper and tied with a yellow ribbon. He hid it from Nana before she could see.

"Is that Nana's Chanukah present?" I whispered.

Papa nodded and held his finger to his mouth.

"Looks like Nana's been a good girl."

We lit the Chanukah candles, said the blessing over the holiday lights, and then sat down to sweet and sour meatballs and potato latkes. I watched the way Papa used his latke to mop up the sauce and then licked his lips and helped himself to another heaping portion. I watched the way that Nana Lena followed his every movement with her eyes.

"So how does Aunt Poogie make her sweet-and-sours?" I asked.

"You won't believe me if I tell you."

"Try me."

She reeled off the ingredients. "A jar of Heinz Chili Sauce, a jar of sweet pickle relish, and a jar of Welch's Grape Jelly."

"You've got to be kidding."

"I told you so."

"Does it taste any good?"

"Oh, it's delicious."

After dinner, we exchanged gifts. I gave Nana a pair of warm slippers and a flannel nightgown, and Papa a scarf and gloves. My gift was from Miller and Rhoads; I could tell by the wrapping. I figured it was probably a sweater because now that I was going to school in Boston, I needed more warm clothes. When I opened the box, I found two bras instead.

"You bought me a bra, Nana?"

"I bought you *two* bras."

"Yes, I see. They are very nice. Why did you buy me bras, Nana?"

She looked at me over her glasses, the way she did when she wanted to make a point. "It looks like you could use a little more support, Amele. The woman at the store said this was the best bra for that."

With logic like that, there was no use arguing. I got up and gave her a kiss. "Thanks, Nana."

"Wear them in good health."

"I feel kind of funny thanking Papa for my bras."

Papa waved his hands; he wanted no part of that. He winked as he cleared his throat and pulled a gift box from its hiding place behind the chair, placing it in front of Nana Lena.

"What's this?" She acted surprised, but I could see she was pleased.

"A little present."

"Looks pretty *big* to me." She hugged Papa and her eyes got all misty. "Thank you, Myer, for all the good years we've shared together, for Elayne, for my beautiful home, for everything."

"No, it's my turn to thank you for being the best wife, mother, and grandmother in the world. Go ahead, open it."

Nana Lena opened the box. Inside, she found a beautiful pair of diamond and pearl earrings. "Oh, Myer, you shouldn't have. They're gorgeous."

"Just like you."

"Don't be silly, I haven't been *gorgeous* in a long time."

"You'll always be gorgeous in my eyes. You'll always be my jewel." And then they kissed, and it didn't seem that forty years had passed. The way they kissed, you would have thought they had just fallen in love.

* * *

Sweet-and-Sour Meatballs

yields 16–20 meatballs

Best when served with potato latkes or potato kugel.

2 lbs ground beef

2 eggs, beaten

1/2 cup water

1 tsp salt

1/4 tsp pepper

1/2 cup minced onion

1/2–3/4 cup matzo meal or flour

Combine the first six ingredients in a large mixing bowl. Then work meal into the mixture until firm enough to make balls that retain their shape.

In a large pot, combine:

1 large diced onion

1/2 cup lemon juice

1/2 cup water

3/4 cup sugar

1 can tomato mushroom sauce

Add meatballs to simmering sauce. Bring to a slow boil. Reduce heat and simmer for one hour, stirring occasionally so balls won't stick to bottom of pan. Add additional liquid if necessary.

Kosher Hot Dogs

also known as The Boys of Summer

It was late one summer afternoon when I called to check up on Nana Lena.

"Amele! I'm so glad you called! I'm just fixing myself some supper."

"What are you eating?"

"You're going to laugh. A kosher hot dog."

"Hebrew National?"

"But of course."

"With mustard and relish and onions?"

"Is there any other way?"

"Has the game been on long?"

"A half hour already. St. Louis is winning, 3 to 1."

"Bummer. I know you're rooting for the Braves."

"I don't know what Bobby Cox was thinking. This whole pitching team ought to be replaced."

"You tell them, Nana. Isn't that what Uncle Coochie would have done?"

"He'd be telling them, 'Boy, you are just wasting my time. You can't pitch. You call that pitching?'"

"Leon was a scout for the Norfolk Tars, the Yankees Triple-A farm team in the 1940s and 1950s. Mike coached City League; Sidney coached Little League for thirteen years. We were all crazy about baseball, even when we were kids. My four brothers and I, we used to play ball in the field behind the house. Leon, being the oldest, was the coach and star player all rolled into one. He was eight years older than Pete, ten years older than Mike, and fourteen years older than Sidney, who all adored him. He was old enough to garner their respect and wise enough to pass on what he had learned. With eight of us, we almost had enough for our own team, but Goldie, Fannie, and Poogie weren't really into baseball. I don't know exactly what it was I liked about it; maybe it's all those memories of playing ball with my brothers when we were kids. Maybe it was the way I felt when Leon taught me how to hit the ball, and I sent it careening over the field, and Leon said,

'The next time I have bases loaded, I'm sending you in, kiddo.' Or maybe it was the way the men looked in their uniforms at the beginning of the game, all shiny and new and filled with hope. But as far back as I can remember, someone in the family was always playing baseball. Now I just watch it on the television. Damn it!"

"What happened?"

"Second foul. Come on, Chipper, just hit the ball!

"We used to go down to the ball field on Saturdays and hang out with the players, who were all friends of Leon. They even gave him his nickname, Coochie, because of the little dance he did before stepping up to the plate. Anyway, Leon made friends with a young ballplayer, a catcher named Yogi Berra."

"You mean, Yogi Berra who was catcher for the Yankees?"

"He was a damn good catcher. And a good manager, too, but that was later. Yogi was more than just a ball player; he was a character. He had a way of turning a phrase that couldn't help but make you laugh. For example, when asked what he would do if he found a million dollars, Yogi answered, 'I'll find the fellow who lost it, and, if he was poor, I'd return it.' Or, 'you can observe a lot just by watching.' Of course, most of his 'Yogi-isms' related to baseball. He'd say, 'Think? How the hell are you going to think and hit at the same time?' Or, 'Baseball is 90 percent mental, the other half is physical.' Or, 'You give 100 percent in the first half of the game, and if that isn't enough, in the second half, you give what's left.'

"Yogi was about twenty years old. This was the year he joined the Yankees. Leon liked Yogi, and especially his wry sense of humor. He was always coming home and telling Mama the latest Yogi tale.

"'Mama, you should have heard what Yogi said today. Yogi had just come back from a game in Atlanta, and I asked him how the hotel was, where the team had stayed. He said his only complaint was 'the towels are so thick I could hardly close my suitcase.'

"And Mama said, 'Sounds like my kind of boy. Why don't you bring him over to supper sometime?'

"This was right after the war, and Mama liked us all to come over on Sundays for supper. On this particular Sunday, it was the triple birthday: Mike, Fannie, and Sidney—you know, they are all born on July 24th, two years apart, in 1916, 1918, and 1920."

"That's pretty amazing!"

"It made the Guinness Book of Records. Bubbie was invited to be on the radio show, but Goldie and I talked her out of it. We were afraid if she were asked how this happened, she would tell the world, 'Well, my husband, Morris, would say to me, 'Come, Minnie, let us get under the featherbed,'' and we'd never be able to show our faces in school again."

"It was 1946, and everyone was home from the war. Sidney, the youngest of the brothers, was the last to return, and he returned a hero. As a corporal and front-line medic in the 12th Armored Division, Sidney was one of five hundred U.S. soldiers attached to the French Army to spearhead the Allied drive to the Rhine. In the Colmar Pocket, enemy machine guns and artillery fire pinned down and isolated thirteen Allied soldiers. Sidney floated across the canal while holding onto a life raft, even though he couldn't swim, and gave first aid to the men. Later he organized and directed the evacuation of the wounded, even though he himself was injured. He was awarded a Purple Heart for bravery and a Silver Star for gallantry in action.

"Everyone admired Sidney's medals. Minnie kept bragging to no one in particular, 'My son, the hero.'

"Pete grabbed Sidney and hugged him. 'Damn it, Goodman. It's good to have you home.' Mike put his arm around Sid, and Pete stood on his other side, as if they were posing for some immortal snapshot in time.

"Sidney had always looked up to his older brothers. Now the war was over, and he wasn't a kid anymore. He was one of them, and the bond they shared—a brotherly bond, strengthened by their common experiences of war—added an air of dignity to these simple brothers, having a family dinner together for the first time in years.

"Leon arrived with Yogi, who took off his cap to shake Sidney's hand. 'Where you back from, soldier?'

"'France, mostly, but we sure did move around.'

"'Kind of like baseball. We're always on the move. Did you see much action?'

"'More than I care to remember.' He and his brothers exchanged knowing glances, confirming they each felt the same.

"'You guys are the real heroes. I just play ball.'

"And then Sidney said, 'In our family, that's as good as God.'

"That broke the nervous tension, and then everybody bombarded Yogi with questions.

"Pete asked him about his batting slump. 'Slump? I ain't in no slump. I just ain't hitting. I never blame myself when I'm not hitting. I just blame the bat, and if it keeps up, I change bats. After all, I know it isn't my fault that I'm not hitting; how can I get mad at myself?'

"Sidney asked about the Yankees' odds in the playoff.

"Yogi answered, 'The other teams could make trouble for us if they win.'

"Minnie stepped up and said, 'I want I should shake your hand, Mr. Yogi. My sons tell me good things about you.'

"'They must be making it up.'

"'My Leon tells me, "That man is going to go far," and I believe him. My son knows a lot about baseball.'

"'Why, thank you, Mrs. Goodman.'

"'Minnie, you should call me.'

"'And you should call me Yogi; all my friends do.'

"'Now that we're friends, Yogi, can I ask you something?'

"'Anything, Minnie!'

"'The next time you go out of town, I could use some new towels.'

Everybody stopped for a moment and stared in shock at what Mama had said. But Yogi started to laugh and shook Minnie's hand. 'If your brisket is as good as your sons say, Minnie, you've got yourself a deal.'

"Later that year, Mama received a whole box of towels that said Hilton Coast to Coast. Every time she used them, she laughed. She was a lot like Yogi. She played dumb, but she was sharp as a whip."

"I guess that's where you get it from, Nana. What's the score?"

"4 to 1. St. Louis scored a home run."

"Why didn't you tell me?"

"It wasn't worth mentioning."

"Look, Nana, it's only a game."

"Only a game! That reminds me of a story."

"What doesn't?"

"What?"

"Remind you of a story?"

"Are you complaining? As I was saying, it's not always whether you win or lose. It's whether they let you in the game."

"Did Yogi say that, too?"

"It sounds like him, but I was referring to another ballplayer, first baseman Jackie Robinson."

"Jackie Robinson?"

"You don't know about Jackie? Why, he changed everything! He was the first player from the Negro Leagues to be invited to the majors. He crossed baseball's color line in '47 when he walked out on first base to play ball for the Brooklyn Dodgers. America was never the same; baseball was never the same! Even though they let him in the game, they didn't always treat him right. He bore the indignities with humility and grace, and in that way did more for his people, and for baseball, than anyone ever imagined. Another thing I liked about Jackie Robinson. He gave back. He opened youth centers and was always working with kids. He once said, 'A life is not important except in the impact it has on other lives.' He had an impact, opening up baseball, and ultimately all pro sports, to minority players.

"You see, that's the thing about baseball. It's as American as apple pie. Some people put cinnamon in their pie, some like it with raisins, some prefer seasoning with vanilla, or rum, and some say lemon. It's the same with baseball. It doesn't matter where your people come from, what your flavor, so to speak, as long as you got what it takes to play ball. And Jackie had what it takes. I'll never forget that day as long as I live; it's like the day Joe Louis knocked out Max Schmeling in the first round. Black people got to walk a little prouder that day, and white people got to practice what they had been preaching about equality and brotherly love. And for one day, it was great to be an American. Baseball did all that."

Nana Lena thought for a moment. "I'll tell you another story, about this pitcher named Catfish Hunter. You ever heard of him?"

"Can't say I have."

"James Augustus Hunter: They called him Catfish. He was the last of eight children, kind of like your Uncle Sid, and he grew up in the small town of Hertford, North Carolina. Coochie had seen him pitch a no-hitter while Catfish was still in high school. He was attracting the attention of major league scouts, when during his senior year, he was wounded in a hunting accident and lost one of his toes. Each time he dragged his bum foot onto the pitcher's mound, his major league prospects seemed to grow dimmer.

"One day, Coochie and Pete were sitting around in Pete's office with Harry Postove, a scout for the Chicago White Sox. Coochie was telling Harry about this gimpy kid who was the best damn pitcher he had ever seen, that you could tell time by his ball, that's how damn accurate his pitch was. But the very day that Coochie drove Harry down to Hertford, Catfish was signed by the Kansas City Athletics.

"My all-time favorite ballplayer was a Jewish boy named Sandy Koufax. He was the closest thing to pitching perfection, and the fact that he was a Jew was hardly overlooked in our family. For five years, Koufax was the dominating pitcher in baseball. In September of 1965, he pitched a perfect game. Twenty-seven Chicago Cubs stepped up to bat that night, and twenty-seven slunk back into their dugout as a Jewish boy from Brooklyn pitched the eighth perfect game in baseball history. Then on October 6th, 1965, Sandy Koufax stunned the baseball world by refusing to pitch the opening game of the World Series because it fell on Yom Kippur, the holiest day of the Jewish year. With Jews across America, we held our breath and then stood proudly by him. And when he returned to beat the Twins in the seventh game of the World Series, baseball reclaimed him as their own. It was another great day for baseball.

"So you ask yourself, what kind of game lets a jokester, a black man, a kid with a bum leg, and a Jew play ball together? Baseball... my kind of game."

* * *

Kosher Hot Dog

What, you don't know how to make a hot dog? You're expecting some kind of fancy recipe or something? You boil a kosher hot dog. Or if you're having a cook-out, you heat it up on the grill. You put it on a bun. Maybe you toast the bun first, maybe not. Then you add some mustard and onions and sometimes a little relish. Then you've got a hot dog.

Sometimes I eat it with just mustard and sauerkraut.

Dee-licious!

Yogi Berra and Leon Goodman, 1964

Blintzes

We were in the kitchen making blintzes. I watched as Nana Lena made the *bletel*, the paper-thin pancakes that form the outside of each blintz. "You pretty much always end up throwing out the first one, Mama always used to say. I think it's an Old Russian saying. Mama was from Kiev, and blintzes are basically what the Russians call *blini*."

Using a thin crepe pan, Nana Lena poured the batter into the pan and swirled it around until it set and was slightly browned on one side, and then she flipped it browned-side-up onto a stack of other crepes. She continued until all the crepes were done.

"I love watching you cook, Nana. The way you do that, it's so graceful."

"What, you think cooking is like ballet? You are the dancer in the family, not me."

"It's definitely an art."

"I'll give you that, and one that takes a lot of practice. You think I was so good at this the first time I tried? Believe me, I threw away more than the first one. I nearly threw away the whole batch."

"I find that hard to believe."

"All right, maybe just a few. Let's get started on the filling. Amele, take out two pounds of the farmer's cheese and the cream cheese. Beat up one egg and combine it with a half a *yahrzeit* glass of sugar..."

"*How* much sugar?"

"Half a cup. Add a pinch of cinnamon and a pinch of salt. Mix it up real good, and put it back in the icebox to chill."

I did as I was told and then returned to watching Nana Lena make the crepes.

"You know, I can't make blintzes without thinking about Mama. She loved to make blintzes. Do you remember your great-grandmother, your Bubbie Minnie?"

"Of course, I do, Nana. I was thirteen when she died."

"She was already a sick woman then. You never knew Mama like I knew her."

Your Bubbie Minnie was born on a ship coming to America in 1886. Your great-great-grandparents, Elka and Muttel Gustomilsky, were traveling by ship to the New World with three of their children—Sarah, Ida, and Joe—when your great-grandmother Minnie pushed and fussed her way into this world. For six weeks, Elka had dreamed of having her baby in a clean, warm place, hopefully in their new home. But Minnie couldn't wait for that luxury. She was born in the ship's hold the day before the boat docked in Baltimore Harbor. Since they had already reached U.S. territorial waters, the captain deemed her a U.S. citizen. Minnie immediately made her presence known on ship. She was a feisty little thing from the start.

Minnie grew up in Baltimore, Maryland, the second largest immigration center on the East coast, second only to New York City in the number of immigrants it received. In the 1880s, wave after wave of Jewish immigrants from Eastern Europe arrived in Baltimore Harbor. Mostly, they were fleeing the pogroms in Russia and Poland. Many of the new arrivals immediately boarded trains for cities like New York and Chicago, but many remained in Baltimore, where there was a thriving Jewish community and a considerable infrastructure to help them find jobs and homes. Jewish educators like Henrietta Szold taught English and civics in night schools. Since everyone in the Gustomilsky family had to work, including the children, night school was their only chance to receive an education. Minnie went to night school along with her parents, brother, and sisters.

Within a few years, four more children were born: Jane, Betty, Bennie, and Moe. Later, Aunt Jane and Aunt Betty moved to Brooklyn. Mama used to go up to see them from time to time. Bennie married a woman named Ruthie. I have their wedding picture around here somewhere. Moe, which was short for Moses, was killed during World War I, when the gas depot he was guarding ignited.

In 1904, Mama went to a dance hall in Baltimore. She was eighteen years old. Morris Goodman also attended the dance hall that night. Now Morris couldn't move his feet, but Mama, she was some kind of pretty, so he walked up to her and told her she was pretty, and he asked her if he could walk her home. On the way, they stopped at a fruit stand, and he bought her a pear. We always laughed at that. He bought her a pear, and he walked her home, and the next day when she came home from work, he was sitting there waiting for her with another pear. Now they had two.

I have a picture of Mama. It's an old picture, from around that time. Mama had a beautiful figure, a beautifully tight molded bust and a teeny little waist and trim hips. She was wearing a fancy lace dress, with a long train. On the back of the picture, she had written "Compliments of Minnie Gustomilsky." It was addressed to my father. So formal: "Compliments of."

They married in 1905, and Leon was born a year later. Bertha was born in 1907 and Yetta in 1908. Yetta only lived a few days, the poor dear. She was born without a tongue. The doctors tried to save her by grafting a chicken tongue. I know it sounds strange, but it's true. They thought she needed the tongue to nurse. The graft didn't take, and Yetta died. Mama rested a few years between babies; in 1911, Goldie was born. I followed in 1912. Then every two years, they made a baby, from 1912 to 1920, with a short pause until 1923. Ten children in eighteen years.

In 1918, we lost Bertha. That was the year my sister Bertha and my aunt Fannie died in the influenza epidemic brought back by our soldiers returning from the first World War. Mama was never quite the same after that. She always worried about the children. Even when we were grown, she worried about our children. Every year she would call me and ask me. "Does Elayne have enough undershirts?" "Does Elayne have galoshes?" "Has Elayne had her flu shot?"

"Years later, when you children were born, she called your mother and repeated the litany: "Do the children have undershirts?" "Do the children have galoshes?" "Did the children get their flu shots?" She didn't want another mother to learn what she had learned in 1918.

Mama had a sense of humor. She liked to have a good time. Every week, Mama had a card game. There was Mrs. Levinson (Izzie's mother), and a Mrs. Levin who lived in Berkley, a woman named Spilke, the real old lady Ehrenworth, and Mrs. Levy and her daughter Mrs. Gamsey. They used to bet a quarter a game, and that was a lot in those days.

There was one window in the living room; it looked out over the front porch. One day, all of a sudden Mama saw something gleaming on the porch. It was a policeman's shield. Calmly she told the others, *"Mir hob'n gest. Di Politseyleyte komm'n."* (We have guests. The police are coming.) Then came the knock on the door. Everyone picked up everything from the table, and Mama found a little prayer book of Papa's that he kept on the sideboard. Mama couldn't read a word of Hebrew, she just knew a few prayers, so she started leading the women in *Havenu Shalom Aleichem* just as the police entered the room. She was standing there holding the prayer book upside down, but the police didn't recognize that because it was in Hebrew. There they all were sitting around like a group of Sunday school teachers singing "Peace be with you."

Every year, Mama used to have a New Year's Eve party. She and her friends would play cards until midnight. When the bells would sound and the Berkley cannon would go off, they would have something to eat and wish each other a Happy New Year. On this particular night, the card game ended before midnight, and everyone was in a low mood. Mama said to her friend Mrs. Fox, "So, Chiala, what did you buy today at Altschuls on Church Street?" Mama knew what her friend had bought, but she played with her, teasing.

"Such a sale they were having. Such good material. How could I say no?" Mrs. Fox told the other ladies.

"Tell us, Chiala. What color was the material?"

"White... naturally."

"White? What? You're getting married again or something?" Mrs. Fox said, "You know, for after..."

"After? After the wedding? For the honeymoon maybe?" And then Mama said, *"Chiala, geh to'n dayn vays kleyd.* (Chiala, go put on your white dress.) Then everyone can see how pretty you'll be."

That was the story in Berkley for years; Mama had tried to get Mrs. Fox to put on her funeral shroud which she had bought that day on Church Street.

Nana Lena looked up at the clock. "Okeydokey. Let's get started on the blintzes. Amele, can you get me the filling?" Nana Lena took the first crepe and flipped it browned-side-up on a plate in front of her.

She placed a large dollop of filling, about a quarter of a cup, toward the top of the circle. Then she folded the top flap down, the side flaps in, and continued to roll from top to bottom—a perfect blintz in less than a minute. She rolled the blintzes without seeming to pay any attention to what she was doing, as she continued to reminisce.

"One by one, each of us got married and moved out on our own to other parts of the city. Mama continued to live with Goldie and Sidney until 1955. That's when everything changed. Goldie got married in June, your mother got married in September, and Sidney married in November. After Goldie and Sidney moved out, Mama was all alone. That was when she came to live with me.

"Now your Bubbie was not the easiest person in the world to live with. She was used to being the boss, and Myer, he had his own way of doing things, so they didn't always get along. For one thing, she was always cold when Myer was hot. She was always turning the heat up, and Myer was always turning it down. She was diabetic and had high blood pressure. Myer had an ulcer. If I didn't salt the soup because of Mama's blood pressure, Myer would complain it had no taste. About the only thing they could agree upon was that they both liked blintzes. Mama liked to make them, and Myer liked to eat them, so at least the days when Mama made blintzes, there was peace in the house."

Nana Lena turned on the stove, placed two pats of butter into the thin metal frying pan, and set it on the burner to heat. She cooked the blintzes on a medium setting until they were lightly browned on both sides, about two and a half minutes on each side.

"Mama had a bad heart. Did I ever tell you about the first time Mama died?"

"The *first* time?"

"Mama had her first heart attack in the early Thirties. She was rushed to the hospital, but the doctors couldn't seem to revive her. She was pronounced dead and wheeled to the morgue. Her good friend Mrs. Fox had come by to visit; when she arrived, they told her Minnie had died. She asked to see the body.

Mrs. Fox lifted the sheet and started slapping Minnie in the face. "Minnie Goodman, how could you! Only half your kids are grown. You leave four little stair steps to take care of."

Imagine her surprise when Minnie opened her eyes and sat up on the edge of the gurney as if nothing had happened."

Mama had heart problems for years. One time, she was in the hospital, and we used to take turns feeding her. One day, it was my turn. When the tray arrived, I could see that a mistake had been made.

"I'm so hungry I could eat a horse." Minnie said. "What's the matter?"

I looked at the plate of pork chops, mashed potatoes, and gravy, and then I looked at my mother. Mama kept kosher. I don't think she'd ever had a pork chop in her life. Pork was definitely not kosher. "Nothing's the matter, Mama." I lied. "These lamb chops look really good."

I bit my tongue and cut the pork chops into little bites. I mixed them with the mashed potatoes and fed them to Mama, bite by bite. When she was finished eating, Mama licked her lips and said to me. "You know what, Lena? Pork is not so bad."

"You couldn't put anything over on Mama. That's for sure." Nana Lena removed the golden-brown blintzes from the pan. She added more oil, let it heat, and then continued with the next batch.

"Later, when Mama was well enough to come home," Nana Lena went on, "Mrs. Fox came to the house to visit. They were good friends, despite the fact that Mama said Mrs. Fox had the evil eye. Mrs. Fox said, 'Minnie Goodman. You ain't gonna get no credit for being sick, you look so good.'

"That's when you jumped up on the bed. You couldn't have been more than three or four years old, and you licked Bubbie's forehead three times and spit.

"Bubbie was ashamed. She said, 'Amy, what are you doing?'

"And you answered so innocently, 'But Bubbie, that's what you always do when Mrs. Fox says something.'

"You had let the cat right out of the bag. Now Mrs. Fox knew Bubbie thought she had the Evil Eye."

Nana Lena turned the blintzes over in the pan.

"I took good care of my mother, but I couldn't stay home all day, every day. Not that she needed that kind of attention. It was more a comfort to her to be surrounded by her family. After all, with all those children, she was used to a noisy home. Sometimes, when I'd leave the house, for a Hadassah meeting or to go grocery shopping, Minnie would get lonely. She would take out her little blue address book, perch her glasses on the end of her nose, and phone her children, starting with her eldest.

"'Leon?'

"'Mama, what's the matter?'

"'Leon, I don't feel so good.'

"'Where's Lena?'

"'I don't know where she is. Oy, the pain.'

"'What is it? Your heart?'

"'Maybe I should have a *glass*l tea. If only I weren't so dizzy, I could get out of bed.'

"'Don't get out of bed! I'll be right there, Mama.' Leon would hang up and run out the door, as Minnie dialed the next number.

"'Mike, I'm so sick...'

"'Goldie, come quick...'

"'Sidney, you'd better hurry...'

"'Frances!'

"By the time I would return home, there would be at least four cars parked outside. My brothers and sisters would be standing around Mama's bed talking at the same time, just like when we were kids in Berkley. And Mama would be sitting there smiling. She just missed the noise."

Nana Lena removed the last blintz from the frying pan and turned off the stove. She prepared two plates and placed one on the table in front of me.

"That looks so *good*."

"Get the sour cream, Amele. You can't have blintzes without sour cream."

I placed the sour cream on the table in front of her. "You know, Nana, it seems to me that you and Bubbie are a lot alike."

Nana Lena looked at me, indignant. "I am nothing like my mother. She was born on the ship. She spoke with an accent. She still had one foot in the Old World."

"Okay, so in that way you're not alike. You are definitely an 'All-American gal,' but both of you are strong, feisty women who love life and family."

Nana Lena took a bite. "And blintzes."

I took a bite and smiled. "I second that emotion."

We both chewed for a moment in contented silence.

"There's just one thing, Amele... Who are you calling feisty?"

* * *

Bubbie's Blintzes

yields 10–12

> *Blintzes are a perfect Shavout meal. Shavous or Shavout is the
> holiday in which we celebrate Moses receiving the Ten
> Commandments on Mt. Sinai. Two blintzes side by side make
> a believable Torah.*

Bletel
("leaves", the outside of the blintz; like a crepe)

2 eggs	3/4 cup flour
2 Tbsp vegetable oil	1/2 tsp salt
1 cup milk	butter for frying

Combine eggs, milk, and oil in a bowl. Add salt and flour. Mix
well. Chill for 1/2 hour. Stir the ingredients again after removing
from the refrigerator.

Melt 1 teaspoon butter in a 7- to 8-inch frying pan. Pour a little less
than a 1/4 cup of batter into the pan and swirl it around to coat the
pan evenly. Recipes always say to fry until lightly brown on one
side. Unfortunately, that is the side you can't see, so watch until
the top side looks spongy—not wet—approximately 20–25
seconds. Shake the pan once during that time to make sure the
crepe isn't sticking. Flip the crepe browned-side-up onto a plate.

Continue adding butter to pan, cooking leaves, and flipping them
onto the stack. This recipe yields 10–12 crepes.

Filling

1 lb farmer's cheese	1 tsp vanilla extract
2 Tbsp sugar	butter for frying
2 heaping Tbsp sour cream	

Combine the farmer's cheese, sugar, sour cream, and vanilla extract in a bowl.

Place crepe, browned side up, on a flat surface. Spoon 1–2 tablespoons of mixture about an inch from the top of the circle. Fold top edge over filling, shaping it into a log about 4–5 inches long. Fold both sides in and roll from top to bottom. The end result should be 4–5 inches long and 1 1/2–2 inches wide.

After the blintzes have been assembled, fry until lightly browned on both sides.

Serve with a dollop of sour cream or sprinkle with sugar and cinnamon.

> *Blintzes can be made with a variety of fillings, including mashed potatoes, kasha, cherries, or blueberries, or combinations such as potatoes and puréed vegetables, such as broccoli or spinach, or potato and onions that have been sautéed until golden brown. Serve fruit variety with sour cream and potato/kasha/vegetable variety with mustard.*

The Bat Mitzvah Table

When we are young, we question everything. Why is the sky blue? Why is the grass green? But we don't really question our religion. Not at first, I mean; that comes later. As children, we pretty much accept the religion we are being raised in. After all, it is usually a close relative whom we love and trust who first introduces us to his or her own faith. Later, when we're older and have been exposed to other religions, we can make a choice. That choice seemed to coincide with my *bat mitzvah* year.

I was seven years old when President Kennedy was shot. An event forever seared in my mind by images on a black and white TV screen: That poor child saluting at his father's funeral; the beautiful grieving widow hovering like an angel nearby. That was all I could grasp at that age, that and the air of sadness that hung over all the grown-ups in my world.

I was twelve when Robert Kennedy was shot. By then, I understood that the Kennedys were Catholic, and that a lot of people thought that a Catholic should not be President, which made me sympathize with the Kennedy family. If it is one thing a Jew understands, it is what it feels like being called *different* from everybody else.

But the event that forever shaped my politics and that area where religion and politics converge was the assassination of Dr. Martin Luther King, Jr. I had heard Dr. King's speeches on the radio. I admired his melodious voice and the passion and dignity of his words: "I have a dream that one day this nation will rise up and live out the true meaning of its creed: 'We hold these truths to be self-evident: that all men are created equal.'" As a Jew, I shared that dream. And when he said, "When we let freedom ring, when we let it ring from every village and every hamlet, from every state and every city, we will be able to speed up that day when all of God's children, black men and white men, Jews and Gentiles, Protestants and Catholics, will be able to join hands and sing in the words of the old Negro spiritual, "Free at last! Free at last! Thank God Almighty, we are free at last!" I added my voice to the resounding chorus of "Amen."

I was keenly aware of racism in the South. It lurked in the background of every Southern encounter. I lived in an all-white neighborhood in an area called Churchland, near an intersection with five churches and one synagogue. The nearest black church was miles away. We got along pretty well in our "separate but equal worlds" until the assassination of Dr. King, which seemed to unleash a new wave of hatred against minorities of color and religion. All across the South, incidents of vandalism and violence were reported. A black Baptist church in Chesapeake had a cross burned outside its front door; the same week, it happened at our Temple. Both communities seemed to take it all in stride, cleaned up, throw their shoulders back, and tried to move on. Then the questions started to build up inside. What had we done? What was so different about us that we deserved to be treated that way? I asked a lot of questions that year as I was preparing for my bat mitzvah.

"Why do I have to have a bat mitzvah?" I asked Nana Lena.
"Because."
"Because why?"
"Because that's what you do. Because I couldn't have one."
"Why couldn't you?"
"Women didn't get bat mitzvahed when I was a girl."
"Why?"
"First, it was an Orthodox *shul*, and only boys were bar mitzvah. And second, that's just how things were done. Bat mitzvahs for girls are only a recent phenomenon. You know, Amele, you're the first girl in our family to have a bat mitzvah."
"Maybe it's not such a good idea to call so much attention to being Jewish, what with all that's going on these days."
"Is that what's bothering you? What happened at the Temple?"
I nodded. "Why do they hate us?"
"Why does anyone hate? Because they don't know any better. That's what they've been taught. We aren't born knowing how to hate."
"But why do they hate Jews? What have we done to them?"
"The Jewish people that I know are law-abiding citizens, contribute to the economy, and promote higher education and family values. They love their children, take care of their parents, band together, and help each other in times of need. I can see

where other cultures might find this intimidating."

"Nana, I'm being serious."

"It's a serious matter, I know, but there isn't any one clear reason: mostly misinformation combined with prejudice and an occasional pinch of jealousy. You know the word 'prejudice' means to pre-judge, to decide in advance what someone will be like and how you will treat them. I try not to prejudge anyone. I treat everyone with the same grace with which I'd like to be treated. And usually, it comes back. I put my best foot forward and hope others see me for who I am. That's all I can do. That's all any of us can do."

Back in Portsmouth, I asked Bessie, the woman who helped raise me, what she thought about prejudice. Bessie was a light-skinned black woman, an integral part of the Ostrower household since I was four.

"Ever seen a smile melt right off a person's face? Bessie answered. That's what happens every time I walk into a new store when folks realize I ain't white. They start out all smiles and 'How can I help you?' and the smile just slides off their faces when I open my mouth. Outside I may look white, but inside, I'm a colored woman, plain and simple."

"It's kind of like being Jewish. They don't like us, either."

"Baby girl, come here. I can hardly call you that anymore. Look at you. You so grown." I moved closer and she took me by the shoulders. "Ain't nothing wrong with either one of us. You or me. Only thing is *they* don't know that. They still feeding on the hate. Sometimes it's easier than changing the way things are. One thing I do know is there ain't nothing Christian about burning no cross. These folks been taught to hate for so long, they don't see it makes no sense. You show me where in the Bible it says to burn a cross. And it ain't Christian, what they done to Dr. King."

"Why do you think people hate?"

"It's what they been learned. I suppose."

"Can't they learn love instead?"

"Now that's a good question, baby girl. That's a good question."

I wanted to understand prejudice scientifically. I devised a science project entitled Racial Prejudice in Mice. I had two groups of white mice, and a group of black mice, which I kept in separate boxes. I fed half the white mice in a white box and starved them in a black box. I fed the other half of the white mice in a black box and starved them in a white box. If I introduced a black mouse into the group box that had been starved in a black box, they would attack the black mouse. But the group that had been starved in a white box, would not attack the new black mouse. It wasn't the color of the mouse that caused it to be attacked but rather the negative association with the color—in this case, *hunger* with the color *black*. In my control group, black and white mice lived together and were treated equally. They got along just fine. My conclusion: Prejudice is a conditioned response.

Then it dawned on me. If mice can be conditioned to attack other mice, and if believers of one faith can be conditioned to think that burning the symbol of their religion on your property is a correct and appropriate religious gesture, does that mean that they will believe that way forever?

I brought this question to the Rabbi. "Can hatred be unlearned?"

Rabbi Turitz responded, "That is an interesting question. Take, for example, your Torah portion, Deuteronomy 34. It is last chapter of the last book of Moses. After all those years of wandering, God brings Moses to the top of Mount Pisgah overlooking the Promised Land and tells him to take a good look. This is as close as he will get. God tells Moses he will die on the mountaintop; he will never enter the Promised Land. Why? Moses, the leader, who had led his people out of slavery. Moses, the Miracle Worker, who parted the Red Sea. Moses, the Prophet, the subject of four out of five books of the Old Testament. You would think God would let him into the Promised Land after all that he had done for the Jewish people. I'll tell you why! Moses was the last of the original slaves that had left Egypt. All of the others had died. During the forty years of wandering, new generations were born and raised, and none of them had known what it was like to be enslaved. They were the ones who would be allowed to enter the Promised Land. Free men, not slaves. So you see… God did not believe that a certain mindset could be unlearned so easily. It takes at least one generation, maybe more."

Armed with this knowledge and my Nana's put-your-best-foot-forward attitude, I threw myself into my bat mitzvah studies and honed my party list. After all, one of the most important parts of the bat or bar mitzvah was the party part of the bat mitzvah "celebration." There was the main party for my family and my mother and grandmother's friends and a separate "happening" down the hall with a live DJ for the bat mitzvah set. I had decided to meld my two worlds, my Jewish friends and family—boys and girls I had known all my life—and my friends from Churchland Junior High. I was pretty sure they would get along together and would not attack each other—like mice.

That was the summer that man landed on the moon, when Neil Armstrong and Buzz Aldrin took those important first steps. I remember Walter Kronkite reporting and the thrill in his voice we all shared. I remember Neil Armstrong's words: "One small step for man, one giant leap for mankind!" That was the summer of Woodstock and anti-Vietnam protests. That was the summer of Chappaquiddick. That was the dawn of the gay rights movement with the Stonewall Riots. To borrow the words of the great poet Bob Dylan, "The times, they were a changin'." And so was I.

As my bat mitzvah date approached, Nana Lena moved into large-scale dessert mode: pecan tassies, rugelach, strudel, date bars, lemon bars, seven-layer cookies, each recipe lovingly doubled and tripled and tucked away in the freezer until the big day. Small family parties of thirty or so Nana Lena could handle on her own, but there were three hundred people coming to my bat mitzvah. For this, Nana Lena called in her youngest sister, Poogie. Poogie was an unfortunate childhood nickname that had stuck. Her real name was Mathilda, like the waltz. She was an effervescent ball of energy, a caterer by profession. She lived with her husband Jack (whom she called Cupcake) and her sons Mark and Norman, approximately four hours away in Durham, North Carolina.

Aunt Poogie arrived a few days before the party, her car heavy with supplies. As always, she traveled with her helpers, Rachel and Dorothy, who had worked for Aunt Poogie ever since I could remember. Rachel was a petite, light-skinned black woman who was Aunt Poogie's right hand and remained her close friend until the day Poogie died. Dorothy, a heavyset, dark-skinned woman, was always smiling and laughing. She looked the other way whenever I snatched something to eat.

"There's the bat mitzvah girl," Aunt Poogie crooned in her

high-pitched voice. "Come over here and give your Aunt Poog a hug." I embraced my aunt, who was actually my great-aunt. In our family, we just dropped the "great" and called people aunt and uncle because it was easier. All my aunts and uncles were actually my Nana and Papa's brothers and sisters and their spouses. I had twenty-two great-aunts and -uncles on my mother's side alone, and a score of first and second cousins, all of whom would all be at the party in two days.

"Is that my Amy?" I hugged Rachel. "My, you've grown." She gave my budding breasts a look and my Aunt Poogie a wink. "In more ways than one."

"Are you wearing a bra?" Poogie teased me. "Let me have a look."

I turned away, embarrassed; Dorothy saved me: "Come here and give Dorothy a hug, chile." Dorothy took me to her ample bosom, and there was no more talk of my breasts.

Nana Lena took one look at the car, which was really weighted down in the back. "Lordy. You sure you brought enough?"

"This isn't the half of it. We haven't even gone shopping for the fruits and vegetables yet, and the meat is being delivered right to the synagogue."

"You better check on that," Nana warned her.

"I spoke to the butcher this morning. He's bringing the meat over to the Temple tomorrow." Aunt Poogie unlocked her trunk. "Alrighty, let's get started. Amy, call your mother and ask her to unlock the back door. It would be a lot easier to bring things round the back."

For the next two days, these women cooked, let me tell you. I could not enter the kitchen without finding at least three women at a time in aprons, hard at work; and sometimes there were as many as six people, including my mother and sisters. Everyone helped.

The morning of my bat mitzvah, my sister Missy, who was three at the time, was in the kitchen helping Rachel. Missy was separating raisins, and Rachel was separating the cabbage leaves to make rolled cabbage, when Missy asked, "Rachel, are you rich or are you poor?"

The rest of us were stunned by Missy's question, but Rachel answered, "I'm not either one, I suppose."

Missy smiled and then pronounced with certainty, "Oh, then you're middle class like us."

After that Rachel always called her "Miss Middle Class."

Aunt Poogie caught me by the arm as I was heading out the door. "I could use another hand in the kitchen."

"You know I'd love to, Aunt Poog, but I've got to go meet with the Rabbi one more time."

"You don't know your Torah portion yet?"

"Yes. I think so. I'm more nervous about the song."

"The song? What do you think this is, Woodstock?" Woodstock, the famed three-day festival of love and music had taken place two weeks earlier.

"I'm going to sing 'Let There Be Peace on Earth.'"

"Sure do sound like it," Rachel chortled.

"I didn't know you could sing." Aunt Poogie teased in her high squeaky voice. "Go ahead, sing." But before I could open my mouth she had already closed her eyes and put her fingers in her ears. "Are you done yet?"

That night before services, I wandered into the social hall while I was waiting for the guests to arrive. Nana Lena and Aunt Poogie were overseeing the finishing touches on the *Oneg Shabbat* that would follow. The tables were beautifully decorated with long, flowing skirts and elegant flower arrangements. Across the front of the room, above the stage, there were poster-sized enlargements of key moments of my (at this point, brief) life. I inhaled deeply, taking it all in.

"It's so beautiful, Nana. Thank you."

"You like the posters? That was your father's idea."

"Can I keep them?"

"Of course, you can, dear; we made them for you. This day is all about you. Of course, it's also about that turning point when you start to think and feel and make decisions on your own. It's a celebration of all you've accomplished and of all the good things to come. It's a time when your friends and family gather together and surround you with their love."

"I never really realized how important a day it is."

"Are you glad you went through with it?"

"Absolutely."

"Are you nervous?"

"A little."

"You'll do fine. You always do." Nana Lena beamed. "It hasn't even happened yet, and I'm already proud."

That night, as I stood on the *bimah* looking out over the audience, I could see my family seated in the first row, my sisters dressed like angels in white dresses with pink sashes, my mother looking beautiful and elegant like Jackie Kennedy, my Dad sporting a dapper goatee, and my two sets of grandparents beaming proudly. Then row after row of aunts, uncles, cousins, members of the synagogue, friends, and family friends. Bessie was there, dressed like a Southern lady, seated next to several of my Baptist, Presbyterian, and Catholic friends from school. Black and white. Jewish and Christian. So far no one had attacked another. Everyone seemed to be getting along.

At the end of the service, Rabbi Turitz announced, "Before the closing benediction, the Bat Mitzvah Girl would like to lead us in a special song."

I stepped up on a small platform behind the podium. "We're going to do something a little different tonight. I have this song I want to sing. You'll find it on the back of the program. I'm going to get us started, but when I say so, I'd like you all to join in."

After a brief moment of everyone fumbling for their programs, I began to sing, my voice trembling at first:

> *Let there be peace on earth*
> *And let it begin with me*
> *Let there be peace on earth*
> *The peace that was meant to be.*

Looking out over the congregation, I could see Nana Lena crying and Papa taking out his handkerchief and handing it to her, my father taking my mother's hand, and my brother David sitting with his fingers in his ears.

> *With God as our father*
> *Brothers all are we.*
> *Let me walk with my brother*
> *In perfect harmony.*

My Jewish friends and Christian classmates had their arms around one another, swaying to the music. My Catholic boyfriend unclipped his clip-on tie and winked at me. Bessie had her hand up in the air swaying from side to side as in her church.

I signaled for the others to join me, my tiny voice merging with the voices of the other participants.

Let peace begin with me
Let this be the moment now
With every step I take
Let this be my solemn vow
To take each moment and live
each moment in peace eternally
Let there be peace on earth
and let it begin with me!

And when the song ended, for a moment there, I could feel that peace and harmony hanging in the air, surrounding us like a warm cloud. Everything was possible. After all, I was only thirteen.

* * *

"Let There be Peace on Earth", written by Sy Miller and Bill Jackson, Copyright 1955 by Jan-Lee Music.

Corned Beef on Wry

It was a week before Passover, and I was helping Nana Lena with her annual spring cleaning. She didn't take a feather and use it to dust out the remaining crumbs of *chumetz*, as Jewish women are instructed to do before the holiday, with a candle to better see the crumbs, a feather to dust them out of cabinets, and a spoon to catch them with, but she did like to have the house all clean for the holiday. As I dusted each antique cup and saucer she had on display in the dining room, I couldn't help but notice the piece of masking tape underneath, each one labeled with someone's name.

"If there is anything you want, put your name on it."

"Nana!"

"I'm serious. Tell me now, and we'll put a tape on it."

"I can't."

"You've got to speak up to get what you want. Go ahead. Pick one."

I point to one of the cups and saucers, Victorian with yellow roses. "I like that one. It reminds me of you."

"A good choice. I was always partial to yellow roses." She showed me another cup in reverse colors. "Take this one, too; they go together."

"Who gets the dining room set?"

"Melissa; she's got a big family now."

"And the Nana Papa chairs?" I said referring to two Danish leather chairs, one with a high back and one with a low one. Nana and Papa used to sit in those chairs and watch TV every night. Now that Papa was gone, Nana Lena sat in the Papa chair so that she could prop up her feet as the doctor had ordered.

"You know how Ed likes to fall asleep in that one. You've got the chairs in my bedroom, and the drop-leaf table and the lamp. That is, if you still want them."

"Of course, I do. I love that lamp, and the story that goes with it."

"That was your Bubbie Gertrude Anna's, your Papa's mother. She died before you were born. Your Hebrew name, Hinda Gittel... you were named for her. And that lamp was once a beautiful crystal vase, one of a pair of vases that sat on your Bubbie's mantelpiece in her apartment in New York. Now this was after your Papa and I had married, and we were living with his parents, and one day I decided to surprise my mother-in-law by cleaning the apartment while she was out. I was dusting the mantelpiece when I accidentally bumped one of the vases and sent it careening to the floor. I was in tears when I told her, and I remember how Myers's sisters, Pearl and Miriam, scowled at me when I begged her forgiveness.

"Gertrude Anna took it all in hand—she was a good woman—and said, 'There's an old German-Jewish expression, *Scherbe brengen glik.*' (Broken glass brings good luck.)

"I thanked her for being so patient with me, and that was that. A few months later, when Papa decided he was taking me back to Berkley to have the baby, Gertrude Anna handed me a package all wrapped and labeled 'Fragile.' When I asked her what it was, she said that I would find out when I got home and not to open it until then. I did as she said, and when we were back in Berkley, I opened the box, and inside was the other crystal vase, with a handwritten note: 'Handle With Care.' Years later, one of Papa's customers turned it into a lamp, and it has sat on my bedside table ever since."

"Do you have anything else from Bubbie Herzberg's house?"

"No." Nana Lena thought for a moment, and then answered. "As a matter of fact, I do." I followed her back into the kitchen and she reached into a cabinet and produced a cracked plate that has been glued back together. "You know what this is?"

"Something for the Goodwill box?"

"Amele!"

"Is it some kind of family heirloom? A special plate that Bubbie used for *Shabbos* dinner?"

"Ha! It was the plate she kept under the kitchen sink to hold the sponges."

"You're kidding me, right?"

"I'm not kidding. When she died, she left Pearl and Miriam everything. All they gave me was this *farshtunkene* plate. I keep it as a reminder."

"A reminder of what?"

"The things that can tear a family apart." Nana Lena whispered. "Can you keep a secret?"

I nodded conspiratorially.

"I broke the plate."

"*You* broke it?"

"One night I was so mad at Miriam that when I hung up the phone, I threw the plate across the room. It didn't break. So I threw it again. Nothing. The third time it broke into three even pieces. I thought maybe Gertie was trying to tell me something."

"And you feel better for having shared this with me?"

"Now don't go getting all smart-alecky with me, young lady, there is a point to my story."

"There always is."

"I don't want you and your sisters fighting over my things when I'm gone."

"But Nana, you're not going anywhere for a long time."

"Only God knows what's in store for me. Now you remember what I said. No fighting after I'm gone."

"I promise, Nana."

"Good; let's eat. How about a nice corned beef sandwich? I need to use up all the bread before *Pesach*."

We sat in the kitchen eating corned beef on rye piled high with sauerkraut, which Nana Lena thoroughly enjoyed. "Now that's a good sandwich! Pass the pickles."

Several years had passed, and Nana Lena was in the hospital for her second cancer surgery. I stopped at Louie's Deli and ordered a corned beef on rye to go. "Extra pickles on the side."

"You tell your grandmother to get well soon."

"Will do, Mr. Eisenberg. I'll tell her you asked for her."

"I put in a cold cream soda. It's on the house."

When I arrived at the hospital, I was surprised to hear laughter coming from Nana's room. Nana Lena was holding court, propped up in bed with an audience of nurses and orderlies. This was a side of my Nana that few people knew about, the bawdy joke teller, completely in contrast to the image she usually projected, but a side of Nana Lena nonetheless.

Gleefully Nana Lena related, "This man and his wife were having a barbeque. The man says to his wife, 'Honey, your butt is getting big as the side of this grill.'"

She sees me. "Hello, Amele." To the others, "You all know my granddaughter?" Nods and smiles all around.

"Don't let me interrupt."

Nana Lena demonstrated as she talked. "His wife gives him a glaring look and turns away, but he repeats it. 'I mean it honey; your butt is getting really, really big.' That night in bed, he cozies up to her…"

One of the nurses started tittering.

"You know this one already?" Nana Lena asked.

The nurse shook her head no.

Nana Lena continued, "…but the wife moves away. 'What's the matter?' he says, and the wife replies, 'I just don't feel like heating up my really big grill for your puny little piece of meat.'"

Everyone burst out laughing while Nana Lena smiled innocently as the doctor entered the room. "What's going on here?"

I explained, "It's just Nana Lena holding court."

"As right she should."

The nurses and orderlies shuffled out of the room without making eye contact with the doctor.

Nana Lena vamped, "Doc, if I'd known you were coming I would have put on some lipstick."

"Well, Mrs. Herzberg, I've come to see how you're healing. Perhaps you could ask your granddaughter to wait outside?"

"And leave you all alone with me?"

The doctor closed the curtain so that they could have some privacy. "Now let me help you put your feet in the stirrups so we can take a look."

And from behind the curtain, I heard Nana Lena say, "So, Doc, do I have my hat on straight?"

"You're healing just fine, Mrs. Herzberg." The doctor pulled the curtain back.

"Doctor, are you married?"

"Yes, as a matter of fact, I am."

"Then you'll appreciate this story.

"A Jewish woman goes to get her portrait painted. She tells the artist she wants him to paint her exactly as she is.

"'Fine, Madam. I would be happy to. Why don't you have a seat over here, and we'll get started.'

"'One thing, I want you should paint me with a beautiful diamond necklace.'

"'Why certainly, Madam.'

"'With stones like this,' she demonstrates, 'and earrings to match.'

"'But, of course, Madam.'

"'And while you are at it, I want you should paint me a fancy diamond tiara.'

"'Pardon my asking, but why do you want all these things, my good woman, when you asked me to paint you exactly as you are?'

"'One day, I'm going to die, and my husband will remarry. I want the second wife to go crazy looking for the jewels.'"

A little while later, the Rabbi stopped by as he was making his rounds, visiting the Jewish patients. "Rabbi, you remember my granddaughter. My first rose."

"Your first rose after your daughter, right?"

"Of course, Rabbi."

The Rabbi smiled at me. "Yes, it's so good to see you. I know you bring your grandmother great *nachas*. She talks about you all the time."

"You know she's single, Rabbi. Maybe you know a nice Jewish boy who will keep her here in Norfolk so she can be near her grandmother?"

"Nana!"

"I'll keep that in mind, Mrs. Herzberg. I'll keep that in mind."

The next day when I arrived, I again heard laughter as I entered her room. This time her audience consisted of one: a gray-haired nun who stood at the side of Nana Lena's bed, holding her hand and laughing.

"Uh-oh, Sister, looks like we've been discovered. Amele, come meet Sister Mary Margaret. This is my eldest granddaughter, Amele, my second rose, as the Rabbi pointed out yesterday."

The nun nodded, "She does go on and on about her roses."

"So, Nana, what's going on here? Are you going through a crisis of faith? Is there something I should know about?"

Nana Lena gave the Sister a sheepish look. "I guess I have to 'fess up."

Sister Mary Margaret corrected her. "We call it *confession*, Mrs. Herzberg."

Nana Lena shrugged and pointed, "She's my supplier. Go on

Sister, tell her. She provides my daily fix."

"Don't tell me you're taking hard drugs now, Nana?"

"Better."

"What?"

Nana Lena urged, "Go on, show her."

Sister Mary Margaret reached into her robes and extracted a handful of small candies in tan and red wrappers.

Nana Lena beamed. "Mary Janes. My favorite candy when I was a girl."

"Mine, too." The Sister offered me one, and I took it.

I examined the neatly wrapped candy, a rectangle slightly smaller than a domino. "What does it taste like?"

Both of them are incredulous. "You never had a Mary Jane?"

"No."

Nana Lena asked, "You don't have any loose teeth, do you?"

I shook my head.

"Go ahead, then. Try it. It's the kind of candy that always sticks to your teeth and can be used to pull out a loose tooth if necessary. The good Sister comes and visits me each afternoon, and she brings me a treat."

"Call it a donation. I call it the price of admission to hear your Nana's stories. She is always telling me about when she was a child. It reminds me so much of the old days, when I was growing up. I came from a big family, too. My people were Irish. My great-grandpappy came over in the 1880s."

"So did mine."

"We both lived in Berkley. Our family lived over near Liberty Street, and I remember going to your father's candy store to buy Mary Janes."

"I know. Can you believe that?"

"Weren't you the same family who had the ice cream parlor?"

"Yes, we were. Isn't it a small world?"

"See, we share a lot of common history, and we would never have known that had I not offered your grandmother a little piece of sugar. Well, I better be getting on, Mrs. Herzberg. I'll stop by and visit with you tomorrow."

"Thank you, Sister, I'll be here."

I took my grandmother's hand. "I love that about you, Nana."

"What?"

"I love that you can make anything into a positive experience, including spending another day in the hospital."

"The way I look at it," Nana Lena said, "another day, another chance to get to know someone, another friend. Dwell in the positive, and somehow you'll get through the negative. Or as Mama used to say, 'When life gives you lemons, make marmalade!' Fooled you, didn't I?"

* * *

Corned Beef on Rye

Take two slices of rye bread. Spread one side of the bread with mustard, pile high with thinly sliced corned beef, and top with cole slaw and the other slice of rye. Serve with a wedge of dill pickle. Now that's a sandwich!

Seder Table

In 1982, I purchased my first video camera, which in those days consisted of a twelve-pound camera connected by cable to a fifteen-pound tape deck, which you carried on one shoulder, while balancing the camera on the other shoulder, all the while making sure that the cable doesn't get caught (say, on a doorknob) and ruin the shot. I had brought the camera home for Pesach to record my grandmother's gefilte fish-making process, a recipe I had heard about and tasted for many years but never actually witnessed... an old family recipe she learned to make as a child.

Nana Lena was a natural in front of the camera. It didn't hurt that I was the operator and, like the youngest child at the Seder, asking all the questions. She entered the room carrying a large white Styrofoam cooler. "Okeydokey, we're on the way to the fish-making, and it's a big thing. This is the fish I got from the market... twenty-two pounds of rockfish, whitefish, and trout, which is about twelve pounds after it's skinned and filleted, and about another pound that I clean off the bones. All that's already taken care of. I didn't want to leave everything to do in one day. Making fish is really a three-day process: a day to shop, a day to cook, and a day to cool."

She took each piece of fish out of the bag and washed it, squeezing off the excess water. "You don't think I'm an old Bubbie, do you?"

"Of course not, Nana."

"You see, I put a piece of waxed paper between each piece. Then I sealed it all inside a freezer bag. What are you doing, closing in on the fish? If Pat sees this, she won't want to eat it."

"Well, then, I won't show the video to Pat until after dinner." I zoomed in on her brown spotted hands, closing in on her big diamond ring. "Aren't you going to take off your jewelry, Nana?"

"So I won't lose it? So it can be yours someday? Oy, your mother would kill me."

"I was just thinking about what Bubbie Sareva would say."

"Sareva definitely wouldn't like that." She removed her ring and placed it in the windowsill next to her violets.

A huge pot of water heated on the stove. Nana started cutting the onions. "I've got five large onions here. Some of them go into the stock; the rest I'll use in the fish later. I don't measure, so I don't know exactly how much I'll be using. I can only tell when I feel the consistency of the fish; then I'll know if I've got it right.

"Let's start with the stock." She cut the onions, skins and all, right over the pot. "So you take the yellow skins and put it in the stock pot. It makes the fish nice and yellow, golden yellow. Now you're going to be showing this to your children fifteen years from now, and they're going to say that this lady must have been crazy putting the peel in the pot. And they probably won't like what I'm going to do next either," she said, as she took three large fish carcasses, heads and all, and dropped them into the steaming water. "The fish heads, that's what gives you a good strong stock."

She looked up at my camera and said with a twinkle, "You know what it smells like?"

I shrugged my shoulders.

"Fish!" She laughed. "Now I'm going to add more onion peel and celery, and we're going to put in the carrots. The carrots are cut thick, so you can take them out of the pot later and use a little slice on top of the fish for decoration. That's how Bubbie always made it, with the carrot on top. You think I'll ever amount to being a cook, Amele?"

"You are the best cook I know, Nana."

"That's music to my ears." She wiped her forehead with her elbow. "With that, I'll tell you another story about when Bubbie was sick; I guess it was thirteen, no, fourteen years ago. It was just this time of year, and I made everything early and took a whole Pesach tray to the hospital to her. She was most appreciative. She took a bite of the fish, and she looked up at me and spoke to me apologetically.

"Lena, you won't mind if I tell you something?"

And I said, "No, Mama, what?"

She said. *"Der fish darf einkoch'n eine halbe sho."*

"Do you know what I said?" Nana Lena asked me.

"The fish has to cook about a half hour longer."

"Very good! I knew it had to cook a little longer, but I didn't think it was a half hour. I was in a hurry because I wanted to get it over to Mama for her Passover meal before we had our Seder. I took the whole Pesach Seder dinner to her, and I know she enjoyed it. Especially my matzie balls."

"All my married years, I've made gefilte fish for the holidays, and when the grandchildren came along and they loved it as much as they did, I felt that as long as I can stand on these two old legs and make it, I will."

"You know we love it, Nana."

"I know."

The next day, Seder preparations continued as three cooks converged on my mother's kitchen: my mother, Nana Lena, and my great-aunt Goldie. Goldie, once known for her curly golden locks, pranced and preened in front of the camera like a Southern Mae West. "Get me. Get me, I'm the prettiest."

"You are not!" Nana Lena elbowed her sister.

"Yes, I am." Goldie leaned into frame. "We are the cooks of 1920."

Nana Lena added, "Or earlier."

"1920, I wasn't old enough to cook."

"You were born in 1900, and you weren't old enough to cook in 1920?"

Goldie flaunted her age proudly, "I was born in 1911."

Nana Lena thought a minute. "I suppose you're right. I was born in 1912." Nana Lena didn't like it when Goldie was right, so she quickly changed the subject. "Watch me make the *haroset*, Amele. I'm making *haroset*, but I never make it this way. I always grate it. But your Mama insisted on putting it in the blender."

"It's the modern way, Nana."

"Blender's in," Goldie quipped.

"But your Nana's not modern. She's old-fashioned."

"Blender's in, grater's out."

"But Nana, you used a blender yesterday to beat the eggs?"

"That was a blender; this is a food processor."

"That's right, processor is in, blender is out," Goldie rolled her eyes.

Nana turned to the camera. "Now I don't hear anyone saying, 'Be careful, Nana, you're going to cut your hand.'"

Goldie mimicked her, "Be careful, Lena, you're going to cut your hand."

My mother chimed in from across the room. "You wouldn't cut your hand if you used the processor, Mother."

Nana Lena turned toward her daughter and then back toward my camera. "I started to say something, Elayne, but Amy's got the video on."

"What were you gonna say, Mother?"

Nana Lena looked straight into the camera and in her best Southern drawl said, "Shut up."

"Nana!"

Nana Lena rolled her eyes for effect. "Elayne, you said you had some open honey?" Mom brought her the honey, and Nana poured it in.

Goldie leaned in and whispered to the camera. "I'm watching so I'll know how to make it when I make it next time. But I won't make it this way, I'll make it *good*."

Nana Lena teased her, "You won't make it this way, you'll make it good, but you'll watch me to learn how to make it?"

"Smart ass." Goldie turned away.

Nana stirred in the nuts. "*Shit arayn*. That's what Mama used to say."

We all joined in saying "*Shit arayn*," not because it is a blessing or anything—we just like the way that it sounds, like throw some shit in, when it just means to shake or pour. Nana Lena poured a little wine into the mixture and then stirred, handing the spoon to her daughter, "You want to be the official taster?"

"I thought that was my job, Nana?" I teased from across the room.

Nana Lena turned right to camera. "Well, who do you think was the official taster before you?"

Mom took a bite. "It needs more honey. No, it's good."

Goldie elbowed in. "Let me have a taste. Let me taste it." She took a bite off the same spoon. "It needs nuts. All I tasted was apples."

"We need a lot of nuts in this family," my mother added.

"We have enough nuts already," Nana Lena concluded as she dumped the rest of the chopped pecans into the bowl. "To hell with the expense. Give the bird another seed. I'll use them all." She took another bite. "*Now* it needs more honey."

We spent the rest of the afternoon preparing the traditional Seder foods: eggs in salt water, matzo ball soup. The brisket, which Nana Lena had prepared in advance, was returned to the oven to heat. Mother made a matzo kugel. Fannie would be bringing her famous sweet potato, carrot, and prune tsimmes. Aunt Thelma was bringing stewed fruit. Eventually, there would be twenty-six people for Seder. For those of you have never attended a Seder, it is a food orgy preceded by a scripted service in which all of the participants take turns reading from a book called the *Haggadah,* which tells the tale of the Jewish exodus from Egypt, over three thousand years ago. It is a celebration of freedom that occurs in early spring and often overlaps with Easter. There is a reason for that. The Last Supper of the New Testament was actually a Passover Seder.

After all the food was prepared and the tables were set, I set up my video camera in the family room to tape the arrivals. My cousins Pat and Ashley were the first to arrive. Ashley was about two years old then, a blonde imp with a thick southern accent. She hopped around the Seder Table on one leg, eating pickles. When I asked her what was wrong with her leg, she said, "I boke it. I boke my yeg."

I played along, "How'd you 'boke' it, Ashley?"

"I don't know. I boke it."

I finished connecting the video camera to the television. Ashley's image appeared on the screen. "How'd you do that? I'm on the TV. Momma, Momma, come quick! Look!" Ashley stood there waving at the television until Pat arrived.

"Who's on the TV? Is it Robert Redford?" My cousin Pat had had a crush on Robert Redford ever since I could remember. Ever since *Butch Cassidy and the Sundance Kid.*

"No, Momma, look, it's me!"

"Amy, you're not taping now, are you?" Pat asked, adjusting her hair and smoothing down her skirt. "Aunt Lena told me how you taped her making the fish." Pat wrinkled her nose.

I lied. "No, I'm not taping. I just set it up so everyone can see themselves when they come in."

One by one, the guests arrived and filled the area in front of the television: Uncle Pete and Aunt Thelma, Aunt Goldie and Uncle Al, Freddie and Sidney, Fannie, Nickie, Aly and Michael.

Everyone just stood there waving at the television. On camera, they were seen in profile. Finally, my cousin Pat—she was always the clever one—turned to face the camera and said, "Shouldn't we be waving at the *camera* instead of waving at the TV?"

This particular year, we dedicated our Seder to the Jews of Russia who still were not free to celebrate this holiday in their homes. Freedom is an underlying theme of many of our holidays. That is because Jews had been enslaved on more than one occasion. On Passover, we celebrate our freedom from slavery in Pharaoh's Egypt.

One of the pivotal moments of the evening is the asking of the Four Questions. Typically, this is the responsibility of the youngest male. Our family, being female dominated, did not discriminate as to gender. All of us learned to ask these important questions in English and Hebrew from the time we were about five. This year, the assignment went to my youngest male cousin, Michael, who performed admirably, as he asked: "Why is this night different from all other nights? Why on this night do we eat only unleavened bread? Why on this night do we dip not one time but twice? Why on this night do we eat reclining?"

The service goes on to explain that on this night we eat matzo to remind us that that was all our forefathers had to eat when they were finally told they could leave Egypt. They did not have time for the bread to rise, so they baked it immediately so that they would have food to take with them into the desert. We dip two times: once, greens in salt water; once, harozet and maror, to taste the bitter with the sweet. And we eat reclining because that is how a free man ate in the time of Pharaoh, not crouching on the ground like an animal, but reclining, like a free man.

Passover is an important holiday not only because it marks our passage from slavery into freedom, "out of the land of Egypt, out of the house of bondage"; it also marks the beginning of our return to the Promised Land, over three thousand years ago. Israel may be a modern state, founded in the mid-twentieth century, but under other names and leaders, it has always been our home.

Tonight, Jews all over Israel and all over the world, gather together to celebrate this happy occasion with their families and loved ones. As we ask the four questions and hide the *Afikomen*, we become part of one enormous family that encircles the globe,

thankful for our freedom and for God's blessings. We give thanks
to our Creator for allowing us to enjoy this meal in freedom, and
we pray for all of those who are still enslaved.

* * *

Lena and her granddaughters, Passover 1992.

Haroset

Haroset is one of the symbolic foods on the Seder plate. We eat on Passover to remind us of the bricks and mortar that the Jewish slaves used to build the pyramids of Egypt. My family loved to eat this as a snack, so we always made large quantities. This recipe should serve 8–10.

4–6 apples

1 cup chopped pecans

1/4 cup sweet red Passover wine

1/2 cup honey

Peel and core the apples. Dice into small pieces the size of a kernel of corn or a raisin. Chop pecans into similarly sized pieces. Add wine and honey. Combine ingredients. Taste. Add more wine or honey or pecans to taste.

Store in the refrigerator until Seder. Serve with matzo.

Birthday Cake

My great-grandmother, my Bubbie Minnie, had ten children. So you can imagine it was not exactly easy for her to remember the birth dates of all her children. Fortunately for my Bubbie, God—Mother Nature, whichever you prefer—had assisted her with an easy birthday memory plan.

Her first son, Leon, was born on June 22, the first day of summer. Another son, Pete, arrived on March 21, the first day of spring, which happened to fall on Purim that year. My great Aunt Poogie can boast that her birthday became a national holiday—April 15, or Tax Day, a day many Americans would prefer to forget. Three of my great aunts and uncles were born on the same date, July 24, a great memory-saving trick for my Bubbie, two years apart, at approximately 4 o'clock in the morning. July 24 wasn't exactly a holiday, but it probably was the result of some private celebration ten lunar cycles earlier.

My grandmother's birthday fell on my favorite holiday, July 4, American Independence Day, a holiday somewhat like Purim. A day of family cookouts, water-fights, and fireworks, when our nation celebrates its freedom and my family celebrates my Nana's birthday.

On that particular Fourth of July morning, a bright sunny day filled with the sound of birds chirping and lawn mowers humming, I was descending the staircase in my pajamas, rubbing the sleep out of my eyes, when I heard my mother scream.

She had stepped outside to get the newspaper. I rushed out to find her staring back at the house, crying, and twisting the newspaper in her hands. As I turned to see what she was looking at, reality closed in. The hatred was there again, scribbled in black and green and yellow spray paint across my home.

Our house, the two-story white house with the blue trim that Dad had so patiently restored for the party was sprayed with Jewish stars with swastikas painted over them. "Hitler Lives" was scrawled on the sidewalk, along with "Jesus Saves," "Van Halen," and other more pornographic phrases. Clutching each other like frightened *Kristallnacht* survivors, we surveyed the damages. "They" had been everywhere, painting the mailbox, the front steps, the trees, the cars.

My mother was shaking. I was angry. After all, this was the United States! We rushed inside to tell the others. Within minutes, my entire family was running around outside in our pajamas. "Who could have done such a thing?" "Was it someone we know?" "Should we call the police?" WHY? WHY? WHY? Shock, tears, and anger shook my body. Why is this happening to us? Why today of all days? Why is this *still* happening?

We were clustered together in the front yard, crying and talking, when we noticed that the neighbors were watching. Quietly, trying not to look at us directly, Mrs. Wiggins watched from her upstairs window. Mr. Gaskins rode his lawnmower over for a closer look. Mrs. Maxwell from across the street, stood there shaking her head. "I'm so sorry, Elayne," she tried to console my mother, as she tried to shepherd her family into a waiting van.

"Why is their house like that, Mommie?" one of the Maxwell children asked, as Mrs. Maxwell climbed into the driver's seat. She started the engine and turned back to my mother, not sure how to proceed. "We'll be back in a little while." Lowering her voice, "I don't think it's good for the children to see." Voice rising: "Can I get you anything from the grocery store?"

We went inside to dress and regroup. What to do first? I wanted to call the police. Mom suggested calling the Anti-Defamation League. Dad said to go ahead and call whomever we liked, but he wanted to get the place repainted in time for the party. My brother David said we should document the damage. So we videotaped and photographed, made the necessary phone calls, supplied the information on vandalism and bias reports, and put on our red, white, and blue. Then, together, as a family, we painted over the fear and ignorance that had terrified us so.

We all agreed on one thing, not to tell Nana Lena. However, keeping a secret does not come easily in our family. "You can't even see where they painted," my great-aunt Goldie whispered so her sister would not hear.

"What's everybody whispering about?" Nana Lena asked. "I've still got my hearing, you know?"

"Ears like a bat," Goldie quipped.

"Nothing, Mother," my mother countered.

"Don't tell me it's nothing, Elayne. I can tell when you say 'It's nothing' that it's something. Did somebody die?"

"No, Nana. Of course not," Donna piped in.

"Do I have a piece of corn stuck between my teeth?" she asked.

"Lena, can I get you another hot dog?" My father presented a platter of juicy dogs from the grill. "What, no customers?"

"How about a piece of birthday cake?"

"Maybe later. After the fireworks."

"What time are the fireworks starting?" David asked without enthusiasm. All the ingredients were there, but our hearts just weren't in it.

That night, as we watched the fireworks from the pier in the Maxwells' backyard, I thought about why it had happened to us and not to them. How would I have felt if the tables were turned? Would it have been any better being on the other side? No matter how I looked at it, it wasn't a pretty picture. Why are we still doing this to each other? When will we learn?

I took my grandmother's hand and gave it a squeeze. "You feel warm, Amele," she said. "I hope you aren't coming down with something?" Sighing, "I hear there's a lot of bad stuff going around lately."

I looked at her with narrowed lids. Did she know?

As the fireworks neared the finale, their size and tempo increased. My relatives oohed and aahed in harmony with the neighbors. When it was all over, we hugged each other, family and friends, maybe a little more tearfully than in past years, and headed home for birthday cake.

"Ya'll coming over for some cake?" my mother asked the neighbors, before we left.

"Thanks, but we're having red, white, and blue shortcake. Are you sure you don't want to stay?"

As we walked home, Nana Lena pulled me aside and said: "You learned a tough lesson today, and I'm proud of you. You were strong. Because in a lifetime, you'll go through a lot of things and you need to be strong to get through them all."

"You knew?"

"You think it's so easy to keep a secret from your old Nana? And besides, I didn't want to spoil the party for your mother. She worked so hard. But tomorrow, you can tell your father I said he did a great job re-painting the house."

* * *

Ambrosia

One bite, and you are back in the 1960s. Ambrosia was a staple of every summer picnic.

2 20 ounce cans pineapple chunks

3 small cans mandarin oranges

3 regular oranges, peeled, sectioned and cut up

1 pint sour cream

1 package miniature marshmallows

1/2 cup coconut

Mix together ingredients and refrigerate overnight. Serve chilled.

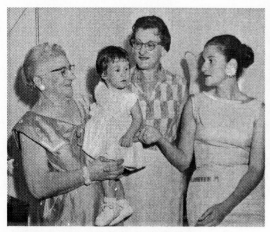

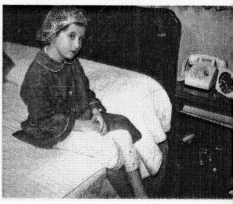

Spending the night at Nana & Papa'

4 Generations: Minnie Goodman,
Amy Ostrower, Lena Herzberg, and
Elayne Ostrower.

Chanukah 1963: David, Amy, and
Donna Ostrower light candles with
their Nana

Chanukah 1968: David, Elayne,
Donna, Amy, and Melissa Ostrower
with Nana Lena

Potato Latkes

The key to a successful Chanukah party is keeping the latkes hot and crisp and keeping the hungry hands out of the kitchen. Latkes are crisp thin potato pancakes, fried in oil, and are best when eaten immediately, which we did every chance we could until Nana Lena slapped our hands and ejected us from the kitchen.

She used several large cast iron skillets for maximum efficiency and superior conductivity. As she spooned the batter into the well-greased and heated pans, she used just the right amount to make six latkes in each pan. Six latkes, three pans, a new batch every five minutes... you do the math. In an hour, she could make ninety latkes, which we would polish off in no time.

Usually about halfway through the batch, after many attempts to get her to sit down and join us, my father would get up and just take the spoon out of her hand. Finally, she would acquiesce and take a seat at the head of the kitchen table.

"Thank you for joining us, mother."

"Elayne, I was—"

Donna, ever the peacemaker, interrupted, "You make the best latkes, Nana."

"You don't think that's music to my ears?" Nana Lena took a bite and surveyed our plates. "Burt, David needs more latkes."

"Coming right up!"

Every year, the same ritual. We would peel a ten-pound bag of potatoes, more if we were having a large group. Nana Lena would grate the potatoes using a triangular-shaped grater that was probably almost as old as she was, even though mom had bought her a food processor, and even though it would save hours of time. Nana Lena was like that. She preferred the old ways. The food processor remained in a box in the garage.

(Nowadays when I make latkes, I use the food processor in a two-step process. First, I grate the potatoes and onions using the grater attachment; then, I process it a second time with the chopper blade. Believe me, it beats grating by hand. The food processor is probably the only thing Nana Lena was wrong about. I promise you, Nana Lena, the food processor is our friend.)

Nana Lena finished grating the potatoes and then she washed her hands. "Let the potatoes sit for a few minutes, then spoon off most of the excess moisture." She took a spoon and pressed down on the mixture, removing the puddle of liquid that had formed in the indentation. "Amele, get me the eggs, baking powder, salt, white pepper, and flour."

I assembled the requested items.

"Beat up half a dozen eggs. I may need more. How many pounds of potatoes did you peel? Ten? Six eggs will do. Hand me the measuring spoons, will you?" She added the baking powder, salt, pepper, and eggs, mixing them thoroughly. "I add the flour a cup at a time, until the mixture thickens enough that it isn't runny. Like this. Now if it was Passover, I'd use matzo meal instead, but it is heavier, so you don't need so much."

After covering the bowl with plastic wrap and putting in it the refrigerator, Nana Lena removed the tray of brisket and put it in the oven to reheat. "There. Now that is out of the way, we can sit until it's time to make the latkes."

"I'll put up the coffee."

"You might as well make a whole pot. Your mother will be here soon."

I put up a pot in the coffee maker. Nana Lena had graduated from percolator to instant to drip, but she used the machine only if she were making coffee for more than just herself. She didn't see the point in making a pot of coffee when all she needed was a cup.

While I made the coffee, Nana Lena got the mail, wiped the counters, and rinsed the dishes in the sink. "No point in leaving them for later. As I always say..."

I chimed in, "Clean it up as you go along."

Nana Lena smiled, "I guess I've told you that one before."

I winked. "Maybe once or twice." I poured two cups and carried them to the table. "Nana, are you going to sit down?"

"I'll be right there." She wiped the front of another cabinet and shined the handles. "I'm coming." She folded the dish towel and hung it under the sink. Finally, she sat down and took a sip of coffee. "So tell me something good."

"Well... I've decided to move to California."

Nana nearly dropped her cup. "I thought you liked New York."

"New York is fabulous."

"New York is closer. A lot closer than California."

"I'm going to take the money that Aunt Goldie left me—"

"*Oleho hashol'm* [May she rest in peace]."

"...and I'm going to do it. I've only been talking about this for seven years."

"What about your work?"

"Don't worry about that. There are more movie companies in one zip code in Los Angeles than in all of the five boroughs. I can always get work in production. My agent said if I want to be a writer, I have to move to L.A. So I've decided I'm moving the first of the year."

"Good. Go to L.A. and become a famous writer. Just make sure you come home for Pesach."

"Passover is too early. How about the High Holidays?"

"Rosh Hashana? It's a deal." She shook my hand. "You'll still call every Sunday?"

"I'm just moving three time zones, Nana, not to a foreign country. Of course, I'll call."

"How many hours is the flight?"

"Five, six. I don't know. You worried I'll have a long flight?"

"I just want to know how long it will take for you to come home."

I didn't make it home for Rosh Hashana that year, or for Thanksgiving. So when Chanukah came around, I was feeling kind of homesick. I called Nana Lena for her latke recipe. "How many eggs should I use?"

She answered my question with a question, "How many potatoes?"

"Six."

"What size?"

"Big ones."

"Two, maybe three. Depends how big the eggs are."

"How much baking powder?"

"One teaspoon."

"How much flour?"

"Until it's firm, but not too firm."

"That's a big help."

"One to two cups."

"Thanks, Nana."

"What kind of frying pan are you using?"

"I don't know. A frying pan."

"You need a cast-iron skillet? I'll get you one."

"Don't be silly. You'll pay more to ship it than it costs for me to buy."

"So, buy one, and I'll pay for it."

"Nana."

"Don't argue with your Nana. You want the world to think I didn't teach you any manners?"

"Okay, Nana. I promise I'll get one soon."

A few months later, I was homesick again and called Nana Lena for another of my favorite recipes, potato kugel, a potato pie that you bake for a long time at a high temperature until it's crispy on the outside and firm, but moist, within. Kind of like a giant potato pancake that's been baked, not fried.

She started reeling off the ingredients: "Potatoes, onions, eggs, flour, baking soda, salt, pepper."

"Aren't those the same ingredients for latkes?"

"The same substance, yes, but not the same form. The same ingredients with a different method of preparation. Another thing they share in common, though: They do require the same pan. Did you get the cast iron skillet?"

"I've been meaning to."

"It won't taste the same in a Pyrex or a baking pan."

"It will be fine, Nana."

"Alright, *ess gezundhayt*."

"Thank you, Nana. I'll pretend I'm eating it with you."

There is silence for a moment at the other end of the phone. "When you come home for Pesach, I'll make you another one."

"That would be wonderful, Nana. It's a date."

Nana Lena was right. My potato kugel didn't taste anything like hers. The crust was too thin, and the middle never hardened. I was a failure as a kugel maker, and I knew it. The next day I went out and bought a cast iron skillet and tried again. This time, it tasted like home.

* * *

Potato Latkes

yields 20–25 small pancakes

5–6 large potatoes, peeled (about 3 pounds)

2 onions

2 eggs, beaten

1 tsp baking powder

2 tsp salt

1/4 tsp white pepper

1 cup flour or matzo meal

corn or peanut oil for frying

Keep peeled potatoes in a bowl of cold water until you are ready to use them; this keeps them from turning black. Grate potatoes by hand or use a food processor with a medium grating blade to grate the potatoes and onions, transferring them to another bowl, as you work in batches. Replace the grater with a chopper, and process the potato and onion mixture a second time, for a short time. Do not liquefy. You want the potatoes to have some texture. Drain excess liquid using spoon or strainer, but don't go nuts about it.

Pour mixture into a large bowl. Add eggs, baking powder, oil, salt, and pepper. Add the flour 1/4 cup at a time. If you use matzo meal, you may not need as much. You want the mixture to be a little firmer than when you started out, but not stiff.

Heat oil in frying pan. Nana preferred using a cast iron skillet, but any frying pan will do. Make sure the oil is hot before spooning batter into skillet to create pancakes about 3 to 4 inches in diameter. Cook 3 to 4 minutes until the bottom of the latke looks golden brown; then turn and fry for another minute or two. Drain on paper towels. Latkes taste best when served immediately, but if you are preparing large batches, you may need to keep them warm in a preheated 400° oven.

Serve with applesauce, sour cream, or a mixture of cinnamon and sugar.

Potato Kugel

serves 6–8

> 3 pounds potatoes, peeled
>
> 2 onions
>
> 2 eggs, beaten
>
> 1 tsp baking powder
>
> 1/4 cup corn oil
>
> 2 tsp salt
>
> 1/4 tsp white pepper
>
> 1/2 cup flour or matzo meal
>
> oil for frying

Keep peeled potatoes in a bowl of cold water until you are ready to use them. This keeps them from turning black. Using a food processor, grate the potatoes and onions, transferring them to another bowl, as you work in batches. Replace the grater blade with a chopper, and process the potato and onion mixture a second time, for a short time. Do not liquefy. [Alternatively, you can skip the grating and just use the chopper blade if you process a few pieces of potato and onion at a time. It's up to you.] Drain excess liquid using spoon or strainer, but don't go nuts about it.

Pour mixture into a large bowl. Add eggs, baking powder, oil, salt, and pepper. Add the flour 1/4 cup at a time. If you use matzo meal, you may not need as much. You want the mixture to be a little firmer than when you started out, not stiff.

Heat baking dish in oven with 1/4 cup of corn or peanut oil. Nana preferred using a cast iron skillet, and to tell you the truth, she was right, but any 2 inch deep oven-safe pan or glass dish will do. Remove heated dish from oven, and pour mixture into pan. Drizzle a little more oil on top and return to oven.

Bake at 400° for one hour until crust is crispy brown, and outer edges detach from pan. Center should be moist, not runny. Serve hot.

BLT

It was a hot summer day, the kind of day when you needed a constant supply of iced tea. Nana Lena was reading the headlines from the morning paper when she exclaimed, *"Oy gutenyu!"*

"What?"

"Another terrorist attack on Israel. Five killed, one hundred eighty-one injured in a pedestrian shopping mall in Jerusalem."

"Which band of hoodlums did this? Hamas? Hezbollah?"

"No group has of yet claimed responsibility." Nana lowered her newspaper. "Ay yi yi. When is the killing going to stop? I tell you, Amele, what really pains me is all this death and dying. Where are the mothers? You can't tell me they are enjoying this, watching their children die. We do not bring children into the world to watch them die. No mother should have to do that. It is up to the women to end this cycle of war. We must bring up our children to understand that you cannot kill in the name of God. That is the ultimate profanity, to kill in God's name. There is no God who calls upon us to kill each other, and if someone tells you there is, maybe you need to ask for a second opinion."

Nana Lena sighed and headed over to the counter. "What should we make for lunch, Amele?" She pointed to some beefsteak tomatoes that had been ripening on the windowsill. "Don't these tomatoes look nice!"

"A tomato sandwich would be all right with me, with fresh basil and a little mozzarella, on a baguette or Italian focaccia bread."

Nana Lena peered at me over her glasses. "Where do you think you are, young lady, California? The only kind of basil I have is dried and comes in a bottle. And the only kind of cheeses I have are cream, cottage, and parmesan. I tell you what I'm in the mood for, Amele."

I was refilling Nana's glass when she dropped the bomb.

"I was thinking about a BLT."

I nearly dropped the glass. "Nana! I thought you don't eat pork."

"I don't eat pork, I eat bacon. It's not the same thing."

"Bacon isn't pork? Since when?"

"Truth is, after your Bubbie died, I figured what the hell. I was only keeping Kosher for her. When I was growing up, if I wanted a BLT, I had to go out and eat it in public, which was so humiliating. After all, what if one of Mama's friends saw me? Most people sinned in the privacy of their home. My sin of consumption could be witnessed by the entire diner, but that didn't stop me. This time of year, when the tomatoes are so ripe like this, a BLT is just what I want."

"Why don't Jews eat pork?"

"The basic rules of *Kashrut* were based on dietary laws that were designed for separation. Milk from Meat. Jewish from non-Jewish. But they were also designed for desert living. There was no refrigeration, and it was an extremely warm climate. Back in biblical times, pork was known to have worms and cause illness. It was declared *treyf*, forbidden. Now in this day and age, it is irradiated, inspected, and declared safe—"The new white meat." So, do you see religious Jews eating pork?"

"Not likely."

"But they'll eat turkey bacon, as long as they call it something else. You know Muslims don't eat pork either. Who do you think they learned that from?

"Do you believe in God, Nana?"

"Of course, I do. I speak to Him every day. I ask Him to look out for my family and keep them safe from harm. And sometimes, if there's a special problem, I ask Him for a little help with that. I have a very personal relationship with God."

"Do you believe in the Bible?"

"Of course I believe in it. But how closely should we follow a document that was written thousands of years ago? Our own religion is sharply divided on that. Orthodox and many Conservative Jews keep Kosher. Reform Jews do not. Orthodox men keep their *payes* and their beards long, and many Orthodox women shave their heads and wear wigs, but not in our family, except for the Royte Bubbie, so-named for her red *shaytl* or wig. Each of us has to find a way to take what is important to us in our religion and make it work in the context of the world we live in. That is the key phrase here, *in the world we live in*. Laws that may have applied two, three, four thousand years ago are not always suited to today's world.

"Sometimes the Bible tries to teach us by making us think. For example, the Bible says that God called upon Abraham to sacrifice his only son, Isaac, and Abraham was tearfully willing to comply, when God basically said, '*Shmok*! What were you thinking? Do you really think I want you to kill your son, your only son whom you love? After I made you and Sarah wait all those years? Don't take things so literally!'"

"Is *that* what the Bible said?"

"Do you really think that in the Koran, where it says, 'Kill the infidel,' that Muslims are supposed to go out and kill eighty percent of the people on Earth because they don't believe in the same God? What if this is another lesson? What if they are *supposed* to defy their God and practice charity and compassion to all their fellow man? What would happen? Maybe we would have peace."

"You see, each religion has its Bible, its blueprint, its set of myths, a particular view of ethics and history suitable for the time it was written. There is no master race, no perfect religion, no absolute truth. There are many countries, many religions, many truths.

"The way I look on it, maybe a BLT is like the Abraham/Isaac lesson. God is just waiting for us to call this into question. Maybe what we need is to make a nice BLT sandwich out of turkey bacon and ripe summer tomatoes and crisp lettuce and a little Miracle Whip."

"That sounds great, Nana. And who should we invite?"

"Why, we'd invite the Pope, the Chief Rabbi, and the Chief Mullah. We'll serve them turkey bacon, lettuce, and tomato sandwiches and iced tea, with plenty of cucumbers and pickles and tomatoes on the side. We'll have a *kum sitz*, and we'll eat sandwiches, and later a little tea and rugelach. We'll just sit here and talk until we work it out. We'll figure out a way for us all to get along."

"If anyone can do it, Nana, it's you. You've always been the mediator in the family."

"That's because I'm a middle child; I had a lot of brothers and sisters, so I learned to get along. Later, people started coming to me for advice. I'll tell you what I told them: When your Papa and I got married, we made a promise never to go to bed angry with each other, no matter what. We didn't fight much, but when we did fight, we always kissed and made up before we fell asleep.

That's what needs to happen in Israel. Enough eye for an eye and tooth for a tooth. It doesn't matter anymore who did what to whom. Enough name calling. Enough death. It is time to get on with the living. It's time to kiss and make up."

"Or no tea and rugelach, right, Nana?"

Nana Lena thought for a moment. "First, I'll give them a little taste so they'll know what they're missing. Then, I'll make my demands. Basic love and tenderness. That's what we all need. BLT."

"That was a good one, Nana. I didn't see that coming. Will there ever be peace in Israel, Nana?"

"From your mouth to God's ears, my Amele."

"I mean, really? Do you think?"

"Not in my lifetime." Nana Lena kissed me on the cheek. "*Halevai*! Maybe in yours."

Lena in Israel

The Mitzvah Table

"Make a mitzvah," I can still hear Nana Lena say, "It will come back to you." Like the karmic boomerang or the Judeo-Christian "Do unto others as you would have them do unto you," making a mitzvah is a guiding principle of Jewish life. *Mitzvah* in Hebrew means both *commandment* and *good deed*. According to the Talmud, it is important that a mitzvah be done with a joyous heart and not out of self-interest. So, buying a temple raffle ticket is not really a mitzvah, but planting a tree in Israel is.

A mitzvah might consist of baking a noodle kugel for a neighbor with a broken arm, or visiting a friend in the hospital, or spending countless hours doing volunteer work for every imaginable cause: Hadassah, Sisterhood, B'nai Brith, Youth Aliyah, American Cancer Society, American Heart Association, Lions Club, the Beth Sholom Home. Nana Lena used to say, "You have to pay for the space you take up on Earth. You can't just give money, you have to give of yourself." Nana Lena gave *money*, don't get me wrong; but one thing I learned from her was that it was more important to give *time*. Nana Lena gave of hers freely.

It was traditional on Friday nights, after services, that the Sisterhood of Beth El Temple would hold an *Oneg Shabbat*, coffee and sweets would be served, and the congregants would greet one another and welcome the Sabbath. The women of Sisterhood took turns preparing the food, and Nana Lena joined in the baking. Attendance was particularly good on the nights Nana Lena's desserts were served. There were strudel and rugelach, and sometimes mandelbrot, date nut bars, lemon bars, and seven-layer cookies, and of course, Nana Lena's pecan tassies. These were the staples of Nana Lena's *Oneg Shabbat* that were also served at every special family occasion, *bris*, wedding, or bat mitzvah.

Pecan tassies were not exactly Jewish treats, but they definitely qualified as a mitzvah because of the time it took to make them. All of these treats were lovingly made and beautifully displayed in little pleated pastel baking cups, colorfully arranged on silver platters.

"Bless you, Lena; you've outdone yourself this year."

"Thank you, Rabbi."

"It's a real mitzvah. All that work. Mrs. Cohen was going on and on about the rugelach, and they *are* wonderful, I tell you, but I prefer the tassies myself."

"*Ess gezundhayt*, Rabbi."

The Rabbi smiled as he took another bite.

Raine Levinson joined them. "Lena, you must give me the recipe for your strudel. Good *Shabbos*, Rabbi."

"Good Shabbos to you, Raine. I'll leave you two ladies to talk shop." The Rabbi took his leave and moved on to greet Raine's husband, Izzie, who was standing nearby thoroughly enjoying a handful of Nana Lena's treats.

One of the organizations she supported was the Beth Sholom Home for the Aged. She was Treasurer of the organization for eighteen years. Every year at Christmas, the Jewish volunteers at the home did—and still do—a group mitzvah they call Switch Day. The volunteers fed, dressed, and cared for the aged so that the nursing home staff could spend Christmas with their own families. Nana Lena was a regular participant, and one year, she brought me along.

We were putting our coats in the volunteers' room when a cheerful, extremely petite blonde-headed woman entered, clipboard in hand. It was Goldie Satisky, a real *balebuste*.

"Goldele. You look so good. I can't believe you just turned ninety-three. *Keyn eynhore*."

"If it isn't my favorite *makher*, Lena Herzberg." They exchanged kisses. "I see you brought us a young one."

"Amy, you know Mrs. Satisky, Gail's grandmother."

"It's so good to see you, Mrs. Satisky."

"Call me Goldie, it makes me sound younger." Goldie consulted her clipboard. "Lena, I've put you in the kitchen, naturally. Amy, maybe you could start off by helping your Nana with that, and at ten o'clock we're having a sing-a-long in the rec room. You can sing, can't you?"

"Not really."

"Don't worry, most of them can't hear anyway."

I followed Nana Lena down the hall and watched as she stopped to greet nearly every person in the hallway, calling them by name, asking after their loved ones. Volunteers, workers, residents, she knew them all. She stopped to greet an old friend, Sara Weinraub, who stood near the lobby, pocketbook dangling from her arm, wearing a winter coat and hat and bedroom slippers.

"Sara, it's Lena."

Sara and Lena had been close friends since they were girls. Now Sara no longer recognized her. But seeing a friendly face, she asked, "Will you give me a quarter?"

"Of course, I'll give you a quarter, Sara."

"I need to make a phone call."

"Sara, you know you're not supposed to use the phone."

"I need to call a taxi, to get me out of here. I've got to go home and fix supper."

"You don't want to leave now, Sara, you'll miss my lunch. You wouldn't want to do that, now, would you?" Nana Lena gently guided her back to her residential unit, handing her over to a nurse.

Eventually we made it to the kitchen. I could hear Nana Lena sigh as we entered the quiet room.

"She was such a vibrant woman, so full of life. It breaks my heart to see her like that."

I gave my Nana a hug and patted her on the back. "I know it must be hard for you."

"I know too many people here."

I found two aprons, tied one around Nana Lena, and tied the other one around my waist. "Okay, boss lady, what are we making?"

Nana Lena consulted a written menu. "Looks like we're making tuna fish."

"Tuna fish on Christmas?"

"The majority of the people here are Jewish. The few Christian folks, their families usually come and pick them up on the holidays." She looked at the menu again. "Tuna salad and sliced tomatoes for seventy-five. We better get to work. Amy, chop the onions real fine. I'll get started on the celery."

We chopped what seemed like a mountain of onions and celery. "How much tuna?"

Nana Lena consulted the recipe card. "It says here three cans."

"That can't be right. Three cans of tuna for all of these vegetables? Where's the tuna?"

Nana Lena pointed to the storage area at the end of the room. There I found three of the largest cans of tuna fish I had ever seen. "Man, these things weigh a ton."

"Three cans will be just fine." Nana Lena located three large mixing bowls. After we opened the cans and drained the water, we emptied one can into each bowl. We divided the minced vegetables into three parts and dumped them in with the tuna. Nana added the low-fat mayo and low-fat sour cream, as called for in the instructions.

"It says here, don't add any salt. Most of the folks here are on blood pressure medication." She handed me a spoon, "Mix it up real good."

Believe me I got quite a workout that morning, between stirring the tuna and scooping it onto the plates. We sliced dozens of tomatoes and arranged them next to the tuna. Then it was time to set the tables, and two other volunteers joined me to help. Being the youngest one, I did most of the lifting.

About ten minutes to ten, Goldie stuck her head inside the door of the lunchroom, "Lena, I hate to take your helper, but I could use a pretty face."

"What? You don't think mine is pretty anymore?" Nana looked hurt.

"Come, Amy, let me show you the way."

I followed Goldie out of the lunchroom. The recreation room was at the end of the blue corridor. The wings were color coded to help the residents find their way "home." In the orange wing were the most active residents, people who were relatively healthy, who did not require constant supervision. The recreation room was a colorful room with artwork on the walls and holiday decorations. There were crafts tables and a game area, with boxes of games like Parcheesi and checkers. Several rows of chairs were grouped around the piano, at the far end of the room, where an older, gray-haired gentleman waited. Goldie introduced us.

"Mr. Konigman, this is Amy Ostrower. She's going to help you today."

"I don't know what help I'll be," I tried to explain. "But I'll do my best." I reached out to shake his hand, but he did not take it.

I whispered to Goldie. "Orthodox?"

"Mr. Konigman is one of our residents. He's a bit..." She discreetly made a circular motion with her finger. "But he can play the piano."

"Oh, I see." That didn't make me any more comfortable.

The doors of the rec room swung open as a battalion of diminutive gray-haired women entered the room, on walkers, in wheel chairs, or on foot. One woman was at least thirty years younger than the others; I wondered why she was there. There were only two men. The audience shuffled to their seats and except for some coughing, there was silence. I could see that they were waiting for me to begin.

"Hi, my name is Amy Ostrower."

Blank stares from the women, smiles from the two men.

"I'm Lena Herzberg's granddaughter."

Now some of the ladies smiled as well, but it was still pretty quiet out there. I tried to get things rolling. "I hope you folks are ready for some music today. What kind of songs would you like to sing? Does anyone have any requests?" Still no response. I cut to the chase. "So, without further ado, I'd like to present the fabulous Mr. Konigman. Take it away, Mr. Konigman."

The ladies started to applaud, and Mr. Konigman began to play, with fervor and relish, like a spring-loaded toy that had just been released. It was a song I did not know, but the ladies in the audience started to sing. No two people were singing in the same key, and I was not sure whether they were even singing the same song, but I saw their faces relax and something resembling laughter behind their eyes. I joined in the song. I figured it didn't matter that I did not know the words; the important thing was that *they* did.

After a while, a tiny, red-headed woman with a bouffant hairdo came over and took me by the arm, guiding me to a seat in the front row. She looked me directly in the eyes, holding her finger to her mouth. I obeyed. Then she took her place next to Mr. Konigman at the piano and burst into song. For the rest of the hour, I watched two entertainers come to life and a room full of people thoroughly enjoying themselves.

When the sing-along was over, I stood in the doorway, saying goodbye. One of the men, the one in the blue polo shirt and the baggy pinstriped pants, reached over and pinched my ass.

"The *alter kaker* pinched me. I couldn't believe it," I told Nana Lena. But she didn't seem surprised.

"You think everything dies when you get old? You're probably the youngest thing he's seen in a long time."

"Nana!"

"And besides, you did a mitzvah. You reminded him of what it feels like to be young."

"But Nana, if that's a mitzvah, then wouldn't prostitutes be the true 'mitzvah girls'?"

Nana Lena scowled and didn't answer me at first. "I suppose you're right. As long as they don't do it on the Sabbath. Or are you supposed to do it on the Sabbath? I can't remember anymore; it's been so long."

Nana Lena folded her apron and hung it on the side of the sink. We made our way out of the kitchen and down the hall, stopping to talk to a dozen or more people on our way.

"Good bye, Mrs. Rosenbaum. Nice to see you, Mrs. Teitelman. Goldie, I'll speak to you next week." As we put on our coats and hats and scarves and braced ourselves for winter, I felt all warm inside. "Thanks for bringing me, Nana."

"Why? I should be thanking you."

"I really enjoyed it."

"That's good. You're supposed to, or else it isn't a mitzvah."

"Come on, Mitzvah Girl," I teased her as I took her arm. "Maybe we can pick up a couple of guys on our way home. You know, do another mitzvah?"

Nana Lena paused a moment. "They didn't call me a Goodman Girl for nothing. You don't believe me? I was quite a fox in my day."

"I'm sure you were, Nana."

We pushed the nursing home doors open and ventured out into the cold and snowy Christmas night, arm in arm.

"Merry Christmas, Nana."

"I can't believe I'm saying this to you, my Amele, but *Merry* Christmas."

And it was, in the truest sense of the word.

* * *

Banana Bread

Four bananas ripened on the windowsill, black and spotted,
filling the room with their strong aroma. "Nana, these bananas
look pretty ripe. Why don't we bake some banana bread?"

"That's your Aunt Goldie's recipe, not mine."

"I know it's Goldie's recipe, but you know how to make it."

"Of course I do."

"When you were growing up, did Goldie like to cook?"

"We all did, all of us girls."

"Who was the best cook?"

"The best cook? I don't know. I suppose we all had our
specialties. Goldie really came into her cooking prime after she got
married. That's when she moved out and didn't have Mama
standing over her shoulder telling her what to do every second.
She started buying cookbooks, Fanny Farmer and Betty Crocker.
She was always trying something new."

"Aunt Goldie was always promising to give me a cookbook. I
think she gave me a Weight Watchers cookbook once, and she
never let me forget it. How long has Goldie been gone now, is it
two years?"

"Two years in November. She was such a pistol. You
remember?"

"Goldie was nineteen months older than me. She had blonde
curls and a winning smile. She was tall and lean and always
smartly dressed. I was always kind of mousy. Goldie got all the
attention. If we walked into a party or dance together, the men just
flocked to Goldie. Remember Mae West? Goldie had her sass.

"Goldie never had a problem getting a date; her problem was
that her relationships never lasted. Something always happened.
There was that fellow, Feinstein, whom she fancied. He finally got
up the nerve to ask her out. They had a lovely evening, but after
that night he never called. He had been hit by a car crossing
Brambleton Avenue on his way to work the very next day. By the
time he got around to letting Goldie know what had happened, he
had fallen in love with one of the nurses at the hospital."

Nana Lena whisked together three eggs, a half cup of butter, a half cup of regular sugar, a half cup of brown sugar, and a pinch of salt while I mashed the bananas. To her mixture, she added the bananas, two cups of flour, and three tablespoons of baking soda. "Amy, look in the drawer over there; see if I have any dates or walnuts?"

"Then there was Mendelbaum. He was a nebbishy accountant Goldie met at work. She was a secretary at a clothing credit company. This was before the days of credit cards and ATMs. If you didn't have enough money to buy a new dress, you could purchase it on credit. Each week, you'd bring in a little money, and eventually, after it was all paid for, you actually got to wear it. I forget what the rate was—I don't know, one or two percent. Anyway, Goldie prided herself on operating the adding machine faster than anyone else in the office. I can tell you Mendelbaum was impressed. They dated for a few months; then Mendelbaum's father died, and he had to move back to Pittsburgh to take over the family business. When he didn't ask Goldie to join him, Goldie pretended she wasn't interested. 'Who wants to live in Pittsburgh? I can't live in Pitts-anything. I'll stay right here in Berkley. Something better will come my way.' And it did. It just took time."

Nana Lena poured the mixture into a greased eight-by-four–inch loaf pan. "I prefer using a loaf pan, but your mother makes the mini muffins, and they are good, too." She pounded the filled cake pan on the counter until hundreds of tiny bubbles rose to the top. "You do that to let the air out."

"Then there was Weingarten, a businessman from Baltimore who wined and dined her all right, until Goldie was so head over heels she nearly popped the question herself. Then one day, she found out from Mama's brother in Baltimore that there was a *Mrs. Weingarten* waiting for Mr. Weingarten back in Baltimore.

"I married Myer in 1934. That must have been hard on Goldie, watching her younger sister get married before she did. For the next few years, Goldie dated several different men who took her to dinner, occasionally a movie or a show, but no one asked her to marry him, and after a while they would move on. When the war came, Norfolk was filled with thousands of soldiers and sailors. Goldie dated a succession of men who eventually went off to war. She wrote to them like a good girl until their letters stopped coming. She never knew if it was because they were no longer interested or because they had been killed. She bore it all with a cheerful attitude and a crackerjack sense of humor. She was the Golden Girl.

"Then the war was over and the men returned. Goldie continued to date through her thirties and into her forties, but never had any luck until she was forty-five years old and met Al Mogul. Al was from Boston, short and loud, with a thick 'Bah-ston' accent. Kind of like that dark-haired fellow on the Three Stooges, I think they called him Moe. Anyway, he and Goldie hit it off like the cat's pajamas. From all appearances, they were total opposites. She was tall, he was short. She had blonde curls, his hair was dark and straight. He spoke "Bah-ston" and she spoke "Naw-fouk." But they had the same sense of humor, and that's what really holds a marriage together through all the years.

"They had thirty happy years together until Al developed Alzheimer's. Thirty years, can you imagine? And she thought she'd never get married."

"Are you trying to tell me something, Nana?"

"I'm just saying that *life has a funny way of ruining your expectations*. At forty-five, Goldie expected she would remain an old maid, then life turned things upside down and she ended up happily married for thirty years."

"And you and Papa?"

"Forty-three, thank God!" Her eyes started to tear up. "I only wish the same for you."

"I know, one day my prince will come. I'd just like to know what's taking him so long."

"You're a lot like Goldie. She was the oldest girl in the family. She had a job that she was proud of, as do you. She worked for almost thirty years, until Al Mogul made an honest woman out of her and she retired, trading her adding machine for a mah jong set, as she graduated to a woman of leisure."

"I don't think I'll ever stop working."

"Good for you. Goldie didn't really want to stop, but she did it because it made Al feel so good to be able to do that for her. He enjoyed being her liberator. He was also her chauffeur."

"That's right; Aunt Goldie never did learn how to drive."

"Al tried to teach her on more than one occasion. I think she didn't learn on purpose. She liked being chauffeured around."

"That sounds like Goldie."

"I have a picture of Goldie sitting on the hood of a sky-blue car with chrome bumper and fins, wearing those big pointy glasses she used to wear. I think she and Al had driven to Atlantic City for their anniversary. Or maybe it was Las Vegas. Goldie loved going to Vegas. She loved to gamble. She was such a sparkplug, your Aunt Goldie; I can't tell you how much I miss her."

"Me too, Nana. That's why it's good that we talk about her. It keeps her alive."

Nana Lena stroked my head lovingly. "Somewhere out there, Amele, there is a man for you. I know it and feel it, as much as I know anything. Any man would be blessed to have a woman like you. You are a good person, a hard worker, you're kind and smart. I don't know where I've ever seen such an inquisitive mind, except for your mother. Your mind is both your blessing and your curse. Most men are afraid of you. They can't compare, and men have a need to dominate, you know. It's in their nature. You're a hard one to dominate."

"So what do I do? Become weak and dependant?"

"Not exactly."

"Then what?"

"Just *appear* that way from time to time. Ask for their help. Pretend you don't know how to do something and let them show you. It makes them feel powerful if they think they know more than you."

"Is it that simple?"

"It's a start."

"And then what?"

"Be a good listener. Men are not by nature as talkative as women, so when they do talk, pay attention. Listen to what they say. You can tell a lot by the way a man talks. Is he a braggart, only talking about himself? Do his stories constantly change? Then he's a cheat. If he starts quoting things you said the last time you were together, at least you know that he's paying attention. You can weed out the good ones from the bad ones pretty quickly, if you're a good listener."

Nana Lena turned on the oven light and peered inside. "About ten more minutes." She removed a cake rack from the cupboard and placed it on the counter along with her aluminum cake tester.

"When I met your Papa, I knew he was a good man. I could

feel it with my heart. I knew he was the one for me, but I was only seventeen years old when I met him, and I knew I was too young to be making such a life-altering decision, so we dated on and off for four years. I had a lot of time to get to know your Papa. That's the one thing you young people don't take enough time to do these days. You jump into bed at the drop of a hat. You need to get to know each other first before you reveal that most personal part of yourself, and then he'll love you even more."

"I think you're right, Nana. Sometimes the old ways *are* best."

"I don't want you thinking, I'm a prude about sex, mind you. I loved your Papa very much. We enjoyed having... relations. That's important, too. It was a gift that we gave each other. It's the gift that keeps on giving, or so they say."

"Nana, you're making me blush."

"Come here, Amele."

I did. She put her hands on both my shoulders.

"One day you'll meet him, your *bashert*. Let's hope I live to see the day."

"Of course you will, Nana. You're going to dance at my wedding."

"Then you better hurry up. I won't live forever."

"That's what *you* say."

"If I don't make it, Amele, don't you worry. Come hell or high water, I'll be at your wedding. A little thing like death won't keep me away."

* * *

Goldie's Banana Bread

3 dozen mini muffins, or 4 tea loaves, or 1 large loaf

1 stick butter or margarine,

1 1/2 cups granulated sugar

2 eggs, beaten

1 tsp vanilla

1/2 cup sour milk, or buttermilk

1 1/2 cups very ripe bananas

2 1/2 cups flour

1 tsp baking soda

1/2 tsp salt

1/2 tsp baking powder

1 cup walnuts or dates, chopped

Whisk together in a medium bowl the butter and sugar, beaten eggs, vanilla, and sour milk, adding mashed bananas at the end. To make sour milk, add 1 teaspoon lemon juice to 1/2 cup milk. Let sit a few minutes until it begins to curdle.

Mix flour, baking soda, baking powder, and salt with fork in separate bowl. Add flour mixture and 1 cup chopped dates or walnuts (or both!) to egg mixture and stir to combine. Do not overmix batter, or bread will be tough.

Pour batter into greased 8 x 4-inch or 9 x 5-inch loaf pan or mini muffin tins. If you use muffin tins, fill cups only 2/3 full.

Bake at 350° until firm to touch and a toothpick inserted in center comes out clean. For a 9 x 5-inch loaf, bake about 45 minutes to an hour. 5 x 2-inch mini loafs, 25–30 minutes. Muffins, 15–20 minutes. Keep an eye on the oven because baking times vary. Bread is done when golden brown and cake tester can be removed clean.

Chopped Herring

"Damn it, Sidney, put the plate down and stop fidgeting," Nana Lena shouted over the grinder.

"I want some chopped herring."

"And I'm making you chopped herring, Sidney. It takes time. It's a good thing I had a jar of pickled herring in the fridge. Amele, hand me the onions and the apples. You put them through the grinder with the fish."

I handed her the bowl of quartered onions and apples. She put in a few pieces, and the dark gray fish mush turned lighter in color.

"Lovely."

"Now peel the hard-boiled eggs and hand me one."

I took the four hard-boiled eggs and cracked them in the sink.

"Sometimes I don't know what's gotten into him lately. He's become so impatient."

Sidney elbowed his way closer. "Is it ready yet?"

"See what I mean? No, Sidney." She talks to him like talking to a child. "Take a slice of challah if you're hungry. How about a piece of noodle kugel?"

Uncle Sidney fumbled with the tie on the challah bag, extracted two slices, and left the bag open on the counter. "Call me when my appointment gets here."

"Will do, Mr. Goodman. I'll let you know when he's here."

Uncle Sidney left the room, and I turned to Nana Lena. "So what's up with him?"

"What do you mean?"

"It's like he's a little kid."

"He's always been my baby brother. I guess I baby him."

"I know, with all those kids, Bubbie Minnie relied on you to help her raise them."

"Only the younger ones—Mike, Pete, Fannie, Sidney, and Poogie. Sidney was such a good boy. Never any trouble. Not like Pete. Pete was always in trouble. Now that Jean's gone, I look after Sid."

Forty years had passed since my Uncle Sidney returned from war a hero. He married Jean Yavner from Norfolk; they had had a son, Freddie, now grown with a family of his own. But Uncle Sidney of the Purple Heart bore little resemblance to the confused and agitated gentleman who burst into Nana Lena's kitchen.

"I can't find the contract. Where's the contract?"

Without missing a beat, Nana Lena answered. "It's on your desk, Mr. Goodman, next to the telephone."

That seemed to settle Uncle Sidney, and he grabbed another slice of challah as he left the room.

"I mean, what was *that*?"

"What?"

"The appointments, the contracts? He doesn't have a desk, does he?"

"He *thinks* he does."

"Must be a bitch finding it."

"Amele! Show some respect for your elders. Sidney's got Old-Timer's."

"You mean Alzheimer's?"

"Alzheimer's/Old Timer's. It's all the same thing."

"Are you sure you can handle this, Nana? After all, you're seventy eight years old."

"I'm no spring chicken if that's what you mean. But he's my brother, and I'm going to take care of him. I always have; I always will."

"Does Freddie know?"

"Of course, he knows. He sees him all the time."

"Is he coming home for the holidays?"

"He'll be here tomorrow night. Come on, let's finish up the herring. Freddie likes it as much as his father does. We'll put the big jar in the refrigerator downstairs; that way, Sidney won't eat it all by tomorrow."

My cousin Freddie was the youngest of my mother's generation, sons or daughters of Goodman sons or daughters, but because Uncle Sidney was eight years younger than Nana and because he married later in life, my cousin Freddie actually belonged to my generation, a year younger than me. Like all Goodman's, he arrived in time for dinner.

Nana Lena placed a large bowl of herring on the table with

some kichel, and Uncle Sidney was chowing down as though it was going out of style. He didn't even look up when his son entered the room. Freddie looked over at his father, who didn't seem to recognize him.

Nana Lena gave Freddie a big hug. "Oh, he's just in love with my herring, that's all. He knows it's you."

"Are you sure?"

Nana Lena nodded. Freddie tentatively inched over to his father. "Dad?"

"Damn it, Goodman, can't you see I'm eating!"

"What you got there, Sid?"

"Chopped herring."

"Mind if I join you, Dad?"

"Suits me; just don't eat it all yourself!"

Later that night, we all piled into Freddie's car and headed over to Ocean View to see the Christmas lights. There was a long line of traffic: Other families were doing the same, in cars, on foot, people dressed in red and green, some with furry white collars, out admiring the colorful lights.

Uncle Sidney sat in the back seat fidgeting with impatience. "Damn it, Goodman, can't you go any faster? You are so slow and deliberate!"

Freddie laughed, and then we all started laughing. "I'd like to see you drive in this traffic, Dad!"

"I'd put my foot on the gas and I'd get the hell out of here!"

Nana stared out the window at all the people walking along in front of the cars, "And he would too, the way he's been driving lately. I've been meaning to talk to you, Freddie."

"About what, Aunt Lena?"

"About your father's driving. I think you need to go for a ride with him. Not now, maybe tomorrow."

Freddie's face tightened. "Is it that bad?"

She sighed with an air of resignation. "I don't think your father should be driving any more."

The next day, the son took a ride with his father.

"What? You think I can't drive?"

"We'll see, Sid. Show me what you got."

"I'll show you. I can still drive. I'll show you, you better believe it."

Freddie climbed into the car and fastened his seat belt. After a while, Sidney did the same. "Let's go over to the Amphib Baseball field, Dad. You know, where we used to play Little League."

"Yeah, the ball field. Sure. We'll go there."

Sidney backed out of the driveway very slowly and began moving down the street with a similar lack of speed. At the first stop sign, Sidney hesitated, then inched the car forward into the intersection, and then hesitated again. At the next stop sign, he cruised through without stopping. When he reached the stoplight, instead of turning left toward the park, he turned right.

"You missed the turn, Dad."

"What the hell are you talking about?"

"The ball field, Dad, it's the other way."

"No, it's not. I know where the ball field is."

Freddie shook his head. "It's the other way. Look, Dad, I hate to tell you, but you drive like a Bubbie."

"Are you saying I drive like a woman?"

"Yes, and an old woman at that, older than Aunt Lena."

"That's old." Sidney did not seem at all perturbed. He spied a fast-food chain store on the corner. "Feel like a milkshake? I'm buying."

"Do you even have your wallet with you, Dad?"

"Hell if I know."

They went inside and each got a milkshake—Freddie, vanilla and Sidney, strawberry—and then headed back toward the car.

"You know, when your mom was still alive, she liked chocolate."

"You want to go back and get a chocolate shake, Dad?"

"No, this is fine."

"We'd each drink a little and then we'd switch. Remember?"

"I remember. Dad, why don't you let me drive?"

"I can drive, goddammit."

"Then you can't enjoy your milkshake."

"That's right; I need two hands to drive."

"Give me the keys, Dad."

Sid gave him the keys and took another sip of his milkshake. "Wanna switch?" Sid handed his milkshake to Freddie.

"Sure, Dad, I guess it's time."

Nana Lena did all the driving after that. Uncle Sidney stayed with Nana for one more year. She watched as Sidney slipped further and further away, each day becoming more childish, more helpless, less able to communicate his needs. She was a patient and loving sister/mother, but there came a time when Nana Lena couldn't handle it anymore. She called Freddie and told him he had to come home. When he arrived the next day, Nana Lena was outside hanging sheets on the clothesline.

"Aunt Lena, let me help you with that."

"I can do it."

"I know you can, but let me do it for you. It's the least I can do after all you've done for Dad. I got here as soon as I could. What's wrong?"

"It's your father. He can't control himself. He keeps having 'accidents,' and I keep having to do the laundry. The neighbors must think I'm running a boardinghouse, as often as I do the sheets. Now don't take me wrong, I love Sidney, he's my baby brother, but I can't handle this anymore. He needs someone who is physically able to bathe him and dress him. I can't do it anymore, Freddie, I just can't."

"So what are we talking here? The Home?"

"Not yet. His doctor thinks he's ready for an assisted-living facility. There's a place I want to show you, off Newtown Road. It's not bad, as far as those places go. They are holding a bed for him."

That night, Nana Lena made a meatloaf and a potato kugel for Sidney because that's what he liked, and Nana spoon-fed him like a child. "Come on, Sidney, you know you like my meatloaf. Open wide the hangar," as she circled the fork and brought it in for a landing. "Remember the Wright Brothers, Sidney? Wilbur and Orville?"

For a moment, Sidney seemed to tune in. "The Wright Brothers? They weren't from Berkley. Now the Goodman Brothers, they were from Berkley."

Nana laughed. "The Goodman boys, they were definitely Berkley."

When it came time to take Sidney to his new home, Nana was in the kitchen packing up all kinds of treats for her brother. "Now you're sure he has a refrigerator in his room?"

"Yes, Aunt Lena, he has a small fridge to keep his favorite things."

"Does he have a microwave? How's he going to heat the kugel if he doesn't have a microwave?"

"There's a microwave in the nurses' station. They promised me they will take care of him. If he wants a snack, he just has to ring a bell."

"I've packed him some kugel, some rugelach, and some strudel. You know how Sid has a sweet tooth. Do you think that's enough?"

"He's only ten minutes away in case you want to bring him something else."

"They won't know how to cook for him, like I do."

"Then you just go on over and show them how."

"Maybe I should."

"Are you sure you want to ride over with us, Aunt Lena?"

"Yes, I'm sure."

They rode over in silence. When they arrived, Freddie got out of the car, opened the trunk, and carried the bags inside. Nana Lena opened Sidney's door and reached in her hand to help him out.

"Come on, Sidney, we're here."

Sidney got out of the car. An aide arrived and waited by the car patiently.

"Now you be a good boy, Sidney. Don't give the woman any trouble."

"Do you think they have ice cream?" he asked. "I like ice cream."

Nana Lena opened her purse, retrieved a twenty-dollar bill and turned to the aide. "You'll see that he has ice cream whenever he wants it."

"Please put away your money, Ma'am. We have plenty of ice cream."

"Well, if he needs anything, you just call me. I'm Lena Goodman Herzberg, and I'll take care of it."

Freddie nodded at the nurse's aide, who took Sidney by the elbow. "Come along now, Mr. Goodman. We're going to take a little walk now."

Freddie turned to Nana Lena. "I think it's better if you wait out here."

Nana Lena nodded, watching as they led Sidney inside.

"What flavor ice cream do you favor, Mr. Goodman?"

"Strawberry."

"Oh, we've got plenty of that."

As the doors closed behind them, Nana Lena stood in the parking lot, dissolved in tears.

The *yahrzeit* candle flickered on the counter. "Uncle Sidney lived for six years after that, three years in assisted living and three in the Beth Shalom Home, in the special Old-Timers wing. I visited him every week, at least once, even when he no longer recognized me, even when he no longer recognized anyone, and I'd sit there and hold his hand and tell him the latest ball scores. He didn't know who the hell I was, but it made me feel better. It's been three years now since he died. Three years. But he was gone long before that. It was like his memories had been put through a grinder. Bits and pieces were still there, but it didn't all fit together anymore."

I took my Nana's hand and gave it a squeeze. "What shall we make for dinner tonight, Nana?"

"How about a little chopped herring? I happen to have a jar in the fridge."

"Uncle Sid would like that."

* * *

Chopped Herring

1 1-lb jar herring filets in wine sauce and onions

3 slices stale challah or other stale unseeded bread

2 Red Delicious apples

4 hard-boiled eggs

Sugar to taste

Juice of 1/2 of a lemon

Dash of white pepper

Pour off wine sauce into bowl, separate onions, and soak two pieces of stale challah or other stale bread in the wine sauce. Grind herring with apples, hard-boiled eggs, and onions, or process in food processor. Add two slices of bread soaked in the wine sauce, using one slice of the dry bread to push the last of the mixture through the grinder. Mix "real good." Add sugar to taste and juice of 1/2 of a lemon. Add a dash of white pepper.

Serve chilled with kichel.

Challah

"I can't tell you how honored I am to have you in my kitchen, young lady." Melissa's three-year-old daughter, Madison, watched intently as her eighty-six-year-old Bubbie, Nana Lena, gathered the ingredients to make bread. "Your mother tells me you are quite a good little cook."

"I like to cook."

Nana leaned in as if to tell a secret. "So do I. Ever since I was about your age, I always felt at home in the kitchen. It was warm, it smelled good, and it was always filled with family. Cooking is a family activity, filled with stories and laughter, not dinner in a microwave, like today."

"We have a microwave, Bubbie."

"I'm sure you do, sweetheart, but… you can't make a proper challah in a microwave. You remember that. You remember what your Bubbie tells you."

Little Madison nodded as Nana Lena finished measuring flour into a bowl. "Do you know what challah is?"

Madison nodded again. "Yummy bread."

"Yes, it is," Nana Lena smiled, "And when do we eat challah?"

"On Shabbat."

"That's right, and on holidays, that's when we use the raisins."

Madison looked up at her great-grandmother with wide eyes, "How do we make challah, Bubbie?"

"Well, let me show you. You start with a little yeast, which we'll dissolve in a quarter-cup of water. It should be warm like a baby's bottle."

"Like Harrison's?"

"Yes, like your brother's bottle: warm, not hot. When I was a child, we bought yeast in fresh cakes; now they have it in a packet like this. So modern."

Madison watched as Nana Lena emptied the packet into the water and small bubbles formed on the surface.

"It smells funny."

"It does, a little, but I kind of like the way it smells."

"Me, too."

Lena continued, "Next, we'll add a half a cup of sugar, a teaspoon of salt, and one-half stick of softened margarine. Do you think you can stir that for me? Stir it up real good."

Madison took the spoon eagerly, stirring slowly, methodically.

"You're a good helper."

"That's what my Mommy says."

Nana Lena couldn't help but crack a smile at the self-assured way her great-granddaughter answered. She took a carton of eggs out of the refrigerator.

"Can I? Can I?"

"I don't know. Can you?"

"Mommy lets me. Please?"

Nana Lena peered into the intent dark eyes of her great-granddaughter and saw her own daughter and her daughter's daughter, asking the same question. She placed an empty bowl in front of Madison and passed her the first egg. "Not too hard, *bubele.*"

Madison tapped the egg against the side of the bowl, gently at first, then a little harder until the egg cracked just a little bit. She handed it to Nana Lena very carefully.

"You did a fine job." Nana Lena removed the top part of the shell. "Now you look inside the egg. Make sure it's good inside. No spots, no surprises." She showed Madison. "See. It's good." She poured the egg into the bowl. "Now, it's your turn," as she handed the child the next egg.

Madison cracked it on the first try, and handed it to Nana Lena.

"Why don't you finish it yourself?"

"Mommy doesn't want me to get my hands dirty."

"I'll make sure we wash real good when we're finished. And if you do it right, you don't even have to get your hands dirty. Go ahead, try."

Nana Lena beamed proudly as she watched her great-granddaughter crack the third egg like a professional, peer inside with a critical eye, pass judgment, and pour the contents into the bowl.

"I did it!"

"You most certainly did. Now, we'll beat those eggs nice and fluffy and add them to the other mixture, and then we'll add the flour, a little bit at a time until the dough is smooth and doesn't stick to the side of the bowl. Like this." She showed Madison. "Now we'll cover it up with a clean dish cloth and let it sit in a warm place for about an hour, so the dough can rise. And while we wait for the dough to rise, we'll have a little tea and rugelach."

"What is rugelach, Bubbie?"

"Cookies, very special cookies."

"I love cookies."

"Let's wash those dirty hands of ours, and then we can have some."

Nana Lena made a cup of tea for her great-granddaughter, using lots of milk. She poured herself another cup and placed it on the table with a plate of rugelach between them. She carefully eased herself into her chair.

"You tired, Bubbie?"

"No, baby, Bubbie's just not as spry as she used to be. Take a cookie. Take two."

Madison didn't need much urging. She picked up a crescent-shaped cookie, dusted with powdered sugar, and took a delicate bite. "These are good, Bubbie. How do you make them?"

Nana Lena couldn't get over her precocious cooking prodigy. "You really want to know, *bubele*?"

The child nodded seriously.

"I use flour and butter and cream cheese to make the dough."

"I like cream cheese. Cream cheese and jelly."

"You know who liked cream cheese and jelly? Your Zeyde."

"My Zeyde?"

"My husband, your great-grandfather Myer Herzberg. He liked cream cheese and jelly, and he loved my rugelach."

"It has raisins, too, doesn't it, Bubbie?"

"What, *bubele*?" She stroked the child's head lovingly.

"The rugelach."

"Yes, it has. Sweet little raisins." Referring more to her great-granddaughter's eyes than the real thing, "So sweet I could eat them up."

"We have raisins at my house. Maybe Mommy and I can make some rugelach, too."

"I'd like that, Maddie. I'd like that very much." Nana Lena used her apron to wipe her eye before dropping the dough on a floured cutting board and punching it with her fist.

"What are you doing, Bubbie?"

"I'm kneading the bread."

"Can I knead, too?"

"Let me see how hard you can punch it."

Madison balled up her tiny fist and punched the dough without making a dent.

"Not, bad, but you have to punch it harder."

Madison punched with all her might.

"So you punch a little, then you fold it over like this and you pinch. Punch and pinch."

Madison punched again, then turned and looked up at her teacher. "It's your turn, Bubbie."

Nana Lena chuckled as they took turns punching the dough. "After you, my dear, after you."

Little Madison rocked her head from side to side as she recited, "Punch and pinch. Punch and pinch. This is fun!"

"The next step is my favorite part. It's called braiding the challah. But first, I'll take the dough and divide it into two parts. I'll take the big ball for me, and give this little ball to you."

"How come?"

"You'll see. Then we take each ball and divide it into three parts. Like this." She pinched off a large piece and began to roll it out like a snake.

"Playdough!"

"Yes, it's like Playdough, only without the colors."

"Let me. I'm very good at Playdough."

"Then, by all means," Nana Lena said.

Madison rolled her piece out on the cutting board, smooth and uniform, like a pro. Nana Lena watched proudly as Madison finished the first piece and began the second.

"You really *are* very good at that."

Madison added, very matter-of-factly, "I know."

Nana Lena smiled at her great-granddaughter's self-confidence; she continued with the lesson. "Then we take the strips and we lay them out side by side and we begin to braid them, threading the left strip over the middle, then under the third, pulling the strips tight, over and over until we reach the end, just like braiding hair."

"It's so pretty, Bubbie."

"It will be even prettier when we are done. Pinch the ends good for me."

"I'm pinching them very hard."

"That's what holds the bread together. That reminds me of a story. I was about fourteen, and Goldie was fifteen. And one day we decided to straighten our hair. Now Goldie had curlier hair than mine, and she wanted me to iron it. I was afraid that I would burn her; I said no. She convinced me that if she braided her hair, and I ironed only the braid, I wouldn't have a chance of burning her, so I agreed. We braided our hair, and I ironed her braid. While she ironed mine, we started talking about the new Valentino movie and how handsome he was, and I guess we got distracted. All of a sudden, I smelled something burning. I said to her, 'Goldie, I think Mama burned the challah again.' And Goldie said, 'Mama always burns the challah.' Then I realized that it was my hair that was burning, and when I jumped up, my braid was still lying there on the ironing board. I wore my hair real short after that.

"That night, at Shabbos dinner, Pete said, 'Pass me a piece of Lena's hair—I mean Mama's challah.' It was a big joke in our family for some time."

Nana Lena handed Madison the second ball of dough. "It's your turn, *bubele*. Now you braid the challah."

Madison divided the dough into three parts. As she rolled out the strips with her tiny little hands, Nana Lena's eyes filled with tears. Slowly, methodically, the child braided the little loaf. It was not as perfect as the other one. It was nowhere near as big, but Madison was prouder of that little loaf of bread than of anything she'd ever done. She pinched the ends and looked up at Nana Lena for approval. Nana Lena swept her up into her arms and smothered her with kisses.

"It's beautiful, Maddie. I'm so proud of you."

That night, at Shabbos dinner, the entire family was blown away by the newest cook in Nana Lena's kitchen. But no one was prouder than Nana Lena.

* * *

Challah

This recipe yields two loaves because what's the point of making just one? Actually, the tradition of making two loaves stems from not working on the Sabbath. Because you couldn't bake on Shabbos, you made two loaves the day before.

If you want to make one loaf, cut the recipe in half. Or if you prefer one large loaf instead of two smaller ones, you will need to bake it longer, say 35–40 minutes.

2 Tbsp fresh yeast or 2 packages of Fleischman's

1 1/2 cups warm water (1/4 warm, 1 1/4 hot)

1 stick of margarine

1/2 cup sugar

2 tsp salt

2 eggs, beaten

6–7 cups of flour

1 egg, reserved for glaze

poppy or sesame seeds (optional)

Dissolve yeast in 1/4 cup of warm water. In another bowl, mix hot water and melted margarine. Blend in sugar and salt and then add beaten eggs. Add yeast mixture. Mix well. Add four cups of flour and mix well. Continue adding flour to make a soft dough. Knead in bowl until smooth and elastic. Place in oiled bowl; cover. When the dough has doubled in size (about two hours), punch it down and divide it in half.

Lightly spray a plastic cutting board with cooking spray or other vegetable oil product. Take the first half of the dough and divide it equally into three parts. Roll out each part onto the oiled board into a long strip, about 15 inches long. Place the three strips on a greased baking sheet. Pinch the ends together and begin braiding. Repeat procedure with other half of dough. Cover. Let the braided loaves rise until they double in size again.

Brush tops with lightly beaten egg. If desired, sprinkle with poppy or sesame seeds. Bake in 350° oven for 20–25 minutes. Cool on rack.

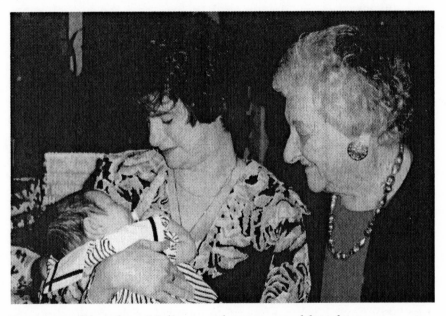

Lena, granddaughter Melissa, and great-granddaughter Madison, 1996.

The Shivah Table

"You better hurry up, or you're going to miss it."

"Miss what, Nana?" I was on location in Las Vegas, in the middle of a busy production office, and quite distracted when she called.

"Donna is here already, and Melissa and the kids. I'm just waiting for you and David. I need you to come home now."

My voice started to quiver although I tried to maintain control. "I think there's a direct flight in the morning."

"You better take one tonight. I don't know if I can make it until morning."

As I started to cry, Nana Lena's voice sharply reprimanded me. "None of that, Amele. It's time to be strong."

That's how Nana Lena summoned each of us. This time, it wasn't for a holiday, a wedding, or anniversary party. This time, she was ready to die. Three times, she had battled cancer, twice surviving surgery and the long recuperation afterward. But this time was different. It was her time, and it was going to be her way.

Four months earlier, the oncologist had told her that she had a difficult choice to make. The cancer was back. She could risk surgery, which at eighty-seven years old was risky enough, and maybe prolong her life a few more months; or she could choose to enjoy the time she had left as comfortably as possible. Either way, her life expectancy was, at the most, six months.

Nana thanked him politely, gathered up her things, and went home to prepare for the inevitable. It was her choice, and this time, she had chosen *not* to fight.

It happened to be Valentine's Day, when she received the news, the same Valentine's Day when my sister, Donna, called to tell her that she had eloped. Nana's curt tone with her darling granddaughter was our only clue that something was amiss. Never one to make a big deal about her personal tragedies, Nana Lena decided not to burden us with this information. She just went along with the process of dying without telling any of the grandchildren. At first, only my mother knew.

So it came as quite a shock when the family got together a month and a half later for Passover. One look at her pale drawn face, the dark circles under her eyes, and I knew that she was very ill. She didn't actually tell me she was dying until one afternoon in her kitchen, and even then I had to pry it out of her. I noticed a counter full of prescription bottles. "What are all these pills, Nana?"

"Oh, I'm just getting old. I've got a pill to make me pee and a pill to make me poop. I got one for my eyes and one for my toes, one for my heart, and one for my nose. I should open up a pharmacy, don't you think?"

"Either that, or you could try vaudeville." I picked up another bottle. "Morphine, isn't that for pain, Nana?"

She bit her lip, ever the stoic. "I don't like to take them; they make me all fuzzy," she paused. "Sometimes I have to."

"It's back, isn't it?"

She nodded. After a minute I could see a tear run down her cheek. "Nothing much we can do about it. Just pray the good Lord takes me soon."

I burst into tears. She tried to comfort me. "That's exactly why I didn't want to tell you, especially on the telephone."

"But, Nana—"

"I've done a lot of thinking. I've had a good life, a husband who adored me, your mother, the four of you, and such b-eau-ti-ful great-grandchildren. I've had my life."

"Don't say that!"

"I don't know how much time I have left on this good Earth. All I know is that I sure as hell don't want to spend it around a bunch of crying faces. You hear me? I just want to enjoy every minute I can with my family, until..."

I started sobbing, hugging her and holding her up at the same time. She was so much smaller than I remembered her, so frail, I could probably lift her. She patted me on the back like a baby, and in typical Nana spirit, rallied. "Now you go wash up, and then come back in here and help me make the matzo kugel for supper. You know how your father loves my matzo kugel."

Over the next few months, we called her all the time. All of us did. We called to see what she was eating, what the doctor had said, whether it was raining—anything, just to hear her voice.

Sometimes she was her usual self, but sometimes there was a stranger on the other end of the phone. As the cancer spread, she took increasing dosages of morphine to manage the pain. The morphine made her slur her words, forget things. Sometimes I almost didn't recognize her.

She had chosen home hospice care. Twice daily, hospice nurses or aides stopped by to check on her, bathe her, take her vitals, and dress her wounds. The cancer spread to other organs, and her system started shutting down. She was no longer able to walk and was sleeping more and more of the time. In addition to the twice-a-day hospice nurses, there was a series of nurses aides who lived in Nana's house to help take care of her.

One thing she was pretty adamant about was that she wanted to die in her own bed. She had made that pact with Papa long ago, and no amount of urging by her doctor, or any of us, could make her change her mind. She had signed a DNR. This meant that if she had a heart attack or if her kidneys failed, nothing would be done to resuscitate her. She had also prepared a living will. She had crossed her T's and dotted her I's. *She* was ready. Not that any of *us* were.

I took the red-eye from Las Vegas to Atlanta, connecting to a Norfolk-bound flight at seven a.m. I wasn't prepared for the wraithlike figure that greeted me from her bed. I wasn't prepared for the morphine drip and the medical paraphernalia that seemed to cover every surface in the room... syringes, medicine bottles, changing pads, diapers.

"Oh, Amele, I'm so glad you've come."

"Of course I came, Nana. I'm so sorry it took so long."

"Sit here," she motioned to a spot on the bed. "Let me look at you."

I looked at the nurse for approval, who said, "Whatever she says; she's the boss!"

I sat on the bed gingerly, watching Nana's face for any sign of pain. "Does it hurt much, Nana?"

"Only when I laugh, which is all the time, right, Cathy?"

"Right. Oh, she keeps us all in stitches all the time."

"You tell her, Cathy. Tell her what I said the first time I met you."

The nurse, a petite, spirited blonde, smiled as she related the story. "I was one in a long line of nurses that the hospice sends to look after your grandmother."

"And who offer excellent care, I might add," Nana interrupted.

"You're just saying that now to make up for what you *said*."

"Am not." Nana rolled her eyes.

"Anyway, she took one look at me when I came in and she said, 'Are you one of those blonde bitches who's come to shove her fist up my ass?'"

"Nana!"

"I was impacted."

"That's exactly what she said," the nurse testified. "I can't say that anyone has ever said that to me before."

My shriveled-up grandmother, with her raisin eyes, smiled like a child caught with her hand in the cookie jar.

"Nana, that's so unladylike of you."

"What the hell. I'm dying; I can say what I want."

"Are you ready for the pain medication, Mrs. Lena?"

"Not yet. When is David coming?'

"In about an hour."

"That's when I'll take the medicine. I want to be awake when he comes."

Nana Lena took my hand, squeezing it tightly. "So, Amele, tell me all about *you*."

A little later, the nurse's aide brought in a bowl with a spoon. "I've brought your favorite," she twinkled.

Nana arched her eyebrow. "My favorite?"

"The cereal you like."

"Grape Nut Flakes?" she squealed with glee.

The aide fed Nana the cereal, which she seemed to enjoy thoroughly. "Delicious! Amy, you've got to try these Grape Nut Flakes."

That was the last meal my Nana ate.

David arrived a short time later. My brother, who is six feet two and built like a football player, immediately burst into tears. He leaned over the bed to kiss her. She lifted herself just enough to smother his cheek in kisses, as she always did. "David! Sit here and tell me all about yourself. How are you? How are the children?"

"They're fine. I brought some pictures."

"Oh, honey, I don't have my eyes in." That's what she called her contact lenses: her eyes. "What's the use? My cataracts are so big, I can't see anymore anyway. Just sit here and *tell* me all about *you*."

David took my place on the bed. As I turned to leave, she said. "Amele, go tell the nurse, I'll take my medication now."

Shortly after that, as if on cue, she began to lose consciousness. The next day she was in and out, opening her eyes from time to time, talking to unseen forces. The nurse said it was from the morphine, but I knew it was more than that. She had called the rest of her family home, too. The first to arrive were her long-gone brothers.

"Hey, Pete, hey, Mike, throw me the ball." She seemed to catch it and threw it back to them. "Come on, Leon, batter up! You think I can play for the Yankees?"

"Goldie, not that dress. Why'd you wear that dress? That's the one that I was going to wear."

"There's my brother, Sidney. Looking good, Sidney, looking good."

She didn't mention any of her living relatives, only the ones who had long since passed. It was if they were there to greet her and escort her to the other side.

At one point Nana said, "Hey you, in the red dress. What are you doing there?"

At first, we didn't know whom she was referring to, but then Mom thought Nana was talking to her dear friend Raine, who often wore a red dress and who had passed away only a week before. No one had told Nana that Raine had died, for fear it would upset her too much. So, of course, she was surprised to see Raine on the other side.

Several times she tried to get out of bed, something she had been unable to do for weeks.

"Where are you going, Nana?" I held her gently as she tried to pull free.

"I've got to cook something for the man."

"What man, Nana? Is it Papa? Or is it the big man up in heaven? You know, God. What you going to cook for him? Are you going to make him a kugel?"

Nana Lena smiled.

That night the rest of my family went back to my parents' house in Portsmouth. I stayed at Nana's, in the den, on the pull-out sofa. The nurse's aide slept in Bubbie's old room. In the middle of the night, I heard Nana Lena talking, so I got up to investigate. She quickly fell back to sleep, so I lay down next to her in that little double bed she had shared with Papa. I never could understand why they didn't have a bigger bed, but Nana used to say, "It was better to cuddle in."

I dozed off for a little while until she woke up again.

This voice of wonder called out, "There you are…"

"Yes, Nana. It's Amy. I'm here."

But she wasn't talking to me. She was in another world. She reached her hand up in front of her as if to touch someone's face. "I've been waiting for you." She continued to stroke the invisible face. "I've always loved you, from the very first moment I saw you…"

It was then I knew that Papa was there, too.

The following day, she started speaking in Yiddish. She was talking to her Mama and Papa and to her sister Bertie. "*Mama, vus makhst du? Papa, varte, ich komme! Bertie, vie sheyn du bist.*" Donna, Melissa, and I had studied German in high school, so we translated for the rest of the family.

"Mom, what are you doing? Dad, wait, I'm coming! Bertie, how pretty you are!"

At one point, Melissa asked, "Aren't you glad we studied German, Nana?" It was a question Nana Lena would never have acknowledged affirmatively in the past. We thought we saw her smile.

Melissa translated: "She's saying it's a good thing."

She was receiving increasingly higher levels of morphine. The nurse told us if we saw that she was in a lot of pain, we could administer an extra boost.

"It won't work every time because the overall amount of drug released is controlled by the equipment, but this way, you have some control over the timing. If she is awake and in pain, press the button, and if she hasn't gotten her required dosage for the hour, you can deliver it then."

"Could we hurt her if we pressed it too many times, you know, by accident?"

"Do you mean, can you kill her? No, it won't let you exceed her dosage. It will just make her more comfortable. That's all we're trying to do here. She's a DNR. We just try to make her as comfortable as possible."

Later that day, Nana Lena started crying out for "the baby." We thought she was talking about Harrison, Melissa's youngest, whose laughter we could hear from the other room. Melissa rushed out, saying, "I'll get him."

Then Nana started screaming and thrashing about from side to side. "Please, Mama, don't take the baby."

I asked my mother, "Do you know what she's talking about?"

"I have no idea."

"Did Nana have another baby? Did someone take away her baby?"

None of us knew what she was talking about, and her screams were so pitiful, like those of a child whose favorite toy was being taken away.

"Maybe she's talking about a doll baby. It's like she's going further and further back in time."

We called the Rabbi to come over and pray. That night, as we all gathered in her room, Mom, Dad, Donna, David, Melissa, and the kids, the Rabbi led us in the *Shema*, the prayer in which we acknowledge that there is only one God. As we sang the *Shema*, we noticed that Nana was singing, too. Not clearly, but audibly, she moaned along in tune.

I stayed with her again that night, but this time I didn't sleep. She had started to make the deep gargling sound they call the "death rattle." Her kidneys were shutting down; the tips of her fingers were turning blue. I pretended the rattle was Nana and Papa snoring, and I was a child again, listening from the other room, wearing footie pajamas and a pink tulle hairnet, listening to the back-and-forth pattern of Nana and Papa's distinctive sounds.

I was three years old and in the bathtub, and Nana was picking me up and wrapping me in a large pink bath towel, drying me off, drying between my fingers and toes. And there on the wall was the toothbrush with a piece of masking tape, my name written on it, in Nana's clear handwriting.

Then I was six years old, performing plays in Nana's living room with my sister Donna who was three at the time. I was the princess, and she was the servant woman.

"Princess, do you have any money?" the servant woman asked.

"For what, my good woman?"

"For my children. They are very, very hungry."

"And where are your children now, my good woman?" the princess asked.

And the servant woman answered with a child's crystal-clear innocence, "They are at home, with the maid."

And I remember Nana laughing so hard she nearly peed in her pants. And then I remembered her telling that story, again and again and again. That night I look a long walk with Nana Lena down Memory Lane. By the next morning, I was ready, too.

Not all of us were ready to see Nana Lena go. There was talk of putting her on a breathing machine, and a suggestion we move her to a hospital bed. I stood up for my grandmother and would not hear of it. "She wants to die in her own bed. She's told us all a thousand times."

"But she can't breathe!"

"No machines. We promised her."

"We can't stand by and do nothing!"

"We have to let her go."

"How can you say that?"

"It's what she wants."

"How do you know what she wants?!"

"She's told us again and again. Remember?"

I can't say we were perfect in those last days. Each of us handled it differently, with anger, tears, depression, or by staying busy. I cooked; Melissa did laundry. We all played with the kids. The children took our minds off what was happening in the next room. At one point, Madison and Harrison both climbed into a laundry basket, and Madison looked up at Melissa.

"Is Bubbie going to die, Mommy?"

"Yes, she is."

"Why?"

Melissa burst into tears. "It's a part of life, honey. A person is born, a person dies."

"Am I going to die too, Mommy?"

Melissa paused for a moment before she picked up her daughter and held her very close. "One day, Maddie. But not for a very, very long time."

Madison seemed to accept that. She wiggled free from her mother and climbed back into the laundry basket with her brother. "Not for a berry, berry, berry long time, okay, Mommy?"

We had all gravitated to the kitchen, as was natural. The kitchen was her domain. There we could remember her vibrant energy, not the pitiful body slowly shutting down in the other room. I was rummaging through the freezer in search of comfort food when I found a tin labeled "Rugelach." I opened the tin; there were just enough pieces to go around. "Isn't it just like Nana; she made sure there was one for each of us."

"Can we make some rugelach, Mommy?" Madison asked her mother as Melissa wiped away a tear. "Bubbie showed me."

"She did? When was that?"

"I don't know. When I was little."

"You still are little."

"Not as little as I was."

Donna said, "I'm sure going to miss Nana's cooking."

"I have the recipes," I told them. "I'll make copies for everyone."

"I propose a toast." My father lifted his cookie, "To Nana Lena."

"To Nana Lena."

We raised our rugelach and took a bite. I remembered what Papa used to say: "It's sweet, twisted, and a little nuts, like my Lena."

We had just finished enjoying the last crumbs of Lena's rugelach when the nurse's aide appeared in the doorway.

"I'm sorry."

The next two days were a blur. Funeral arrangements were made. The telephone never stopped ringing. Neighbors started showing up with trays and trays of food. Friends and family and even former nurses stopped by to pay their respects. Mama wrote the obituary. I prepared the eulogy. We went through all the motions in a trance.

The morning of the funeral, Oliver's Funeral Home sent over two classic black limos to carry the family. Mom, Dad, my brother and sisters, and their spouses and older children, Aunt Poogie, Aunt Thelma, and I piled into the limos. The rest of the family, the cousins and nieces and nephews, climbed into their own cars to follow on the drive to the synagogue.

We had decided to hold the funeral at Beth El rather than at Oliver's Funeral Home, as we always did. Because Nana was such an active part of Beth El, we decided that was what she would have preferred.

It was mid-June, and the heat was unbearable. While we were standing outside the synagogue, Rabbi Ruberg pinned black ribbons on my mother and my Aunt Poogie as he recited a prayer in Hebrew. Then he tore each ribbon, a gesture that dates back to biblical times when you actually "rent your garments," to represent the grief of having a loved one torn from your life.

The next thing that I remember, I was standing on the *bimah*, shaking, as I looked down on the closed coffin and out at the sea of people below. I watched as particles of dust danced in the light that filtered through the stained glass windows. I thought about how many times Nana Lena had stood on that platform, and I did my best to make her proud.

"We are gathered here today," I began, "to honor a remarkable woman, my grandmother, Lena Goodman Herzberg. When I look out over this room, I see just how many lives she touched. If all her friends and admirers were still alive today, this synagogue would be packed to the rafters, and we'd have them lining up around the block outside, because that was the kind of person that Lena was. She was everybody's friend. She judged you for what you had inside, not what you looked like. Some people operate from the head; with Nana it was all *heart*, and *family*; that was the most important thing.

"Lena loved family. One of ten siblings, she grew up in the Berkley section of Norfolk with her parents, Minnie and Morris Goodman, who emigrated to the United States in the 1880s. She lived next door to her maternal grandparents and several aunts and uncles. She grew up in a traditional, one-generation-removed-from-the-Old-World-family, and they had taken on the mores of the South, their new home. Lena was as proud of being an American as she was of being a Jew. Of course, that might have something to do with being born on the Fourth of July.

"Lena met and fell in love with my grandfather, Myer Herzberg, in 1930. Myer was a Merchant Marine from Lynn, Massachusetts. They fell in love at first sight. But Minnie and Morris weren't very keen on the idea of their daughter marrying a "Yankee." Actually, they used a phrase a little more colorful than that. So my grandmother did something very bold for her time: She eloped to Rabbi Steinbach's house with her friend Mitzi Laden and Myer's best man, Julius Lowenthal. And who does she see at the Rabbi's? Why, her uncle Zachariah. You see, wherever she was, she was surrounded by family.

"The following year marked the arrival of the second great love of her life, the first rose in her garden, her beloved daughter Elayne. Lena loved her daughter fiercely. She gave her everything she herself hadn't had. Elayne went to college; my grandmother had only had a high school education. Lena taught her daughter about Judaism, and to give of your time, if not your money. She also taught her about the importance of family. Mama said Lena was her best friend.

"She was godmother to her nephews Bobby Zucker and Norman Margolis, an aunt to her numerous nieces and nephews on the Goodman side and on the Herzberg side, and then, later on, great-aunt to another generation.

"When Elayne married, Lena welcomed Burton into her heart. But the 'great love machine' that was Lena Herzberg really hit its stride with the arrival of her grandchildren: Amy, Donna, David, and Melissa. We were the next four roses in her garden. We were her 'precious cargo.' We had our little Nana rituals. She used to say, 'Remember what you're driving: Precious cargo.' We used to honk our horns twice before driving away from her house while she waited on the front doorstop to give us a wave. Nana never said she loved us; she always used the word *adore*. But that's how she was with everyone. She made you feel as if you were the most special person on the planet. She loved unconditionally.

"Everyone in this room has heard her brag about her grandchildren. She was so proud of her granddaughter Donna De La Paz, Director of the Houston Chapter of the American Jewish

Committee, for continuing her commitment to Jewish causes and social justice. She *kvelled* when her granddaughter Melissa Hinkle received a degree in Psychiatric Social Work and was thrilled by her commitment to the Jewish education of her own children, Madison and Harrison Hinkle. And she couldn't stop bragging about her grandson, David Ostrower, the telecommunications entrepreneur, and his boys, Shane, Ryan, and Hunter, and about her granddaughter Amele, the writer. And when she was finished bragging about the grandkids, it became the great-grandkids. That's the way she was: classy and unpretentious, kind and hospitable, loving and gracious, with a strict sense of what was proper and a bawdy sense of humor. In the midst of the indignities her illness forced her to bear, she handled that illness with dignity and a joke. Her doctors, nurses, and caregivers know how she kept them laughing. I have great Nana stories about that, but they aren't exactly fitting for a house of worship.

"Lena was an avid baseball fan. She loved the Atlanta Braves. She never missed a game on television. Nana, you'll be happy to know the Braves won last night 8 to 4 over Pittsburgh.

"Lena knew how to apply the right amount of Jewish guilt to bring us all home for the holidays whenever possible. She was the family matriarch. It was not unusual for there to be thirty people at the Seder table.

"I could go on and on.

"A week ago, Lena summoned her family to her once again, to say goodbye. She told us how much she loved us and hugged us with all her might. And in the last few days when she was slipping into the other world, a remarkable thing happened. All the family members who had predeceased her came back to take her home. She began talking to them in Yiddish. She played ball with her brothers Leon, Mike, Pete, and Sidney. She talked to her parents, her grandparents, her sisters, and her beloved husband Myer. At one point, I saw her lift her hand as if to stroke his face. I heard her say, 'I loved you since the moment I met you.'

"I think we could all say the same about Lena."

* * *

As the Beth El Sisterhood honor guard rose and escorted Nana Lena's body out of the synagogue, we stumbled to the cars. I remember a blur of faces: people I hadn't seen since childhood, neighbors, and old friends. Several of her nurses were there, even the young woman who cleaned her house

The hearse, followed by the two black limos, led a long procession of cars from the red brick neighborhood of Old Ghent to the other side of town, where the cemetery was located. Motorcycled policemen stopped traffic at large intersections to let the procession pass. All along the way, cars pulled to the side and men removed their hats. This was the custom down South and had nothing to do with my grandmother, but at the same time, I felt it had everything to do with her.

At the cemetery, it was close to one hundred degrees. My knees buckled as my family and I were led to a small tent that had been erected by the side of her grave. Inside were two rows of folding chairs for the immediate family. Close friends who had accompanied us to the cemetery stood just behind and all around us. As we said the *Mourners' Kaddish*, I was touched when a clearly non-Jewish man from Oliver's Funeral Home began intoning the prayer in perfect Aramaic. He was crying as he said the Kaddish, for he had known my grandmother for many years. She was one of the last surviving members of an extremely large family, and an active member of the Jewish community. I remembered the story she had told me about Great Aunt Bertha and the flu epidemic of 1918. Oliver's was the only funeral home in Norfolk that would bury Jews at that time. Ever since then, local Jews have given Oliver's their business. I'll always be grateful to them, and to the young non-Jewish man who joined us in the Kaddish to honor Nana Lena.

We returned home to sit *Shivah*, to begin the official seven-day mourning period that I used to feel was a barbaric custom until I realized the value of taking seven days to think about the person and adjust to life without her before returning to our everyday lives. As was also the custom, there was a pitcher of water outside the front door so that we could wash the cemetery from our hands. The mirrors had been covered so that we would not be concerned with our appearance during this time of mourning. We removed our shoes and sat on low chairs.

Food is also a part of the tradition. The Shivah table was piled high with symbolic foods with which we were supposed to restore our bodies and spirits: a dairy meal composed of hard-boiled eggs, a symbol of birth and rebirth; bagels, which are round, like life;

lox, whitefish, and herring; and, on the sideboard, an abundance of noodle kugels. After giving so many kugels during her lifetime, it was fitting that Nana Lena would receive so many when her time had come.

The Rabbi raised a slice of challah to begin the blessing over the bread, when three-year-old Madison looked at him and said, "I can make that."

And the wise Rabbi answered, "You're Lena Herzberg's great-granddaughter. Why doesn't this surprise me?"

THE END

May her memory
be for a blessing

The Recipes

After Nana died, my mother inherited her box of recipes. I raided Nana's recipe box and extracted these gems. Whenever possible, I also included several variations of a recipe, from my grandmother, my great-aunts, my mother, or my own kitchen. Unfortunately, Nana Lena did not write down all of her recipes, so I have tried to re-create the missing ones as best as I could through trial and error.

For the most part, these are not foods you want to eat if you are trying to lose weight. During the time that I was growing up, they were considered healthful—as in sticking to your ribs and putting weight on you. This was my grandmother's goal in life until I was eight years old. Hard to believe, I was once a scrawny child, and my grandmother actually paid me to gain weight.

Nowadays, we tend to eat less fat and sugar. I often substitute low-fat versions of milk, cottage cheese, and sour cream, and use egg substitute, without doing much harm to Nana Lena's recipes. The nonfat products don't work as well and tend to be runny. For those of you who don't use sugar, Splenda will work, or you can use fruit juice or applesauce or raisins to sweeten a recipe.

I'm not saying that you should eat this way every day of the week, but once in a while, a nice noodle kugel, or a hearty brisket and potato kugel, can do no harm. I hope these recipes will bring you as much pleasure as they have me—the scents, the tastes, and the comfort that was Nana Lena's Kitchen.

Ambrosia

One bite and you're back in the 1960s. Ambrosia was a staple of every summer picnic.

2 20-oz cans pineapple chunks

3 small cans mandarin oranges

3 regular oranges, peeled, sectioned and cut up

1 pint sour cream

1 package miniature marshmallows

1/2 cup coconut

Mix together ingredients and refrigerate overnight. Serve chilled.

Apple Cake

1 1/4 cups vegetable oil

2 cups sugar

3 eggs

3 cups flour

1 tsp baking soda

1 tsp salt

1 tsp vanilla

3 cups apples, chopped or grated

1 cup nuts

Cake

Mix oil and sugar. Add eggs one at a time. Sift flour, soda, and salt together and add to egg mixture. Combine remaining ingredients and bake in greased and floured pan. Bake at 325° for 1 1/2 hours in a tube pan or 40–45 minutes in an oblong pan.

Glaze

1 cup brown sugar

1/2 cup margarine

1/4 cup milk or non-dairy creamer

Combine butter and sugar and milk. Bring to a full boil and stir. Set aside and stir every 15 minutes. Pour over cooled cake.

Apple Crisp

4 cups peeled, sliced tart apples

1 cup water

1/2 cup butter

1 cup white or brown sugar

3/4 cup flour

1/4 tsp salt

1 tsp cinnamon

Butter a deep baking dish and put the apple slices and water into it. Mix together remaining ingredients and spread over apples. Bake at 350° about 30 minutes, or until apples are tender and crust is brown. Serve warm with vanilla ice cream.

Goldie's Banana Bread

makes 3 dozen mini muffins, 4 tea loaves, or 1 large loaf

1 stick butter or margarine

1 1/2 cups granulated sugar

2 eggs, beaten

1 tsp vanilla

1/2 cup sour milk or buttermilk

1 1/2 cups very ripe bananas

2 1/2 cups flour

1 tsp baking soda

1/2 tsp salt

1/2 tsp baking powder

1 cup walnuts or dates, chopped

Whisk together in a medium bowl the butter and sugar, beaten eggs, vanilla, and sour milk, adding mashed bananas at the end. To make sour milk, add 1 teaspoon lemon juice to 1/2 cup milk. Let sit a few minutes until it begins to curdle.

Mix flour, baking soda, baking powder, and salt with fork in separate bowl. Add flour mixture and 1 cup chopped dates or walnuts (or both!) to egg mixture and stir to combine. Do not overmix batter, or bread will be tough.

Pour batter into greased 8 x 4-inch or 9 x 5-inch loaf pan or mini muffin tins. If you use muffin tins, fill cups only 2/3 full.

Bake at 350° until firm to touch and a toothpick inserted in center comes out clean. For a 9 x 5-inch loaf, bake about 45 minutes to an hour. 5 x 2-inch mini loafs, 25–30 minutes. Muffins, 15–20 minutes. Keep an eye on the oven because baking times vary. Bread is done when golden brown and cake tester can be removed clean.

Bubbie's Blintzes

yields 10–12

> *Blintzes are a perfect Shavout meal. Shavous, or Shavout, is the holiday in which we celebrate Moses receiving the Ten Commandments on Mt. Sinai. Two blintzes side by side make a believable Torah. Nana's recipe went something like this. I say 'something like' because it seems she never wrote down the recipe for Bubbie's Blintzes, as Nana Lena used to call them, long after Bubbie was gone.*

Bletel
(the "leaves", the outside of the blintz; like a crepe)

2 eggs

1 cup milk

2 Tbsp vegetable oil

1/2 tsp salt

3/4 cup flour

butter for frying

Combine the eggs, milk, and oil in a bowl. Add salt and flour. Mix well. Chill for 1/2 hour. Stir ingredients again after removing from refrigerator.

Melt 1 teaspoon butter in 7–8-inch frying pan. Pour a little less than a 1/4 cup of batter into pan and swirl it around to coat the pan evenly. Recipes always say to fry until lightly brown on one side. Unfortunately, that is the side you can't see, so watch until the top side looks spongy, not wet, approximately 20–25 seconds. Shake the pan once during that time to make sure the crepe isn't sticking. Flip the crepe browned-side-up onto a plate. Don't worry if the first one doesn't turn out.

Continue adding butter to pan, cooking leaves, and flipping them onto the stack. This recipe yields 10–12 crepes.

Filling

1 lb farmer's cheese

2 Tbsp sugar

2 heaping Tbsp sour cream

1 tsp vanilla extract

Combine farmer's cheese, sugar, sour cream, and vanilla extract in a bowl.

Place a crepe, browned side up, on a flat surface. Spoon 1–2 tablespoons of mixture about an inch from the top of the circle. Fold top edge over filling, shaping it into a log about 4–5 inches long. Fold both sides in and roll from top to bottom. The end result should be 4–5 inches long and 1 1/2–2 inches wide.

After the blintzes have all been assembled, fry using butter or margarine until lightly browned on both sides.

Serve hot with a dollop of sour cream, or sprinkle with sugar and cinnamon.

Blintzes can be stuffed with a variety of fillings, including mashed potatoes, kasha, cherries and blueberries, or combinations of potatoes and pureed vegetables, such as broccoli or spinach, or potato and onions that have been sautéed until golden brown. Serve fruit variety with sour cream, and potato/kasha/vegetable variety with mustard.

Brandied Compote

2 large cans pear halves

2 large cans peach halves

1 can apricots

1 large can pitted black cherries

18 coconut macaroons

1/2 cup brown sugar

1 cup brandy or wine

Drain fruit well. Crumble macaroons in separate bowl and mix with sugar. Grease shallow Pyrex dish well (with butter or margarine). Alternate layers of fruit and crumbled macaroons. Save some crumbles for the top.

Pour 3/4 cup brandy over fruit 2 hours before baking, and then the remainder at baking. Bake at 350° for one hour.

Fresh alternative: Substitute fresh peaches, pears, and apricots peeled and cored.

Brisket, a.k.a. Damn Yankee Pot Roast

Brisket, at least 2 lbs

1 cup ketchup

1/2 cup steak sauce (Heinz 57 was Nana's choice)

1 packet dry onion soup mix

4 cups water

salt and pepper to taste

Put brisket in roasting pan. For sauce, mix one cup of ketchup, 4 cups of water, 1/2 cup of your choice of steak sauce, and one package dry onion soup mix. Warm until mixed. Pour sauce over brisket and cover. Cook 2 hours at 325°. Uncover, baste, and add more water if necessary. Cook one hour more or longer until tender. Remove meat from pan. Let cool ten minutes. Slice against the grain in long, thin slices and return meat to remaining sauce in pan. Return to oven for at least one hour before serving. It the meat is chewy, it hasn't cooked enough. Eventually, it softens so you can cut it with a fork. Remember, the longer it simmers, the better it tastes.

Variation

Add peeled potatoes cut in wedges, thick slices of carrot, fresh minced onion, and a can of crushed tomatoes. Use at least three cups of water to start. Set the meat on top of the vegetables and let it steam. Keep an eye on your pan; make sure that there is always enough liquid so it won't burn. Cook uncovered for last hour before slicing.

Challah

This recipe yields two loaves because what's the point of making just one? Actually, the tradition of making two loaves stems from not working on the Sabbath. Because you couldn't bake on Shabbos, you made two loaves the day before. If you want to make one loaf, cut the recipe in half. Or if you prefer one large loaf instead of two smaller ones, you need to bake it longer, say 35–40 minutes.

2 Tbsp fresh yeast or 2 packages of Fleischman's

1 1/2 cups warm water (1/4 warm, 1 1/4 hot)

1 stick of margarine

1/2 cup sugar

2 tsp salt

2 eggs, beaten

6–7 cups of flour

1 egg, reserved for glaze

poppy or sesame seeds (optional)

Dissolve yeast in 1/4 cup of warm water. In another bowl, mix hot water and melted margarine. Blend in sugar and salt and then add beaten eggs. Add yeast mixture. Mix well. Add four cups of flour and mix well. Continue adding flour to make a soft dough. Knead in bowl until smooth and elastic. Place in oiled bowl and cover. When the dough has doubled in size (about two hours), punch it down and divide it in half.

Lightly spray a plastic cutting board with cooking spray or other vegetable oil product. Take the first half of the dough and divide it equally into three parts. Roll out each part onto the oiled board into a long strip, about 15 inches long. Place the three strips on a greased baking sheet. Pinch the ends together, and begin braiding. Repeat procedure with other half of dough. Cover. Let the braided loaves rise until they have doubled in size again.

Brush tops with lightly beaten egg. If desired, sprinkle with poppy or sesame seeds. Bake in 350° oven for 20–25 minutes. Cool on rack.

Chopped Herring

1 lb jar of herring filets in wine sauce and onions

3 slices of stale challah or other stale unseeded bread

2 Red Delicious apples

4 hard-boiled eggs

Sugar to taste

Juice of 1/2 of a lemon

Dash of white pepper

Pour off wine sauce into bowl, separate onions, and soak two pieces of stale challah or other stale bread in the wine sauce. Grind herring with apples, hard-boiled eggs, and onions, or process in food processor. Add two slices of bread soaked in the wine sauce, using one slice of the dry bread to push the last of the mixture through the grinder. Mix "real good." Add sugar to taste and juice of 1/2 of a lemon. Add a dash of white pepper.

Serve chilled with kichel.

Chopped Liver

3 large onions

1 lb liver (chicken, calves, beef)

4 hard-boiled eggs

margarine as needed

salt and pepper to taste

Sauté onions in margarine until very dark but not quite burned. Remove from pan and sauté liver until well cooked in a small amount of margarine. (The old recipes called for cooking in chicken fat, or *schmaltz*.)

Cut liver and put onions, liver, eggs into food processor to chop. (It will have to be done in small batches.) Transfer to bowl and add salt and pepper to taste.

Eingemachts (Beet Conserves)

Eingemachts is a term that encompasses all sorts of jams and candies. This recipe made from beets was popular at Passover. Eingemachts can also be made from radishes, carrots, or cherries.

4 cups shredded beets

4 cups sugar

1/4 cup water

1 tsp ground ginger

2 small oranges peeled and sectioned

2 lemon slices, unpeeled

1/2 cup almonds

Combine all but nuts. Cook slowly, about one hour, or until jellied. Cool and then add nuts just before serving.

For jam: Pour into glass jars.

For candy: Spread hot mixture on a moistened cookie sheet. Let cool. Cut into diamond shapes and roll in powdered sugar.

Fig Conserve

Fresh figs

1/2 pound sugar to each pound of figs

sliced lemons, seeds removed

whole cloves

a slice of fresh ginger

Stick clove into lemon skin for easier removal later. Cook about 10–15 minutes. Drop a spoonful of hot syrup into old water to see whether it sets. If it hardens, no more cooking is necessary.

Remove lemons, cloves, and ginger. Pour into jam jars for storage.

Flat-top Eggie

Beat one egg lightly with a touch of milk. Add butter to preheated 6-inch skillet or crepe pan. When butter sizzles, add egg mixture. Distribute egg evenly so that it heats uniformly. Salt and pepper to taste. Using a spatula, flip egg over and cook briefly on other side. Remove to plate. Serve with bread.

Can be served with two slices of challah and a slice of tomato as an egg sandwich.

Gefilte Fish

This is a loose translation of Nana's fish recipe. Nana didn't measure; she did everything by touch and taste. All I can say is that if you are brave enough to make this recipe, "Ess gezundhayt": "Eat it in good health!" And invite a lot of people. This recipe feeds 20–30 people.

Fish

Ask the nice man at the fish counter to filet 20 lbs of rockfish, trout, and pike. This yields about 9–10 pounds of fish meat. Keep the heads and bones, and scrape the remaining meat from the bones. (Don't be wasteful! This can yield up to another pound.) The fish heads will be used to prepare the stock and give it a strong flavor. If you aren't making the fish the same day, you can buy it in advance and freeze it, separating the fish filets between pieces of waxed paper. Make sure the fish is completely defrosted before grinding.

Stock

Fill a large 5-gallon pot about two-thirds full with water. While you are waiting for it to boil, add the following ingredients and let them simmer for about 1/2 hour.

2 onions, cut up, including skins

3 fish heads

3 stalks of celery

4–5 carrots, peeled and cut into thick chunks

salt and white pepper to taste

Skim off the brown foam that accumulates on the top of the water. After broth has achieved a golden-brown color, remove the carrots and set aside for later.

Carefully remove the fish heads and strain all remaining items from the broth, twice. Return the clear broth to the large pot and bring to a boil.

Fish Mixture

fish filets from above, and bits of fish culled from the bones

3–4 onions (no skins!)

2–3 stalks of celery (peeled)

1 dozen eggs

2 cups water

salt and white pepper

matzo meal

Before you begin to grind the fish, check one more time for bones and bits of skin. Rinse each piece and squeeze off the excess water with your hands. Set up your grinder. Nana Lena had the old-fashioned kind you clamped onto the kitchen counter, the kind you could take apart and clean thoroughly before and after making the fish. You'll need a large mixing bowl positioned under the grinder and a small pushing tool. Alternate inserting the three types of fish with pieces of onions and celery until all the fish has been ground. Mix it well so that there are no dark areas or white areas—just a uniform mixture of fish, onions, and celery.

Beat a dozen eggs in the blender. (It makes them fluffier this way.) Alternate adding the eggs and the water to the fish mixture. Mix thoroughly. Salt and pepper to taste.

Now add 1/2 cup of matzo meal and mix well. Keep adding a little at a time until you feel that the fish is firm enough to shape into balls. Nana would pick up a handful and shape it into a ball; if it was too runny, she'd add a little more matzo meal until it was right. Somewhere between one and two cups, you will find the right texture.

Shape a golf-ball-sized "tester" and drop it into the boiling stock. If you see a flake or two rise to the top, that's okay; but if you see the ball break up into several parts, you don't have enough matzo meal.

Keep a dish of water handy to dip your hands in between balls. Drop the balls in one at a time. At first, they will fall to the bottom, but eventually they will rise to the surface. Bring to a boil. Cover and simmer for 2 1/2–3 hours. Shake the pot from time to time so they won't stick.

Carefully remove the gefilte fish from the broth with a slotted spoon. Store in air-tight containers in the refrigerator. Serve chilled with a slice of carrot and a sprig of parsley on top, and a dollop of horseradish on the side.

Hamantaschen

Hamantaschen are small triangular pastries with a sweet filling, a Purim treat. Also known as Haman's hats, after Haman, the evil prime minister of Persia, who plotted to exterminate all the Jews. The plot was foiled, so when we symbolically eat his hat, it has a "happy ending"—a sweet filling, often poppy seed, prune, or apricot. Nana Lena made hers with prunes.

Dough

3/4 cup sugar

2 cups flour

2 tsp baking powder

1/4 tsp salt

1/2 cup vegetable shortening (*or 1/2 pound butter or margarine)

1 beaten egg

2 Tbsp orange juice

Sift dry ingredients. Work in shortening. Put orange juice into beaten egg. Add to dry ingredients. The dough will be very sticky. Cover. Chill 4 hours.

Roll out dough on well-floured board. Cut into rounds using the plastic top of a coffee tin. Let rounds sit for 15 minutes before forming into cookies.

Prune Filling

1 pound sweet prunes (no pits)

3 slices of orange

1/2 lemon

1/4 cup sugar

1 Tbsp oil

dash of nutmeg

Cook prunes with 3 thin slices of orange, half a lemon (use both rind and juice), sugar, oil, and nutmeg, over a low heat until jam-like. Or skip all that and buy puréed prune filling.

Forming the Cookies

Spoon a teaspoon of filling into each cookie. Fold up three sides to form a triangle, pinching the corners, like a three-cornered hat. The filling peeks through only the center of the cookie. Bake at 400° for 10–15 minutes.

Haroset

Haroset is one of the symbolic foods on the Seder plate. We eat on Passover to remind us of the bricks and mortar that the Jewish slaves used to build the pyramids of Egypt. My family loved to eat this as a snack, so we always made large quantities. This recipe should serve 8–10.

4–6 apples

1 cup chopped pecans

1/4 cup sweet red Passover wine

1/2 cup honey

Peel and core apples. Dice into small pieces the size of a kernel of corn or a raisin. Chop pecans into similarly sized pieces. Add wine and honey. Combine ingredients. Taste. Add more wine or honey or pecans, to taste.

Store in refrigerator until Seder.

Honeyed Carrots

A typical Rosh Hashana side dish, the round carrot slices symbolic coins of good fortune that should come to you in the coming year.

3 Tbsp vegetable oil

5 cups sliced carrots

3 Tbsp orange juice

1/2 tsp salt

1/4 tsp dried ginger

1/4 cup honey

Combine all ingredients in a saucepan, cover, and cook over a low heat for 25 minutes, stirring occasionally.

Lemon Bars

yields about 30

1 1/2 cups all-purpose flour

1/2 cup powdered sugar

3/4 cups butter (1 and 1/2 sticks)

Blend together. Press into 13 x 9-inch pan. Bake at 350° for 15–20 minutes.

> 4 eggs
>
> 1/2 cup lemon juice
>
> 1 1/2 cups sugar
>
> 1/2 tsp baking powder
>
> 3 Tbsp flour

Beat eggs until fluffy and then add remaining ingredients. Pour over hot crust and bake 20 minutes. Sprinkle with powdered sugar and cut into bars. Freezes well.

Lox Eggs and Onions

> onions
>
> eggs
>
> lox
>
> butter
>
> salt and pepper

Proportions vary as needed. For two people, I would use four eggs, one onion, and 1/8 of a pound of lox.

Dice onions and sauté until golden brown. Cut lox into small pieces. Add to sauté pan. The salmon will turn opaque. Add more butter if necessary; let melt. Add the beaten eggs, a dash of salt, and a dash of white pepper. Scramble until eggs congeal. Serve hot with matzo, challah, or a sliced toasted bagel

Macaroni and Cheese

> 2 Tbsp butter or margarine
>
> 2 Tbsp flour

1 tsp salt

1 tsp dry mustard

2 1/2 cups milk

8 oz shredded cheddar cheese

8 oz macaroni

paprika

1/4 cup buttered bread crumbs or matzo meal (optional)

In saucepan, melt butter. Remove from heat. Blend in flour, salt, and mustard. Add milk and then heat, stirring constantly until sauce thickens a little and is smooth. Add 1/2 cup of shredded cheese; heat until melted, stirring occasionally. Meanwhile, cook macaroni and drain. Combine with sauce in a 2-quart casserole. Top with remaining cheese, paprika, and bread crumbs. For a little spice, add a dusting of cayenne pepper.

Bake 20–25 minutes at 375° or until top forms a crust.

Lena's Mandelbrot

1 cup oil

3 eggs

1 cup sugar

1 tsp vanilla and 1 tsp almond extract

3 cups flour

1 tsp baking powder

1 cup chopped almonds

3/4 cup glazed fruit (optional)

Mix eggs, oil, sugar, vanilla, and almond. Add nuts and fruit to flour and baking powder mixture. Add slowly to egg mixture. Mix well. Refrigerate uncovered overnight.

Divide into four parts and put into freezer trays. Evidently, before the advent of aluminum mini loaf pans, my grandmother used freezer trays—the metal bottom half of an ice cube tray—to bake in. It made a perfectly sized Mandelbrot, but any 4 x 6-inch baking pan with sides will do.

Bake 30 minutes at 350°. Let cool. Slice 3/4 inch thick and toast on both sides. Store in airtight containers.

Poogie's Mandelbrot

1 cup oil

6 eggs

2 cups sugar

2 tsp vanilla or almond extract

5 cups flour

2 tsp baking powder

1 cup slivered almonds

3/4 cup glazed fruit (optional)

Mix eggs, oil, sugar, and vanilla (or almond extract). Add nuts and fruit to flour and baking powder mixture. Add slowly to egg mixture. Mix well. Refrigerate uncovered overnight.

Divide batter into 6–7 mini loaf pans.

Bake 25–30 minutes at 350°. Let cool. Slice 1/4 inch thick and toast on both sides. Store in airtight containers.

Matzo Ball Soup

Chicken soup is Jewish penicillin. Great for a cold. Matzo ball soup adds stomach-calming qualities, with the addition of matzo dumplings. Nana Lena was a purist. She always served her matzo ball soup in a clear broth with one or two slices of carrot. Matzo ball soup, the only soup that clears the sinuses, calms the stomach and is good for your eyes.

Stock

1 chicken, whole or in pieces

2 medium onions, quartered, with skins

2 stalks celery, including leaves

2 parsnips (optional)

2–3 carrots, peeled

water

salt and pepper to taste

Fill a 5-gallon pot about 2/3 full with salted water. Bring to a boil.

Add chicken and remaining ingredients. Cover, reduce heat, and simmer for one hour.

Remove chicken from pot. Set aside. You can shred some of the white meat and add it to the soup later, or you use the boiled chicken to make a nice chicken salad.

Strain the broth before storing in glass jars in refrigerator. When it has cooled, remove the later of fat that accumulates at the top.

When ready to serve, add previously cooked matzo balls to broth to warm briefly.

Optional: Sprinkle with freshly chopped dill and/or parsley to garnish.

Matzo Balls

Starting with one pre-packaged matzo ball mix, follow the directions on the box, substituting carbonated water or seltzer for tap water to form the mixture. One box yields about one dozen balls.

Remove balls from cooking water and add to soup before serving.

Matzo Brei

serves 1, double or triple recipe as needed

Passover breakfast food. Can be served scrambled or as a pancake.

2 slices of matzo

1 egg

pinch of salt

pinch of cinnamon

tsp sugar, honey, or sweetener

Crumble matzo in a colander or mesh strainer. Do this in the sink so you don't make a mess. Wet matzo with warm water. Drain.

Beat egg and add sugar and spices. Add drained wet matzo to egg mixture and stir.

Melt butter in a non-stick frying pan. Add egg and matzo mixture. Scramble until dry, or let it set like a pancake and flip it carefully to cook on the other side.

Serve with a mixture of sugar and cinnamon sprinkled on top.

Alternate method: Skip the sugar and cinnamon and use salt and pepper instead.

Lena's Noodle Kugel

There are as many kugel recipes as there are cooks. You can pretty much interchange what dairy products you use, whether you use applesauce, fresh apples, or apple pie filling. I've used currants or dried cranberries instead of raisins. Some people prefer to cook their noodles first. Experiment! A successful kugel can be made with pretty much anything.

12-ounce package medium or wide egg noodles

6 well beaten eggs

2 cups milk

1/2 stick melted margarine, cooled

1 1/2 tsp vanilla

3 tsp lemon juice

3/4 cup sugar

3/4 cup raisins, steamed in a small amount of sherry, then drained

1 can pie-sliced apples, drained, or 4 apples grated on medium grater, or 2 cups applesauce

Boil noodles and drain. Or not. Lena boiled her noodles, while her sister Poogie insisted there was no need to precook the noodles, as long as the milk and egg mixture covered them.

In a large mixing bowl, combine the eggs, milk, margarine, vanilla, lemon juice, sugar and raisins. To this mixture, add the drained apple slices, grated apples or applesauce. Add the noodles. Mix thoroughly.

Butter a 9x13 pan or Pyrex dish or two 8x8 pans. Pour the kugel mixture into the pan. Sprinkle with sugar and cinnamon. Bake in preheated 325° oven for one hour, or more, until firm and golden brown on top.

This dish can be prepared in advance and returned to a 325° oven for half an hour before serving. Also good served at room temperature.

Poogie's Noodle Kugel

1 12-oz carton cottage cheese

8 oz sour cream

1 tsp vanilla

4 eggs

1 stick melted butter or margarine

1 can crushed pineapple with juice

2 1/2 cups milk

10 oz medium noodles (uncooked)

Golden raisins, sugar, and cinnamon to taste

Grease a 9 x 13-inch pan, or two 8 x 8-inch pans, with butter or margarine.

Place the first five ingredients in a large bowl and mix well. Add pineapple, noodles, and raisins. Add milk last. Pour mixture into prepared pans.

Bake at 350° for 1 hour, or longer, until firm and golden brown on top. Can be partially cooked, stored in refrigerator and then reheated in 325° oven for 1/2 hour before serving.

Orange and Honey Glazed Beets

1 16 oz can sliced beets

1 orange, grated and juiced

2 Tbsp honey

1 tsp fresh lemon juice

1/4 tsp grated nutmeg

salt and pepper to taste

Drain beets and arrange in baking pan. Grate and juice one orange, combine with remaining ingredients. Spoon this mixture over the beets.

Bake at 375° about 30 minutes, basting once or twice with orange juice mixture. Serve hot.

Fresh alternative:

Bring 2 large beets to a boil for about 30 minutes. Peel when cool and slice 1/4 inch thick. Proceed with directions above.

Pecan Tassies

Yields 36

Pecan tassies are little pecan pies, made in mini muffin tins. They take time to make, but one bite, and you'll be hooked. I double the recipe and freeze the rest for later.

Dough

1 stick unsalted butter

3 ounces cream cheese

1 cup flour

1/2 tsp grated orange or lemon peel

Cream butter and cream cheese together. Add flour and orange or lemon peel. Knead together until bowl is clean. Cover and refrigerate overnight.

Filling

2 beaten eggs

2 Tbsp melted butter

1 1/2 cups light brown sugar

a pinch of salt

1 1/2 cups chopped pecans

Press a marble-sized ball of dough into miniature muffin tins using your thumbs. Use only enough dough to cover the bottom and sides of each cup, removing any excess dough with the side of a spoon for a good edge. Spoon a heaping teaspoon filling into each cup. Fill about 2/3 full. Batter will rise slightly. Bake 20–25 minutes at 325°.

Pierogi

These Polish style dumplings are a favorite among Eastern European Jews, including the Lithuanian branch of the family. They can be served boiled or pan-fried. Nana Lena filled hers with potatoes and onions, and served them with lots of sautéed onions and a dollop of sour cream.

Dough

2 cups all-purpose flour

2 eggs

1/2 tsp salt

1/3 cup water

Spoon flour in a mound onto bread board; make a well in center. Drop eggs and salt into the well. Add water and work from center toward the outside of the flour mound with one hand to mix liquid and flour. Keep flour mounded with other hand. After liquid is mixed with flour, knead until dough is firm and well mixed.

Alternate method: Use a large bowl instead of mixing on a board. Add the flour first, make a well in the middle, and add the egg mixture. After the liquid is mixed with flour, knead until dough is firm and well mixed.

Cover dough on board with a warm bowl or a hot towel. Let rest about ten minutes.

Filling

1/2 stick of butter

4 onions, diced

4 cups potatoes, mashed

2 tsp salt

1/4 tsp white pepper

Sauté onions slowly until golden brown. In a bowl, add one-fourth of the cooked onions with the remaining ingredients; mix thoroughly.

Forming the Pierogi

2 egg whites

2 Tbsp water

flour for board

sour cream

In a small bowl, mix the egg whites and water. (This will be used to seal the pierogi.)

Gather a rolling pin, a pastry brush, a fork, a flatware teaspoon, and a 2 3/4-inch cookie cutter or small plastic lid to create circles.

Divide dough into three parts. Roll out dough on a well-floured board. Cut out circles of dough. Put a heaping flatware teaspoon of filling in the center of each circle. Using the pastry brush, brush one-half of the circle with the egg white and water mixture. Fold over and crimp with a fork. Place the completed pierogis on a floured surface. Do not stack.

Fill a large pot with salted water and bring to a rapid boil. Add pierogis a few at a time and bring to a boil. Cook for 4 minutes.

Serve with reheated sautéed onions and a dollop of sour cream.

If you prefer them fried, boil for two minutes and then sauté in butter until golden brown.

Plum Spice Cake

2 1/2 cups sugar

2 1/4 cups self-rising flour

1 tsp each, cinnamon, allspice, and nutmeg

1 cup salad oil

3 eggs large, or 4 small

1 8-oz jar plum or apricot baby food and one 8- oz jar tapioca

4 oz black walnuts, chopped (Black walnuts or American walnuts grow in the Eastern and Midwestern United States. They are rich and nutty in flavor.)

Combine sugar, flour, and spices. Blend together eggs, oil, and prunes. Add flour mixture to prune mixture and beat until smooth. Add nuts and mix well.

Pour into a greased and floured tube pan or Bundt pan, or two 9-inch loaf pans. Bake at 350° for 1 hour, 10 minutes. Freezes well.

Also good with apricot baby food instead of plums.

Poogie's Poppy Seed Sherry Cake

4 eggs, beaten

1/2 cup buttery oil

1 cup sour cream

1 package yellow cake mix

1 package instant vanilla pudding

1/3 cup poppy seeds

1/2 cup cream sherry wine

Mix eggs, oil, and sour cream. Add remaining ingredients. Pour into greased and floured Bundt pan. (Or, it can be baked in 9 x 13-inch pan and cut into small squares.) Bake at 350° for 1 hour. (Baking time is shorter for a 9 x 13-inch pan.) Ice with lemon glaze.

Lemon Glaze

1 1/4 cups confectioner's sugar

1/4 stick of melted butter

juice of one lemon

2 Tbsp water

(Optional) Sprinkle with 1/2 cup chopped nuts or 1/3 cup coconut.

Potato Kugel

serves 6–8

3 pounds potatoes, peeled

2 onions

2 eggs, beaten

1 tsp baking powder

1/4 cup of corn oil

2 tsp salt

1/4 tsp white pepper

1/2 cup flour or matzo meal

oil for frying pan or baking dish

Keep peeled potatoes in a bowl of cold water until you are ready to use them. This keeps them from turning black. Using a food processor, grate the potatoes and onions, transferring them to another bowl, as you work in batches. Replace the grater blade with a chopper and then process the potato and onion mixture a second time, for a short time. Do not liquefy. Alternately, you can skip the grating and just use the chopper blade if you process a few pieces of potato and onion at a time. It's up to you. Drain excess liquid using spoon or strainer, but don't go nuts about it.

Pour mixture into a large bowl. Add eggs, baking powder, oil, salt, and pepper. Add the flour 1/4 cup at a time. If you use matzo meal, you may not need as much. You want the mixture to be a little firmer than when you started out but not stiff.

Heat baking dish in oven with 1/4 cup corn or peanut oil. Nana preferred using a cast iron skillet, and to tell you the truth, she was right, but any 2-inch deep oven-safe pan or glass baking dish will do. Remove heated dish from oven and pour mixture into pan. Drizzle a little more oil on top and return to oven.

Bake at 400° for one hour, until crust is crispy brown, and outer edges detach from pan. Center should be moist but not runny. Serve hot.

Potato Latkes

yields 20–25 small pancakes

5–6 large potatoes, peeled (about 3 pounds)

2 onions

2 eggs, beaten

1 tsp baking powder

2 tsp salt

1/4 tsp white pepper

1 cup flour or matzo meal

corn or peanut oil for frying

Keep peeled potatoes in a bowl of cold water until you are ready to use them; this keeps them from turning black. Nana Lena grated her potatoes by hand, but that's a sure way to ruin a manicure, so I suggest using a food processor instead. First, use a medium grating blade to grate the potatoes and onions, transferring them to another bowl, as you work in batches. Replace the grater with a chopper and process the potato and onion mixture a second time, for a short time. Do not liquefy. You want the potatoes to have some texture. Alternately, you can skip the grating and just use the chopper blade if you process a few pieces of potato and onion at a time. It's up to you. Drain excess liquid using spoon or strainer, but don't go nuts about it.

Pour mixture into a large bowl. Add eggs, baking powder, oil, salt, and pepper. Add the flour 1/4 cup at a time. If you use matzo meal, you may not need as much. You want the mixture to be a little firmer than when you started out but not stiff.

Heat oil in frying pan. Nana preferred using a cast iron skillet, but any frying pan will do. Make sure the oil is hot before spooning batter into skillet to create pancakes about 3 to 4 inches in diameter. Cook 3 to 4 minutes until the bottom looks golden brown, and turn and fry for another minute or two. Drain on paper towels.

Latkes taste best when served immediately, but if you are preparing large batches, you may need to keep them warm in a preheated 400° oven.

Serve with applesauce, sour cream, or a mixture of cinnamon and sugar.

Sweet-and-Sour Meatballs

yields 16–20 meatballs

2 pounds ground beef

2 eggs, beaten

1/2 cup water

1 tsp salt

1/4 tsp pepper

1/2 cup minced onion

1/2–3/4 cup matzo meal or flour

Combine the first six ingredients in a large mixing bowl. Then work meal into the mixture until firm enough to make balls that retain their shape.

In a large pot, combine:

1 large diced onion

1/2 cup lemon juice

1/2 cup water

3/4 cups of sugar

1 can tomato mushroom sauce

Add meatballs to simmering sauce. Bring to a slow boil. Reduce heat and simmer for one hour, stirring occasionally so balls won't stick to bottom of pan. Add additional liquid if necessary.

Best when served with potato latkes or potato kugel.

Amy's Sweet Potato Latkes

serves 4–6 people

> *These Asian-influenced latkes can be served with a tamarind or soy dipping sauce.*

3 large sweet potatoes, peeled

6–8 scallions, sliced

3 eggs, beaten

1 tsp baking powder

2 tsp salt

1 tsp cumin

1 tsp paprika

1/4 tsp cayenne or other red pepper

1 cup flour or matzo meal

corn or peanut oil for frying

Peel sweet potatoes and shred using a food processor or grater. Leave half the batch shredded, and put the other half back in the processor with the chopping blade for a finer texture. Cut scallions into 1-inch pieces. Combine with sweet potatoes. Add remaining ingredients, stirring as you add each item. Heat oil in frying pan. Spoon mixture into 3-inch circles. Brown until crispy on both sides. Drain on paper towels. These latkes are so good, they don't need anything, but they can be served with a variety of Asian dipping sauces.

Rice Pudding

makes 8 servings

4 cups milk

1 package (4 serving-size vanilla, or coconut cream flavor pudding

1 cup instant rice

1/4 cup raisins (optional)

1 egg, well beaten

1/4 tsp cinnamon

1/4 tsp nutmeg

Combine first five ingredients in a saucepan and heat until mixture comes to a boil. Sprinkle with cinnamon and nutmeg. Serve warm.

Elayne's Rolled Cabbage

makes 20–24 rolls

Cabbage rolls

2 large heads cabbage

3 lbs ground meat (lean)

3 large eggs

1 cup water

1 cup matzo meal

1/3 cup ketchup

3/4 cup diced onions

salt to taste

Sauce

Remaining cabbage, chopped

20 gingersnaps, crushed

2 large sliced onions

1/2 cup raisins

2 cans diced tomatoes with 2 cans water

1 cup brown sugar

1 tsp Kosher Salt

1/2 cup maple syrup

cabbage leaves to cover all the rolled cabbage

1/2 cup ketchup

4 Tbsp lemon juice

Core the two heads of cabbage and then either boil until the leaves can be separated (and burn your fingers separating them), or you can freeze the cored cabbage overnight (and freeze your fingers separating them). Either way, you need about 30 large leaves.

When you finish separating the leaves, chop the broken pieces and smaller leaves and place them in the bottom of an 11 x 17_x_3-inch pan. Top with one thinly sliced onion. Cover with crushed gingersnaps.

In a large bowl, mix the meat, eggs, water, matzo meal, ketchup, diced onions, and salt. Place a large meatball-sized portion on each leaf, starting on the thicker end, folding up the sides as you roll. Seal by placing the end flap down when you place it in the pan.

Place cabbage rolls on top of the cabbage mixture. Sprinkle with raisins.

To make sauce, combine all remaining ingredients and pour over the rolls. Cover with tough outer leaves. Cover tightly with foil or roasting pan lid. Bake at 350° approximately three hours.

Rugelach

yields 48–64 pieces

Dough

> 1 cup butter
>
> 8 ounces cream cheese
>
> 2 cups unsifted flour

Cream butter and cream cheese. Add flour. Knead until the bowl is clean. Refrigerate two hours or overnight.

Filling

Strawberry, raspberry, or apricot jam. I prefer the apricot because it doesn't turn dark in color when cooked. I have also heard of orange, cranberry, or currant jam being used, or a thin chocolate spread. Look in your refrigerator, see what you have, and use that.

> 6–8 oz of desired jam
>
> 1 1/2 cups of sugar
>
> 1 tsp of cinnamon
>
> 1/2 cup finely chopped walnuts
>
> 1/2 cup golden raisins

Divide the dough into four parts. Keep the other parts in the refrigerator until you are ready to use them. Roll out each part on a floured cloth to 8 inch rounds. Spread dough with jam of choice. Sprinkle with 2 tablespoons of the sugar and cinnamon mixture. Then sprinkle the nuts and raisins around the outer edges of the circle. Leave the center clear except for the jam and sugar.

With a sharp knife, divide the circle in half, then again into quarters, and again into three or four pieces depending on size of dough. You will end up with 12 or 16 wedges. Roll up from the wide end to the center. Curve to form a crescent. Space slightly apart, pointed side down, on greased cookie sheet or on parchment paper.

Bake at 375° until lightly browned, 20–25 minutes. Using a wide spatula, remove to wire rack to cool. If you use parchment paper, they will just slide off the tray.

Roll in powdered sugar and store in freezer for a party.

Seven-Layer Cookies

1 stick of butter melted

1 1/2 cups graham cracker crumbs

6 oz chocolate bits

6 oz butterscotch bits

1 cup shredded coconut

1 cup chopped pecans

1 can Eagle brand sweetened condensed milk

The seven layers are actually the seven ingredients and the order is very important. Melt a stick of butter in a 9 x 9-inch pan. Sprinkle graham cracker crumbs over butter and press into butter to form a crust. Add 6 oz of the chocolate bits, 6 oz of the butterscotch bits, and 1 cup of coconut. Drizzle 1 can Eagle Brand sweetened condensed milk over other ingredients. Sprinkle 1 cup finely chopped pecans on top.

Bake 30 minutes at 350°. Cool and then refrigerate. Cut into 1-inch squares or 1 x 1/2-inch bars. Can be frozen.

Variations: Use white chocolate chips instead of butterscotch.

Or skip the coconut and pecans and add 1/2 box of dark raisins before topping with condensed milk.

Or try adding a layer of peanut butter.

Lena's Strudel

makes 4 dozen bite-sized pieces

Dough

1/2 pound melted butter

1 Tbsp sugar

3/4 tsp salt

1 cup sour cream

2 1/4 cups flour, sifted

Mix together. Stir until it forms a ball. Roll in waxed paper and refrigerate for an hour.

Filling

1 lb dried citrus fruit, diced

1 small can flaked coconut

1/2 box of golden raisins

2 lb chopped pecans

6–8 oz jar strawberry preserves

3 lemons, rinds and juice

sugar, to taste

Chop dried fruit, coconut, raisins, and pecans by hand into small pieces. Combine in bowl with remaining ingredients.

Remove dough from refrigerator. Put a little oil on your hands and start working the ball. Divide it into four parts. Roll it out 1/8-inch thick, about four inches wide, and 12 inches long. Trim the edges of the rectangle with a knife. Save excess to patch holes.

Spoon the filling down the middle of the roll. Fold one edge over filling and shape evenly. Try to pack the filling in as closely as possible. Fold other edge over middle, sealing the log by smoothing out the dough, pinching off any extra. Place logs sealed-side down on a greased and floured cookie sheet or on parchment-lined baking sheet. Leave a little space between the rolls; they should not touch the sides of the pan.

Bake at 325° for 30 minutes. Let cool. Roll in confectioner's sugar. Slice into 1-inch pieces.

Poogie's Strudel

yields 4 dozen bite-sized pieces

Dough

1/2 pound melted butter

1 Tbsp sugar

3/4 tsp salt

1 cup sour cream

2 1/4 cups flour, sifted

Mix together. Stir until it forms a ball. Roll in waxed paper and refrigerate for an hour.

Divide dough into four equal parts. Roll out each on floured wax paper to form a rectangle about 4 inches wide and 12 inches long.

Filling

6 oz orange marmalade

6 oz apricot preserves

1/2 cup brown sugar

1 Tbsp cinnamon

1 cup chopped walnuts

1/2 cup golden raisins

Combine preserves and marmalade. Spread on each rectangle. Combine sugar, cinnamon, walnuts, and raisins. Sprinkle 1/4 of the mixture on each rectangle. Roll up like a jellyroll and place on greased floured cookie sheet or use parchment paper. Bake at 325° for one hour. Baking times may vary.

When cool, sprinkle with confectioner's sugar. Cut each roll into 1-inch pieces.

Sweet Potatoes and Apples

8 sweet potatoes, cooked

4 baking apples

1/2 cup honey

1 tsp sea salt

1/2 tsp mace

2 Tbsp vegetable oil

Peel 8 cooked sweet potatoes, cut into 1/2-inch slices and place in a 2 qt casserole.

Peel 4 apples and cut into rings. Combine honey, salt, mace, and oil. Layer potatoes, apples, honey, and seasonings.

Bake at 350° for 30 minutes.

Taiglach

makes about 8 dozen

4 cups all-purpose flour

1 Tbsp sugar

1/2 tsp baking powder

1/4 tsp ginger

6 eggs

1/4 cup oil

chopped nuts or coconut

Dough

Sift flour with sugar, baking powder, and ginger twice. In a large bowl, beat eggs with oil; gradually add the flour mixture.

Pinch off about one-tablespoon of dough and roll on counter to form a thin rope; tie in a knot. Repeat with rest of dough.

Drop Taiglach into hot syrup (recipe to follow) and simmer, covered about 30 minutes. Shake pot often to prevent sticking; do not remove cover. When syrup has been absorbed, remove cover and pour the boiling water over top and shake pot well.

With slotted spoon, remove Taiglach from pot and place on platter sprinkled with nuts or coconut; separate while still warm. Let cool and dry.

Syrup

In a large heavy pot, preferably cast iron, combine 3 1/2 cups honey, 2 1/4 cups sugar, and two teaspoons ginger. Bring to a boil, lower heat, and drop in Taiglach, as directed in above recipe.

Tongue with Apricot Sauce

1 boiled pickled beef tongue, cooked

1 cup hot water

1 can apricot nectar

juice of one lemon

1/4 cup golden raisins

10 crushed gingersnaps

1/2 cup brown sugar

1/4 cup white vinegar (optional)

arrowroot for thickening

Stir all ingredients except tongue together in a saucepan until smooth. A little arrowroot may be used for thickening if needed. For a sweet-and-sour taste, add 1/4 cup vinegar to sauce.

Slice peeled, cooked tongue, very thin. Pour sauce over all. Keep warm in oven. Serve hot.

Fannie's Tzimmes

serves 10–12

A sweet dish of stewed fruits and vegetables, usually served on Rosh Hashana. Over the years, the word tzimmes has taken on another meaning—trouble, a big deal, a mess. As in "Don't make a tzimmes over this." My Aunt Fannie's tzimmes contained meat and was a complete meal in a pot. What made her tzimmes so special was a layer of matzo balls on top.

8 sweet potatoes

5 white potatoes

2 lbs chuck

8 carrots

1 1/2 cups matzo meal

5 eggs

2 1/2 cups of water

salt

Take the eggs, well beaten, and the matzo meal and mix it all together. Put it in the refrigerator until later.

Peel the potatoes and carrots and then cut them into chunks. Place potatoes, carrots, and chuck in a large pot on the stove, with 2 1/2 cups of water and let cook for 1–2 hours.

After the meat and potatoes look cooked, salt to taste, and then mash up all of the above and put in a roasting pan. Let it cook at 300° for 1–2 hours.

Take the matzo meal mixture out of the refrigerator and make it into little balls. Put the matzo balls on top of the potatoes and meat and return roasting pan to the oven for the last 1/2 hour before serving.

Glossary of Terms

Afikomen, the piece of matzo that we hide and let the children find during the Seder: one of the ways we keep children involved in the service.

Alter kaker, old fart

AMG, American military government

Ashkenazim, Jews from Northern France, Germany, Poland, Russian, and Eastern Europe (my family). As opposed to *Sephardim,* Jews from Portugal, Spain, and southern France, as well as Jews with roots in mostly Arabic countries, also known as Mizrachi Jews.

Baby naming, the smaller naming ceremony when the child is a girl. See *bris.*

Balebuste, a real go-getter; someone who takes authority, a head of household, f. balebuste, m. balebos)

Bar mitzvah, bat mitzvah. When Jewish boys (bar) or girls (bat) reach age thirteen, there is a religious ceremony, followed by a party, to celebrate their entry into adulthood.

Bashert, beshert, beloved; destined one

Berches, sweet rolls; alternate name for challah

Berkley, a neighborhood of Norfolk, Virginia (not to be confused with Berkeley, California, which is on another coast entirely)

Bimah, pulpit; a platform where the Rabbi stands and where the Torah is read.

Bisele, a little bit

Bris, the traditional ceremony eight days after a Jewish boy's birth, during which the infant is circumcised; the family usually throws a big party.

Brokhe, blessing

Bubbie (rhymes with Tele-tubbie), another word for grand-mother. In my family, we used Nana for grandmother and Bubbie for great-grandmother.

Bubele, a term of endearment for anyone you like, regardless of age

Bubkes, bobkes, in effect this means nothing, but this is very euphemistic—it literally means dung of sheep or goats.

Chai, (rhymes with high) in Hebrew, the numerical equivalent of eighteen is chai, or life. It is customary to make charitable contributions in multiples of eighteen. There is also a **Chai Ceremony** that is part of a Havdalah ceremony, when a child is eighteen, sending him or her out into the world.

Challah, a braided egg-based bread used on Shabbos and holidays.

Chevra Kadesha, volunteers who clean and dress the dead, to prepare them for a Jewish burial. They also sit with the body so that it is never alone. It is an honor to be among this group.

Chumetz, leaven, any food prohibited on Passover for containing leavening

Chupah, the ceremonial bridal tent, usually a piece of cloth suspended by four poles, a symbol of their new home together

Daven, to pray by swaying back and forth with the body. My Uncle Pete davened as he talked, fast and furious. He always finished davening before everybody else.

Dinnerboard, a large menu

Esrog or etrog, the special citrus used on Succot, slightly larger than a lemon, and more bitter

Ess gezundhayt. Eat in good health.

Farmer's cheese, also known as pot cheese, resembles a dry, large-curd cottage cheese

Farshtéy? Farshtéyst? Do you understand?

Farshtunkene, stinking

Flaschl shnaps, small bottle of schnapps

Fleysh, meat

Galicia, Galizia, a region in which many Jews lived, between Eastern Poland and Western Ukraine

Geh to'n dayn vays kleyd, Go put on your white dress

Gezundhayt (Yiddish), **Gezundheit** (German), literally, health; you say this when someone sneezes

Glassl, Yiddish for small, or little, glass. In the old country, tea was often served in a glass, not a cup.

Good Yontif, Happy Holiday

Hadassah, Hebrew for Esther; also name of the Women's Zionist Organization of America founded by Henrietta Szold in 1912

Hadassah Hospital on Mount Scopus, From its dedication in 1939, this modern health care facility served Jews and Arabs alike, until April, 1948, when 78 doctors and nurses were massacred going through the Sheikh Jarrah neighborhood, on their way to work. The hospital was cut off from Israel until it was recovered in the Six Day War in June 1967. It required complete renovation and was reopened in 1978.

Halevay, halevai, alevai, rhymes with mollify. An Aramaic word that has several meanings, such as *if only, I hope, I wish*. It is liberally sprinkled in conversation.

Harozet, a mixture of apples, nuts, honey, and wine; an important part of the Seder meal, a symbol of the mortar that was used to build the pyramids.

Havdalah, the ritual farewell to the Sabbath, performed with a braided candle, a saucer of alcohol, and an ornamental spice box

Hebrew National hot dogs, a Kosher all-beef hot dog brand that advertises, "We answer to a higher authority."

Ich bin Jude, I am a Jew.

Kalookie, a rummy game, popular during the 1930s, in the U.S. and Britain

Ketubah, marriage license; usually a painted scroll made of parchment, signed by the bride and groom, two witnesses, and the officiating Rabbi

Keyn eynhore, kineahora, an expression said to ward off the Evil Eye, as in, "You don't look a day over forty-five, keyn eynhore."

Kichel, technically, it means cookie. Kichel is used to scoop up chopped herring; it is slightly sweet but more of a cracker than a cookie.

Kinder, children

Kneidlach, dumplings made out of matzo meal

Kovno, a Jewish village in Lithuania, once located where the city of Kaunus exists today

Kristallnacht, the Night of Broken Glass. November 9th, 1938, the night on which Jewish-owned property was destroyed and Jewish people were attacked and humiliated all over Germany.

Kuzines, cousins

Kvell, to swell with pride or happiness

Lulav, the dried branch made up of palm, myrtle and willow used on Succot that made a noise like a rattle

Mah Jong, a Chinese tile game appropriated by American Jewish women during the 1950s

Makher, do-er, someone who gets things done; if a woman, she is sometimes known as a balebuste

Mazel Tov, congratulations; literally, Good Luck!

Med, also known as mead, an alcoholic beverage made from fermented honey and water

Meshuge, crazy

Milkhik, made with milk products, as opposed to fleyshik, made from meat or meat by-products. Jews who keep Kosher never combine milk and meat products in the same meal.

Mir hob'n gast. Di Politseyleyte komm'n. Yiddish for "We have company. The police are coming."

Mishpokhe, family; often, extended family

Mitzvah, good deed; literally, commandment

Motzi, short for hamotzi, a blessing over the bread said before every meal

Mourners' Kaddish, a prayer recited by a mourner to honor the dead

Nachas, joy

Nebbish, a nothing of a person, a loser, an unlucky person

Oléyohashol'm, Olevhashol'm, may she/he rest in peace

Oneg Shabbat, joyous Sabbath; a reception held after Friday night services during which sweets are served and the congregants greet one another and welcome the Sabbath.

Oy vey iz mir, "Woe is me!"; literally it pains me.

Pareve, foods that are pareve contain neither animal nor dairy products and can be eaten with either, in keeping with Jewish dietary laws that do not allow meat products to be eaten with milk or dairy products. Margarine is pareve; butter is not.

Payes, the long sideburns of Orthodox Jews

Pesach, Passover, a spring holiday that often overlaps with Easter. The Christian Last Supper was probably a Passover Seder.

Pisher (m), **pisherke** (f), young squirt, someone who's wet behind the ears. Also used for someone who wets the bed.

Pope Pius XII (1876–1958; Pope from 1939–1958). It was implied by playwright Rolf Hochhuth in "The Deputy" that Pope Pius XII did nothing to save the Jews, and that was the prevailing opinion during and after the war. In hindsight, it appears that more than 860,000 Jews were saved by the Catholic Church. "That is not bubkes," as my Nana would say: A double negative, meaning that is something.

Purim, The word "Purim" means "lots" and refers to the lottery that Haman used to choose the date for the massacre of the Jews. The festival, celebrated in March on the 14th of Adar, the day that was chosen for the extermination, celebrates the heroism of Esther, who went to the king at great risk to herself and saved her people.

Pushke, a small metal box in which charitable contributions are collected. Each time she put a coin in the pushke, Nana Lena said a prayer for one of us. "Please God, take care of Myer. Please God, make sure that Melissa's baby comes out all right. Please God, let Amy sell her screenplay or find a husband. Something!" She always put in eighteen (chai) cents, or a multiple of eighteen, such as thirty-six, double chai, on special occasions.

Rebbetzin, Rabbi's wife; often, today, a female Rabbi

Rosh Hashana, The Jewish New Year, one of the High Holidays; the other being Yom Kippur

Royt, royte, red

Shabbos, Shabbat. The Jewish Sabbath, from sundown Friday to sundown Saturday.

Shande, shame

Shaytl, wig, worn by Orthodox Ashkenazic Jewish women after they are married so that they will not be attractive to other men

Shema, one of the central prayers of the Jewish religion in which we acknowledge that there is only one God

Sheynele, derivation of Sheyn, Yiddish for pretty

Shidduch, arranged marriage, as in "make a Shidduch"

Shivah, the first seven days of mourning

Shivah Table, the ceremonial meal after a funeral

Shmok, alt. **Schmuck,** in this context, idiot, although it also refers to the male organ

Shtetl, small town or village

Shul, Yiddish for synagogue

Succos (Ashkenazic), also **Succot** (Sephardic), the Feast of Tabernacles, which coincides with the fall harvest

Synagogue, a Jewish place of worship, or as my Baptist friends tell me, a Jewish church

Tallis, also **tallit**, prayer shawl. **Taleysim**, plural.

Tante, aunt

Treyf, unsafe, used to refer to foods that are not Kosher

Tu Bishvat, the 15th day of the month of Sh'vat, Arbor Day, a day to plant trees and appreciate nature

Tzimmes, a stewed mixture, usually of meat, carrots, and prunes. Alternate meaning: trouble, a big mess. (Not to be confused with **Tsouris**, trouble, worry, suffering).

Vunderkind, Wunderkind, young genius, child prodigy

Yahrzeit candle, a memorial candle burned on the anniversary, usually according to the Jewish calendar, of a loved one's death

Yahrzeit glass, the glass that holds a yahrzeit candle, the candle burned on the anniversary of a loved one's death. It is a common item in most Jewish homes. It holds about one cup.

Yiddish, Traditional language of East European Jews. A combination of German, Hebrew, and Slavic words, written in Hebraic characters.

Yom Kippur, the Day of Atonement, the most holy day of the year. One of the High Holidays, the other being Rosh Hashana.

Zeyde, (sounds like lady, with a "z") grandfather

Zisele, sweetie, sweetheart

Index of Recipes

9 781598 580563